THE
STRUGGLE
FOR
WHOLENESS

MARTTI SIMOJOKI

Former Archbishop of the Church of Finland

THE STRUGGLE FOR WHOLENESS

Daily Briefings
for the Spiritual Journey

Translated by
Walter Jacob Kukkonen

POLARIS PRESS
Tucson, Arizona

ISBN 0-9622985-0-6

Published by POLARIS PRESS
1281 W. Elko Street
Tucson, AZ 85704

Printed in the United States of America.

Translator's Foreword

THE STRUGGLE FOR WHOLENESS is your invitation to engage in serious spiritual self-direction, the heart of mature Christian spirituality. These daily inspirational readings will involve you personally in the struggle of faith. If we are conscious of the power struggle within us, we will benefit from other forms of Christian ministry: counseling, spiritual growth groups, and corporate worship. Spiritual self-direction means accepting our freedom and responsibility in matters of the spirit, taking time for regular reading of Scripture and edifying literature, meditation, contemplation, and prayer. We do that believing God's promise that everyone who seeks will find.

The Struggle for Wholeness was first published in Helsinki, Finland in 1961 with the title Paivan sana (Day's Word) by Kirjapaja Publishers. The author, Dr. Martti Simojoki, is respected and loved in Finland for his many years of Christian service to his church as pastor, professor, bishop, and archbishop. Thousands more know and love him as a spiritual writer. His spiritual roots are in Finland's spiritual awakening movement known as Awakenism. This movement emphasizes simultaneously in a unique way the mystical dimension of an inward knowledge of Christ, the believer's waiting for God to take and maintain the initiative in matters of faith and life, and the small group as setting for spiritual nurture and growth through the ministry of all believers in Christ's body. In Finland both clergy and laity participate together in this mutual ministry producing through inner spiritual renewal a kinder and gentler church and society.

Simojoki's spiritual heritage is expressed in the readings of this volume. Describing his personal faith recently, Simojoki declared that "knowing oneself as ungodly is not learned from books. The doctrine of justification says explicitly, 'God justifies

vi THE STRUGGLE FOR WHOLENESS

the ungodly.' In doctrinal matters the Awakened have various opinions, which is all right. Just so we remember that God is everything and man is nothing."

"The struggle for wholeness" involves the soul in the conflict between the flesh and the spirit. The soul sides with the Spirit of God, whose goal is to turn the management of the "mission control center" over to Christ, to whom God has given "all authority in heaven and on earth." The Christ dwelling in each disciple seeks to gather all into one body uniting them with himself, with the Father, and with one another in the "communion of saints." On this foundation God seeks to build the "community of nations or peoples."

Jesus states the primary goal of the struggle of faith: "I am the vine, you are the branches. If a man remains in me and I in him, he will bear much fruit; apart from me you can do nothing" Jn 14:5. Asking Jesus to heal his son, a father expressed the nature of the struggle, "I do believe; help me overcome my unbelief" Mk 9:24. "The struggle for wholeness" is between faith and unbelief, between God in Christ and forms of piety that idolize doctrines, rituals, rules, and regulations making "means" into "ends."

The creative core of Christianity is the faith that believes. Paul states succinctly: "I have been crucified with Christ and I no longer live, but Christ lives in me. The life I live in the body, I live by faith in the Son of God, who loved me and gave himself for me" Ga 2:20. In my opinion Martin Luther stated it well in a postscript to a letter written by Melanchthon to a mutual friend:

> "Remember that he himself says, 'I am the way, the truth, and the life.' He does not say, I give to you the way and the truth and the life, as if he effected all this in me from without. It is within me that he must be, stay, live, speak, so that we are righteous in God's sight in him and not in love and in the gifts that flow from faith."

This book comes to you with the prayer that it will serve you as an effective tool of spiritual direction, involving and sustaining you in the very personal struggle for wholeness. May it help you to join Paul, who wrote to his spiritual son and comrade, "Fight the good fight of faith. Take hold of eternal life to which you were called when you made your good confession in the presence of many witnesses" 1 Ti 6:12.

Martti Simojoki has been one of my spiritual mentors. This translation gives me deep satisfaction. It is an honest and serious effort on my part to share with others "the faith that believes." My prayer for you and me is that when our struggle for wholeness draws to an end as death approaches, we may say with Paul, "I have fought the good fight, I have finished the race, I have kept the faith" 2 Ti 4:7. Good reading; good struggling!

I acknowledge with gratitude the assistance of others, especially family members, in the preparation of this book, the initial publication of Polaris Press, founded to promote evangelical spirituality.

July 4, 1989   W. J. K.
Tucson, Arizona

To the Reader

THE APPEARANCE of a fifth printing of a book of daily meditations is an indication of the number of people looking for this type of reading. All kinds of fears, a sense of guilt, and the difficulty of finding a purpose for one's personal life weigh upon us. The higher standard of living cannot meet the deepest need of the soul. We yearn for a new, living relationship to God, who alone can drive away our fears, forgive us. and give substance to our lives. God-fearing people used to say that God has only day-old children. Rightly understood this thought suggests that God's grace is new each morning. "Yesterday is gone, we know nothing about tomorrow, today the Lord takes care of us."

The short meditations collected in this book were written during the years 1939-1951. They represent simple talk about our most important concern. Since they continue to meet a need, the author feels justified in thinking that there still are many whose only security is Jesus Christ. My sincere prayer is that he himself will speak to the reader. Then the new printing will have been done for a good reason.

Helsinki, Finland   M. S.
June 5, 1961

January

1 / New Hearts for the New Year

"Look, the Lamb of God, who takes away the sin of the world" Jn 1:29.

A NEW YEAR reminds us that our hearts need renewal. Unless we deal with the evil inside us, in the form of lust, envy, bitterness, malice, unkindness, fault-finding, greed and materialism, our new year will surely be ruined. Sins of the past year will follow us into the new year, and God's wrath will be like a curse upon us. Our inner life must be renewed.

As the new year begins we look to "the Lamb of God, who takes away the sin of the world." The removal of sin is not only necessary, it is also possible. Sin is not just our concern; Christ is also concerned about it. On Golgotha he acted to purify us from our sins (He 1:3). "God made him who had no sin to be sin for us, so that in him we might become the righteousness of God" 2 Co 5:21.

The year we have now entered is, therefore, a year of grace. No matter what lies behind us, we know it is the Lamb of God who is waiting for us. "The Lamb of God, who takes away the sin of the world" welcomes us into this new year.

Let us pray for God's Holy Spirit to fix our eyes upon the Lord Christ, so that in living faith we might share in his work of grace which removes our sins and renews our hearts.

2 / Help Comes from the Lord

"I lift up my eyes to the hills--where does my help come from?" Ps 121:1.

GOD HAS DONE marvelous things. We begin to realize this if we look back on events of the past year. Last year's challenges sometimes loomed like high hills in front of us, filling us with awe and amazement. At other times we became depressed by our helplessness and inadequacy in overcoming these obstacles in our path. But we do not expect help to come from the hills. We wait for help only from the Lord. A person who trusts in God can face the hills along life's journey, praying for the help that "comes from the Lord, the Maker of heaven and earth" Ps 121:2. Obstacles in life need not depress us if we know of the marvelous works of God. We can learn from the psalmist's experience and faith and turn our gaze upon the Lord himself.

We have focused our eyes upon the visible rather than the invisible. We try to tackle the mountains of insurmountable problems on our own, sink into despair, and complain about them. But the person who believes in God knows his source of help. "My help comes from the Lord, the Maker of heaven and earth" Ps 121:2.

With the start of the new year, let us approach this source of help. Many high hills may lie ahead of us, but we can look to God, believe in Him, and trust in Him as we walk into the unknown future. "He will not let your foot slip--he who watches over you will not slumber" Ps 121:3.

3 / Nobody Believes for Nothing

"They replied, 'Believe in the Lord Jesus, and you will be saved--you and your household'" Ac 16:31.

WHEN PAUL answered the panic-stricken prison guard of Philippi, "believe in the Lord Jesus, and you will be saved--you and your household," he knew what he was speaking about. He and his travel companion, Silas, had just experienced the miraculous help of the Lord Jesus. In the darkness of prison Paul and Silas had directed their fervent prayers to the Lord and received new evidence that Christ is truly the Lord for whom nothing is impossible.

We may assume that they prayed for delivery from prison in order to continue their ministry on behalf of the gospel. Incapable of freeing themselves, they believed in the Lord and turned the matter over to him. In fact, so sure were they in their faith that they thanked God in advance, with no idea of how the Lord would help them. They simply committed the matter to the Lord.

Having obtained their freedom, they met the panic-stricken guard and recommended what had worked so well a moment ago for them. "Believe in the Lord Jesus, and you will be saved--you and your household." As far as they were concerned anyone, even this guard, could put their hope in the Lord's help. His whole family could be saved as well if he sincerely left them in the Lord's hands.

This story has been preserved so that we, who are enslaved in many ways and cannot see very far ahead, might be encouraged to leave all of our concerns with the Lord Jesus. We will stubbornly try to help ourselves and our loved ones with our own resources, but the Lord Jesus is the only true helper. Let us believe in him and leave all our concerns with him. Let us believe in his help even when we are in the dark and have no idea how he can help us. "The one who trusts in him will never be put to shame" Ro 9:33. Just as God answered the prayers of Paul and Silas with His "Amen," shattering the walls of the prison, so will he answer all who, in their despair, leave matters in his hands. You may have to wait a long time. God's answer may not come until you close your eyes in death, but it most certainly will come. No one believes in him in vain.

4 / We Can Depend on God Totally

"God gives grace to the humble" 1 P 5:5.

"A MAN CAN receive only what is given him from heaven" Jn 3:27. Everything in life is dependent on God "from whom all blessings flow." We do not always remember this, but it is true. Whatever we have is from God. But why doesn't God, whose resources are inexhaustible, give me more? Why doesn't God let his power show more in my life? Why am I not given power against sin? I have seen often enough what Satan can do; why doesn't the Lord Jesus show what he can do?

The Bible answers, "God opposes the proud but gives grace to the humble" Jas 4:6. Pride stands in the way of God's giving. Perhaps you have struggled with a particular sin. God seemed to answer your prayers for help, but you fell into the same sin again. Why doesn't God help? Because God doesn't help us piecemeal. He helps us as whole persons. We need help not just in one thing; we need help in everything. Our total selves need renewal. God is waiting for us to humble ourselves, not in one or two areas of our lives, but in everything.

Many people want to be disciples of Jesus, but are not ready to humble themselves before other people, especially within their families. Yet, is it not in our homes that we yearn most deeply for God's power to be evident? In the eyes of strangers we manage to look important. In our homes, in relationship to our spouse, parents, children and others, it is more difficult. But unless we humble ourselves among our family members, we wait in vain for power from God. "God opposes the proud but gives grace to the humble." We can take nothing from God. But when God wants to give, no one can stop him. And the Bible says he gives "richly" 1 Ti 6:17.

5 / Christianity Starts in the Heart

"Find rest, O my soul, in God alone" Ps 62:5.

CHRISTIANITY must become a matter of the heart. On this assertion the Bible seems clear: The Spirit of wisdom and revelation are to open the eyes of our hearts (Eph 1:18). Christ should dwell in our hearts through faith (Eph 3:17). In our hearts we should sing and make music to the Lord (Eph 5:19). With sincerity of heart we should perform our services (Eph 6:5). "Whatever you do, work at it with all your heart, as working for the Lord, not for men" Col 3:23.

Thinking of the Christians in Rome, Paul thanked God that they, who earlier had been slaves to sin, now "wholeheartedly obeyed" the teaching of Christ (Ro 6:17). They now had an inner desire to do God's will in all things. And so Paul shares with them his own heart: "For in my inner being I delight in God's law" Ro 7:22.

The life of the heart remains hidden, demanding quietness in order to grow and mature. The heart becomes a prayer chamber in which the soul quietly listens to God's voice. Like a tender plant which remains stunted unless it can draw upon the power of life, the soul requires peace and quiet for growth. If we become quiet, the Lord can speak to us about our condition and we can know of our sin. Likewise, we will not know the grace of God and the fulfillment of his will in the course of history and the end of time unless we learn to listen to the still, small voice of the Lord.

The one requirement for Christianity to become a matter of the heart is quiet, secret conversation with the Lord. Only then will Christianity take root in us. Be still before the Lord and wait for Him!

6 / God's Word Is a Source of Joy

"When they saw the star, they were overjoyed" Mt 2:10.

THE WISEMEN of the East gazed longingly, but faithfully, at the heavens, seeking light and enlightenment. As we again celebrate Epiphany, we learn from them to lift our eyes toward the heavens! God is the God of revelation, giving light for us, too. Viewing the lights of the heavens is not a vague speculation about "signs." The Finnish poet Elias Lonnrot states the matter succinctly in his Epiphany hymn: "The bright star of heaven is the word of God."

The "heavens" we are to search are found in God's Word. When we search the Word the lights of heaven will reveal new insights. In the searching of our prayers, God will kindle his holy word as a light in the darkness of our world. And once again there is joy in the discovery of the bright star of the Word.

A painting of Rembrandt shows a monk reading in his monastery cell. The background is in total darkness, but a bright light bathes the monk's face. Closer study of the painting reveals that the light shining through the window of the cell is reflected onto his face from the pages of the book he is studying.

Sitting in darkness, our faces begin to glow when we study the Word. Why sit in darkness, without the true light, when it is to be found in God's Word? Our faces, too, will glow when we study the Word.

There are times when God's Word is scarce. Revelations do not happen, no stars are kindled. At these times, the lights that were lit for us in earlier times become precious. We honor them now by following the teachings of the Word.

7 / Word and Spirit Belong Together

"Do not go beyond what is written" 1 Co 4:6.

IN THE HISTORY of the Christian church, Spirit and Word have often been separated. In the name of true Christianity, spirit-filled religion has been emphasized and the Bible set aside. Simple living, guided by reading and treasuring the Word, has been looked upon as less valuable than powerful emotional experiences. Our experiences are made more important than study of the Word, and the Word becomes interpreted in light of those experiences. This approach is wrong. Spirit and Word belong together, with experiences evaluated in light of the Word. Without the Word, the Spirit remains only a confused human emotion. Without the Spirit, the Word is mere letters and lifeless, external law. Word and Spirit go together, but the Word comes first.

The Spirit is revealed in the Word. Jesus says, "The words I have spoken to you are spirit and they are life" Jn 6:63. We must remember that he is referring to the words we now have in the New Testament. We who wait for the Spirit to enter our lives and give guidance and counsel must keep faithful company with the Bible. The Spirit will reveal Christ to us in the written Word. Study and treasure the Word. Note even its smaller details. Handle the Bible with respect and submit to it in all matters. It is not just another book. As Christians we are bound to the written Word. "Do not go beyond what is written."

8 / Find Your Place of Prayer

"When you pray, go into your room, close the door" Mt 6:6.

WHEN JESUS told the person who wanted to pray to go into a room and close the door, he used a term which meant a storeroom. In many small homes of his day this was the only room that could be locked from the inside. Perhaps you can think of a special place for prayer in your home, a quiet place set aside for devotional purposes. You are fortunate if you have such a place, but many do not. However, the Lord takes our difficult living conditions into consideration and shows how a place for prayer can be found even in adverse circumstances.

Certainly there is some spot or corner where the Lord wants to meet you, and it is essential that you find this quiet place. It will enable you to really withdraw from the hustle and bustle of daily life and the distractions of the world so that you can hear God's voice and converse with him.

In the final analysis, this quietness is not something we can achieve. Becoming still happens only by God's grace. The psalmist is right in saying that his soul is satisfied only in the presence of the Lord (Ps 63:5). Jesus instructs us to be personally involved in our prayer. Whoever heeds the word of the Lord and goes into his "room" and closes the door will experience renewal in his prayer life.

9 / Love Refuses to Judge

"Love never fails" 1 Co 13:8.

IMAGINING THAT WE are important and clever, we easily become arrogant and judgmental toward one another. In our assumed wisdom we seek to lord it over other people and conflict is inevitable.

The Bible calls such wisdom worldly. "Who is wise and understanding among you? Let him show it by his good life, by deeds done in the humility that comes from wisdom...true wisdom is first of all pure, then peace-loving, considerate, submissive, full of mercy and good fruit, impartial and sincere" Jas 3:13,17.

Being thoughtful of others may appear at first as weakness. After all, we say a person must stand for something and strongly defend it. As a result, even hardness of heart and lack of mercy can sometimes look like Christian virtues.

But, let us remember that love is the greatest virtue. And when our Lord loved he never condemned, leading some to think he was weak. In fact, this non-judgmental love led him to shame, to the cross, and to death. But that was his road to victory. Through his suffering and death he introduced the world to God's way, a way from a totally different world.

Peter, a zealous disciple who once tried to advance the cause of the Lord with a sword, learned about God's way of love. He later wrote about Jesus, saying that "when they hurled their insults at him, he did not retaliate; when he suffered, he made no threats" 1 P 2:23. Our Lord left us a sacred and precious example of how God loves. Let us not judge one another; let us not be offended by one another's faults. Let us love, for love is the source of true wisdom.

10 / Acceptance by God and Surrender to Him

"Offer yourselves to God, as those who have been brought from death to life" Ro 6:13.

IT IS FOOLISH to invite people who do not acknowledge God to surrender to Him. Unbelievers simply do not surrender to a God they do not know. We must not urge just anyone to give themselves to the Lord, for it is impossible to turn to God on our own. Paul wrote: "Offer yourselves to God, as those who have been brought from death to life." The order is crucial. You must first be brought from death to life; only then can you offer yourself to God. Our own attempts to surrender to God will only leave us exhausted, and we will never totally submit to God.

In the Letter to the Hebrews we read that the blood of Christ will "cleanse our consciences from acts that lead to death, so that we may serve the living God" He 9:14. "Where there is forgiveness of sins, there is also life and salvation," says Luther in his Small Catechism. Surrender, without a conscience cleansed and forgiven by the blood of Christ, cannot bring us from death to life.

We can offer ourselves in service to the Lord only if we know that we have been accepted by Him. Our desire to surrender will not help us feel worthy before God. Only Jesus Christ and his reconciling blood can accomplish that. And once we have been reconciled with God, His urgent call applies to us: "Offer yourselves to God, as those who have been brought from death to life."

In what way do you need to offer yourself to the Lord? What does God expect of you today?

11 / Jesus Is a Friend of Sinners

"Here is a friend of sinners" Lk 7:34.

JESUS IS a friend of sinners but not of sin. He is an unrelenting enemy of sin in every form, favoring sin under no circumstances. Still, he is a friend of sinners. He will not condemn the poor sinner, neither will he force himself on him. There is never a poor time to come to him. Nor are we ever too poor to come. He is truly a friend of sinners.

Friends are important to us, a fact we understand best only when we are without friends. As the friend of sinners, Jesus is our best friend. He takes our concerns upon himself. "Surely he took up our infirmities and carried our sorrows" Is 53:4. "He himself bore our sins in his body on the tree" 1 P 2:24. When even our best friends cannot help us, he stands beside us.

> Jesus will not forsake us
> When troubles overtake us.

Why do we think so little about our best friend? Why do we so seldom, and even then hurriedly, visit Jesus in prayer? Why can't we forget everything else in order to be with Christ? When Paul said, "For me to live is Christ" Phil 1:21, he wanted to point out that Christ meant everything for him. That's what happens when we discover that Jesus is the friend of sinners. How meaningful these three words are, "friend of sinners."

> Friends have forsaken;
> You have stood fast.

That is what the "friend of sinners" is like; that is why sinners have always been drawn to him.

12 / Faith Is Realistic

"Yet he did not waver through unbelief regarding the promise of God, but was strengthened in his faith and gave glory to God" Ro 4:20.

FAITH DOES NOT require that we close our eyes to the severity of life. In turning to heavenly things we need not ignore the afflictions and sufferings of this life.

It is said of Abraham that he did not waver in his faith, even though he and Sarah, because of their age, could no longer have a child. Abraham, the father of faith, was realistic and accepted this cold fact. "Yet he did not waver through unbelief regarding the promise of God, but was strengthened in his faith and gave glory to God, being fully persuaded that God had power to do what he had promised." Abraham looked the facts straight in the eye, but he kept one eye on the promise of God. Thus he hoped when there was no hope (Ro 4:18), when the facts seemed contrary to God's promise. In this way he gave glory to God and was strengthened in his faith.

We must live by our faith, just as Abraham did. The facts must not be ignored; life must be accepted as it is. But we must cling to God's promises, even when they seem as impossible as the birth of a child to the elderly Abraham and Sarah. Living faith has power; it can move mountains. Believers stand with both feet in this world, yet leaning with their whole weight on God and his promises.

Modern life seldom proclaims the glory of God; the power of evil is overwhelming. But where people live in absolute dependence upon God's promises, there God is glorified.

13 / Righteousness Follows
Wretchedness

*"What a wretched man I am! Who will rescue me from
this body of death?"* Ro 7:24.

"WHERE GOOD PEOPLE walk, there are the roads of God." In
light of the Bible, this anonymous saying is questionable. The
Spirit of God does produce good fruit, the very best being love.
But this does not happen so that we might become good, for all
that is good continues to be the work of God. We always remain
evil. Our sinful nature continues to live out its devious designs,
and the enemy of our souls continues its dirty work with ugly
results. The life of the Christian, therefore, is warfare to the
very end, marked by struggle, affliction, and toil.

Perhaps you have been deeply depressed by the awareness
that evil still clings to you. You can complain with the apostle,
"What I do is not the good I want to do; no, the evil I do not want
to do--this I keep on doing" Ro 7:19. How can people like us be
children of God? "What a wretched man I am! Who will rescue
me from this body of death?" Ro 7:24. Compelled to examine our
motives, we must bow our heads in shame.

However, Romans 7 is followed immediately by Romans 8.
"Therefore, there is now no condemnation for those who are in
Christ Jesus" Ro 8:1. Likewise, on the Christian journey there is
an inexplicable connection between wretchedness and
righteousness, between sin and grace. Judgments abound, but
there is no condemnation. "In him we have redemption through
his blood, the forgiveness of sins, in accordance with the riches
of God's grace" Eph 1:7.

There is hope for all who are tempted but put their trust in
the Lord. As the saying goes, "There must be war and struggle
against temptation. War shows who is a true Christian and a
servant of the Lord." Do not look upon your cause as lost. Do not
lose hope when the war continues, when you are tempted and
when you fall in defeat. As long as we are on the road, the fight
continues. The war will cease when we reach our destination.
But, we see our victory in the sign of the cross which guides our
way. Feeble fighters though we be, let us gather around the
cross and fix our eyes upon it. Then we shall obtain the final
victory, no matter how things seem now.

14 / The Lord's Work Is Not Seasonal

"Yet I am always with you" Ps 73:23.

OUR FAILURE to be awake in our faith results in our being unprepared for assignments from God. When a need arises we want to serve the Lord, but at other times we forget God and live for ourselves. Our readiness to take on our assignments in times of need depends on what we have learned in between those times.

The Lord's service is not seasonal work. He does not use us occasionally; he wants us as full-time employees. This is what Paul has in mind when he says that believers are "God's fellow workers" 2 Co 6:1. God wants us as his own, living in unbroken relationship with him, obedient to his will each day. We can never know how today's business, no matter how insignificant it may appear, will decide our future.

What God wants to teach you today is necessary, if you are to serve him tomorrow. That in which he tests you today, asking for your obedience, is essential if you are to withstand temptation someday in the future. What he whispers to you in your prayer room today is of such importance that irreparable damage will be done if you let the moment pass without responding to him. We are to live each moment for the Lord. Otherwise we will never be prepared for his service.

15 / Times of Awakening, Times of Judgment

"His winnowing fork is in his hand to clear his threshing floor and to gather the wheat into his barn, but he will burn up the chaff with unquenchable fire" Lk 3:17.

JOHN THE BAPTIST announced that Jesus was coming to baptize with the Holy Spirit and with fire. This baptism first took place on Pentecost and many times since. In times of awakening in the church, when "the wind of heaven blows across the earth," the Lord himself has baptized people with the Holy Spirit and with fire.   We hope for these times of awakening, but let us remember that they are critical times for God's people, times of great division. The Lord clears his threshing floor, gathering the wheat into his barn, but burning the chaff. It becomes clear who God's people really are. Others take offense at awakenings, criticizing them, and opposing the work of God. They smugly pass judgment and vainly reject the new teachings of God which disturb their peaceful but worldly Christianity. Times of awakening are dangerous times, when those who do not belong to the Lord's people will be revealed for who they are.

Stephen had to say about the pious people of his day, "You stiffnecked people, with uncircumcised hearts and ears! You are just like your fathers. You always resist the Holy Spirit" Ac 7:51. Do these words sound a sharp judgment against us, too? Unless the Lord can change us inwardly into new people, we will be found among the wretched opponents of the Holy Spirit. Times of awakening, if sent by God, are times of judgment. They can peel away our external piety and churchliness, and reveal that we have never truly belonged to the Lord's people.

There are rumors that the Lord is again baptizing people with the Holy Spirit and with fire. The wind is blowing in the treetops, and there is movement on the road to church. Let us pray for the grace of inner repentance. Otherwise, guilty of resisting God's work, we will be separated from the awakened and cast as chaff into the fire.

16 / We Stay on the Road by Faith

"You stand [stay] by faith" Ro 11:20.

HOW CAN I stay on God's road? The question is serious, for there are many who stray, beginning in the Spirit but ending in the flesh. It is a matter of life and death for those who want to stay in the Lord, but too often fall to Satan's temptations.

Paul answers, "You stand [stay] by faith." You cannot stay by actions of your will, on the basis of moral or spiritual achievements, or on the basis of zeal. Neither will other people be able to help you stay on God's road. "You stand [stay] by faith."

We misunderstand Paul, however, if we think of faith as the basis of Christianity. Faith is not a merit we can present before God. We do not believe in our faith; we believe in God. That's why the apostle adds, "...provided that you continue in his kindness" Ro 11:22. Here is the heart of the matter. Faith is not a question of our goodness. Faith is a leap into the net of God's kindness. Close your eyes and lean with all you have upon the kindness of God. Let all the concerns that weigh upon you gravitate to the goodness of God. We stay on God's road when, again and again, we trust ourselves to God's grace. Then the power of Christ's resurrection begins to work in our lives. "Taste and see that the Lord is good, blessed is the man who takes refuge in him." Ps 34:8 Blessed, indeed, is the person who trusts everything that he is to the kindness of God. He will stay on God's road.

"You stand [stay] by faith."

17 / A Good Death Is God's Gift

"If it is difficult for good people to be saved, what, then, will become of godless sinners?" 1 P 4:18 (TEV).

HAVE YOU seen a good person die? Bishop Jacob Gummerus breathed the words of a hymn on his death bed:

When memories of my journey come to mind,
They fill me with sorrow,
For few of my works have been of the kind,
Which I would dare to show my Lord.
And perhaps in the eyes of the Righteous One
That which I thought right is wrong,
And perhaps I'll be judged for the things for which
I received the praise of men.

Salvation is troublesome business even for a good person. The King James translation says that good people are "scarcely" saved. There is nothing in the life of even a good person that is of value for salvation.

It would be worth our while, therefore, to look closely at how we live. Consider that what you do today may turn out to be an obstacle to your salvation. Perhaps that which you seek after today, hold dear, rejoice over, and feel that you absolutely need, turns out to be the cause of bitter tears? Think not only of what you do, but also of what you leave undone. Sins of omission are more dangerous.

I have witnessed Christians fighting their last battles in this life and been reminded of these words, "If it is difficult for good people to be saved, what, then, will become of godless sinners?" This doesn't mean that God's grace is "hardly" enough for the poor sinner. Not at all! Grace is always sufficient. But the Bible says that grace must be accepted in such a way that it becomes a part of us.

Even then, salvation is not easy, for grace means that it is impossible to be saved on our own. We are saved with difficulty, for it requires a miracle -- the gracious work of God himself.

18 / The Inside Is What Counts

"They followed the stubborn inclinations of their evil hearts. They went backward and not forward" Jr 7:24.

WE THINK we are not responsible for our wrongful actions if we did not intend to offend or hurt. The Bible, however, teaches otherwise. "For from within, out of men's hearts, come evil thoughts, sexual immorality, theft, murder, adultery, greed, malice, deceit, lewdness, envy, slander, arrogance and folly" Mk 7:21f. Evil is not something external and occasional. It resides in the heart.

The boundary between living faith and dead faith lies inside of us. A Christian in name only is concerned about his evil deeds, particularly when they cause him to lose face with others. But a true Christian is concerned about the wickedness of his heart, knowing that the Lord "desires truth in the inner parts" Ps 51:6. He is to love the Lord with all his heart and all his soul and all his mind (Mt 22:37). It is not enough to draw near to the Lord with one's lips when one's heart is far from him (Mt 15:8). Faith comes alive when it becomes a matter of the heart. The prophet spoke about the difficulty of life: "The heart is deceitful above all things and beyond cure. Who can understand it?" Jr 17:9.

Christians must accept the fact that life is hard. In despair we pray for help from God. But sometimes we complain only about our misfortune and the burdens of life; we do not always get our own way. We ought to be horrified by the wickedness of our hearts and outraged by our evil thoughts.

As long as we are unaware and unconcerned about the wickedness of our hearts, we turn our backs to the Lord. We may be close to the Lord, but we are in the wrong position. It is our faces that we should turn to God. You may feel close to the Lord, but you should examine your "attitude." Is it your face or your back that is toward Him?

> If I cannot raise toward your great glory
> My sin-dirtied face,
> You will let me, Jesus, at your feet
> Sit in all my emptiness and filth.

19 / A Refuge in Times of Temptation

"Therefore he is able to save completely those who come to God through him, because he always lives to intercede for them" He 7:25.

THE LORD INVITED his disciples to rejoice in the fact that their names were written in heaven. He said this, knowing the fires of temptation into which they would be thrown. Because of pride and other sins they would have to endure the winnowing action of Satan. Much of what was inside of them would have to be burned away. They would not know to be on their guard when temptations came, and they would be in great danger. Therefore, the Lord urged his disciples to rejoice that their names were written in heaven. Why?

We hear the answer as Jesus speaks to Peter: "Simon, Simon, Satan has asked to sift you as wheat. But I have prayed for you, Simon, that your faith may not fail" Lk 22:31f. Without the Great Intercessor, who would never tire of praying for him, nothing would be able to save Peter. The names of Peter and the other disciples were written in the Intercessor's book; for that reason they could take heart and rejoice.

If you are depressed or tempted, you know of no reason to rejoice. Weighed down by the circumstances of life around you and by your own wickedness within, you find no encouragment that can help. But your name, too, was written in heaven when you were baptized, and Jesus intercedes on your behalf. In the midst of your troubles you can put your full trust in the Lord who bears you in his arms in times of distress. You need no other refuge.

20 / Have I Ever Come to Faith?

"Our salvation is nearer now than when we first believed" Ro 13:11.

IT IS A GREAT comfort to be able to join with the apostle in confessing that "our salvation is nearer now than when we first believed." How wonderful it is to be able to trust, in the midst of trials and temptations, that we are close to salvation.

But notice that the apostle points to the time when he came to faith. What comfort can I find in the nearness of salvation if I have never come to faith? The word of the apostle does not comfort me; it makes me restless and drives me to self-examination. What is there in my life to suggest that I have come to true faith?

Nevertheless, there is comfort in asking this question. When I am forced to examine myself to see if I have I ever come to true faith, I am closer to salvation than when I live in false peace. The Lord's presence shatters the peace of indifference.

"How can we get near salvation?" Let us read Paul's words very carefully. He speaks of salvation coming near us, making a very important point. I cannot approach salvation even with my very best efforts; salvation comes to me! Salvation is in God's hands; from Him I can expect everything!

Self-examination is the most important thing for me: have I ever come to faith?

21 / True Fear Is Life

"The fear of the Lord is a fountain of life" Pr 14:27.

THERE IS much false fear that robs our lives of its joy. But the Bible speaks also of true fear, the fear of God, which is the power of life. "The fear of the Lord is the beginning of knowledge" Prov. 1:7. "I know that it will go better with God-fearing men, who are reverent before God" Ec 8:12. "He fulfills the desires of those who fear him; he hears their cry and saves them" Ps 145:19. "The fear of the Lord is a fountain of life."

People are eager to believe in their own and other's ideas, but fear of the Lord will help us live according to God's word. Whoever lives in fear of the Lord will honor God's ideas. He will be protected from his own interpretation of matters pertaining to God and eternity, and will be satisfied with what God says in His word. He will not follow his own ideas of what is right and wrong, but will follow God's will.

Fear of the Lord enables a person to accept the portion in life that God has given him. Many of us waste our lives in constant conflict with God; but fear of the Lord leads us to humble acceptance of God's way, which is, after all, the best way.

Fear of the Lord makes us careful not to oppress and harm others, for God is the protector of all people. Therefore, we must be reconciled to others, knowing that we will all appear before the same Judge.

In all these ways "the fear of the Lord is a fountain of life."

22 / Aglow in the Lord

"Keep your spiritual fervor" Ro 12:11.

MANY ARE lukewarm; few are fervent. Those who are lukewarm will experience the Lord's rejection, but not just as a future possibility. The lukewarm make wrong choices already in this life and so lose the blessings of God.

Luther says the Christian is like a wet log, which will not burn. But if the wet log comes in contact with a red-hot iron, it will eventually begin to glow. In an apocryphal saying of Jesus we are told that "he who is close to me is close to fire." Living close to Christ, our ruined and worthless being encounters a spiritual fervor; but apart from him we are like a wet, cold log.

Spiritual fervor is due to the presence of Christ in my life. It is not a Christian characteristic, growing as a result of some change in me. Christ is like fire, and anyone close to him will begin to glow. We must get close to Christ, for, as Paul says, "Christ's love compels us" 2 Co 5:14. This is spiritual fervor, and it happens through the gracious work of the Spirit.

An essential part of this work is that the Lord removes from us everything we have, even our piety, so that Christ becomes absolutely necessary.

But we will not easily admit that Christ is our only help. Without misfortune and problems it seems impossible to come to knowledge of self and knowledge of the merciful Lord Jesus. But, most of all, we need the word of the gospel. When we are moved by the Holy Spirit, through inward promptings and gospel promises, we live in constant fellowship with the Lord. We find inner spiritual fervor, which is not a natural enthusiasm, but the glow of the fire of the Lord Christ.

23 / To Believe Is to Love

"Now that you have purified yourselves [your souls] by obeying the truth so that you have sincere love for your brothers, love one another deeply, from the heart" 1 P 1:22.

LIFE HAS so many facets that we cannot squeeze it into any single form. We cannot understand the nature of reality by living in an ivory tower and spinning theories about how things should be.

The diversity of life is expressed also in spiritual matters. God seems to have all kinds of children, and we should not expect everyone to think as we do.

Does this mean that everyone is saved by his own faith? That would be a great misunderstanding! There is salvation only in Jesus Christ. "There is no other name under heaven given to men by which we must be saved" Ac 4:12.

What then are we to think of the diversity that prevails among people who confess the name of Christ? The writers of the Bible answer: Speak the truth in love (Eph 4:15). Do not compromise the truth; act honestly and with integrity. These are basic guidelines for those who confess the name of Christ. Falsehood of any kind is not to be permitted in Christian relationships.

Christians in New Testament times were tempted to reject those who behaved shamefully and deviously. But, God lets His sun shine on the wicked as well as the good. Even when we cannot accept the ideas of other Christians, we must walk in love, thinking and speaking only good about each other and explaining everything in the best possible light. We must be patient and bear one another's burdens. Whoever acknowledges his own wickedness and experiences God's love in spite of it cannot help but love others. If we look to our own convictions as final we will easily ignore the Bible and its truth for us. "Whoever does not love does not know God, because God is love" 1 Jn 4:8.

24 / The Old Self Is to Be Crucified, Not Changed

"For we know that our old self was crucified with him so that the body of sin might be done away with" Ro 6:6.

WE THINK our old self needs to be changed into something pious and innocent. Some who have been awakened by God begin to clean up their lives, change their habits, and practice piety, so that they might be what God wants them to be. But, all of this is hopeless. Even the most sincere strugglers will become exhausted, frustrated, and, finally, depressed. Some of us may try to compromise our principles and deceive ourselves in order to look good. But we end up living schizophrenically, believing one thing and doing another.

The Lord does not intend our old selves to be changed into something else. The old self must die; it must be crucified.

In daily sorrow and repentance our old self must be drowned together with all its wicked desires. But how? By being buried into Christ's death. The old self is buried at the foot of the cross. Therefore, Christians seek to take their place at the foot of the cross, every day, just as they are.

But, how does one get there? Only through sorrow and repentance. You must let the Savior know the truth about yourself. You do not try to change yourself, adorning yourself with piety so as to focus on your faith and holiness. You must approach your Savior each time as though for the first time. Prior acts of devotion mean nothing. We are fallen creatures, but we approach Christ and ask him once more to receive us. We can tell him everything, even that which we are too embarrassed to tell anyone else. It is in coming to Christ every day that the old self is crucified and a new self is born.

25 / Whose Praise Do You Seek?

*"How can you believe if you accept praise from one
another"* Jn 5:44.

LUST FOR PRAISE can drive people to do things that turn out
to be a blessing to others. More often, however, it brings a curse.
A person sick with lust for praise is irritable, oppressing and
envying others. The lust for praise is destructive because it
violates the law of love.

The greatest tragedy, however, is that lust for praise
prevents a person from truly believing in God. By violating the
law of love a person who is possessed by lust for praise reveals
that he does not believe in God. "Whoever does not love does not
know God, because God is love" 1 Jn 4:8. Likewise, "Anyone who
does not love his brother, whom he has seen, cannot love God,
whom he has not seen" 1 Jn 4:20.

A person possessed by lust for praise is unwilling to
acknowledge what God's Spirit wants to reveal about him. "God
opposes the proud but gives grace to the humble" 1 P 5:5. A
sinner must be ready to be humbled before God, but a person
seeking his own glory will resist such humbling experiences.
With all of his good qualities, talents, busy activities and zeal he
tries to hide his misery from God and others. Seeking his own
glory he compromises with the world, wanting to be an
enlightened Christian in step with the times.

We must be ready to accept being broken by God as evidence
of His mercy, regardless of how painful it may be. For without
such humbling, we cannot believe in God. This holds true for all
Christians, even the best.

26 / We Are Still on the Way

*"Not that I have already obtained all this, or have
already been made perfect, but I press on to take hold of
that for which Christ Jesus took hold of me"* Phil 3:12.

"WHEN THE HOUSE is ready, death arrives," says an ancient
adage. A person who feels that he has made it, who no longer
needs to learn but thinks he is capable and knowledgeable in all
things, is inwardly dead. He no longer exudes natural,

spontaneous joy. He rules over everything. In self-sufficiency he sets himself above others, lacking humility and love. He is dead, fruitless and cold. A Christian is never complete. "Not that I have already obtained all this, or have already been made perfect, but I press on." To keep His own in a constant sense of incompleteness, God undresses them, humbling them, often in unexpected and unpleasant ways. We need to clearly understand that the Lord is protecting us in this way from spiritual death. Real life, including the life of faith, goes together with an abiding sense of incompleteness.

"When the house is ready, death arrives." It would be easy to think that we do not need to take the present moment seriously, since we are not yet complete. After all, we are not yet living our full lives. What difference does it make what we think or do, how we spend our time, since we are not yet what we shall one day become. We rationalize that sometime in the future, when we are fully capable, we shall really apply ourselves. But our entire life is nothing but continuing incompleteness. If we do not give ourselves to the present moment and assume responsibility now, our entire life will be wasted and we will never accomplish anything worthwhile. To the very end everything will seem temporary, until we are called to appear before the judge. "When the house is ready, death arrives."

27 / Christ Is the Light We Need

"In him was life, and that life was the light of men" Jn 1:4.

YOU YEARN for the light. You are uncertain how to make the decisions you face. It is difficult to distinguish between right and wrong. You are sensitive to the influence of others and adjust to their points of view, because you yourself lack clarity about the right road. Often you agree with the last people you met, and yet you heard a variety of different views.

Do we recognize ourselves in this picture? We are like leaves blown this way and that way in the wind, leaves that drop to the ground in the fall and are scattered.

"Life was the light of men." What life? That which is among us in Jesus Christ! By reason alone we can never achieve true knowledge of how we are to live. We can never possess truth just with our thoughts. Truth seeks to possess us, to govern us. Christ seeks to give himself to us and become our life. To the extent that Christ finds room in our lives, we have the true light for life's various decisions.

This applies to everything, not just to spiritual life. If Christ rules over us, he directs us into the proper paths. In this way he is our light. "For with you is the fountain of life; in your light we see light" Ps 36:9.

But do we want to step forward into Christ's light? Dare we permit him to illumine the darkest corners of our lives?

28 / The First Love Needs Renewal

"You do not want to leave too, do you?' Jesus asked the Twelve" Jn 6:67.

PERHAPS THE GREAT CROWD of people who withdrew from Jesus in the incident recorded in John 6 did not fall into any particular sin. Very likely they were the kind of people we are: good, God-fearing people; devout and enthusiastic about good things in life. But they no longer followed Jesus. Enthusiasm for the Lord had disappeared; the first love was lost.

We cannot stay with Jesus unless we are renewed in our admiration and enthusiasm. We cannot continue to be enthusiastic about his cause, because the passing of time seems to distance us from Jesus. Therefore, a disciple always looks for something that will renew his faith. Jesus promised, "You shall see heaven open" Jn 1:51. But, we cannot merely enjoy our glimpse of heaven and let it go at that. Over and over again we must let go of things in our past and live for the great treasure which we have glimpsed.

We live in a time of apostasy, and many people are leaving Jesus. The true disciple, however, remains enthusiastic about Jesus' cause and his heart is aglow. From the signs of the times and the promises of the Word, we can conclude that significant events of God's Kingdom are taking place. We are living in the spring of God's Kingdom. Summer will not come unless the dirt and debris are cleared away, but we are beginning to see this happening. Disciples are looking for the restoration of all things, for which their hearts are on fire.

29 / Our Power Source Is Christ

"I want to know Christ and the power of his resurrection"
Phil 3:10.

IN THE BIBLE "to know" does not mean simply to have
information and knowledge about something; it means
possession, being in a living relationship. To know the power of
Christ's resurrection does not mean we know this or that about
such power but that we experience it, are sustained by an inner
relationship to it, and possess it. Paul's struggle of faith had as
its daily goal the knowledge of the power of Christ's
resurrection.

But what is this significant power of resurrection? It cannot
possibly be anything other than the living, risen, and present
Lord himself. Paul strives to be constantly near the living Lord.
In other words, he wants the Lord to direct him, counsel him,
have mercy on him, raise him, take care of him, rule over him,
and sanctify him. For Paul, Christ was not a distant historical
character, someone written about between the covers of a book.
Christ was a living reality for Paul. "I no longer live, but Christ
lives in me" Ga 2:20. Paul lived in the Lord Christ. The goal of
his struggle was not that Paul might become something in
himself, on his own, but that he might be dependent upon Christ
in everything. "In Him we live and move and have our being" Ac
17:28.

The struggle for wholeness of Paavo Ruotsalainen, the great
19th-century lay spiritual leader in Finland, had to do with
gaining this inward knowledge of Christ and living in it daily.
His struggle was the same as Paul's, to know the power of
Christ's resurrection. According to Ruotsalainen, we need to be
engaged in this struggle of faith on a daily basis. When the poor
sinner seeks to draw close to Christ and appeals to his divine
promise of grace, the living Lord receives him, raises him,
carries him, and saves him.   The more willing we are, like
Paul, to consider everything as rubbish, both our piety and
perversity, and surrender to Christ alone as lost sinners, the
more powerfully will we experience the power of the resurrection
of our Lord.

30 / The Promise and the Blessing

"I will not let you go unless you bless me" Gn 32:26.

BY WHAT RIGHT did the patriarch Jacob demand a blessing in
his night struggle by the river Jabbok? We could point to Jacob's
persistent, fervent prayers. Jacob prayed with great devotion
and concentration. There is no reason, however, to assume that
his prayers qualified him for the blessing. During his long years
of exile Jacob had prayed much, always remembering his crime,
and he was unable to consider himself guiltless before God. Now
in his night struggle he did not expect his prayers or his piety to
bring God's blessing.

Where did he find the courage to say, "I will not let you go
unless you bless me?" From God's promise. In Bethel, on his way
to the foreign country, he had received from God the promise: "I
am with you and will watch over you wherever you go, and I will
bring you back to this land" Gn 28:15. Jacob had some good
points along with his faults and failures, but God had stamped
him with His blessing. "I will not leave you until I have done
what I have promised to you" Gn 28:15. God's promises are
stronger than our failures. Sin cannot nullify what God has
promised. Jacob clung to the promise God had made to him. In
spite of obvious facts to the contrary, he appealed to it, and
received the blessing.

This shows how we too can become partakers of God's
blessing. It is comforting to know it does not depend on what we
are but on God's will and promise. God's promises have been
given to us in Christ. According to God's word Christ has come
to seek and to save that which was lost. Already in holy baptism
Christ was given to us, and in His word God offers His Christ to
all poor and condemned sinners. In Ro 8:30 we are told that
those whom God has called he has also predestined or chosen.
Behind our being called is the eternal decision of God's grace.

May all today's deceitful Jacobs, solitary wrestlers in the
night, take hold of God's promise in Christ and hang on to it, no
matter what. Then they too will be blessed.

31 / To Pray Is to Live

"They will pray as I bring them back" Jr 31:9.

IN THE JOURNAL of J. Fr. Bergh, a young Finnish pastor who died in 1866, we find the prayer: "Guide me every blink of the eye, that you may be able to take as your own all my words, thoughts, desires, and deeds and that they may be pleasing to you."

Do we really ask for anything when we pray? A minute after we pray we barely remember our prayer. Is that praying? We lazy and worldly Christians should listen to the prayers of those who pray to God in spirit and in truth.

A person who asks the Lord to take possession of his words, thoughts, desires, and deeds, is not praying absent-mindedly or carelessly. He really asks for something. He is afraid of his own thoughts, words, and deeds, and asks the Lord to make him a living member of his Body. He knows that his entire life belongs to the Lord. And so he leaves himself in the Lord's hands.

"All my words, thoughts, desires and deeds!" A person who prays in this way has no idle time. There is not even a moment when he does not turn to the Lord. Is there anything he does, any situation he encounters, that does not call for prayer? Such a person is very brave in thinking the Lord cares about his thoughts, words, and deeds. He assumes the Lord is able to use him in his service.   Do you have this kind of sensitivity and courage, this kind of trust and struggle in your prayer life? Consider what someone has said, "We pray as we live."

February

1 / We Are Called to Be Devout

"He was righteous and devout" Lk 2:25.

THE WORD DEVOUT can make us uncomfortable if it brings to mind an image of a person who talks piously but walks without purpose. When used to describe such a person the term really means "hypocrite." In the Bible, however, "devout" originally meant sensitive or cautious. A devout person, thus, is sensitive to God's holy will. A godly person is wary about contradicting God's will through carelessness or ignorance.

Simeon was a devout person. His sensitivity had often caused serious conflict with his contemporaries, especially the temple priests. While others went along with so-called enlightened thinking and bowed to popular opinion, Simeon sought to do God's will in all things. He especially wanted to be faithful to the sacred writings. Such was his piety by which he served the Lord. God revealed His will to Simeon and directed him through His Holy Spirit.

We, too, can be called devout. We will never experience the gracious influence of the Holy Spirit unless we are sensitive to God's will and careful about following it in all things. When we do, we may run into trouble and experience conflict with the people closest to us. We may find ourselves distressed when others are happy and happy when others are distressed. But we find our reward in the Lord, in the awareness of his presence, in the inner witness to the Spirit, and in the marvelous hidden power with which the Lord cares for his own.

The apostle urges us, "Train yourself to be godly. Godliness has value for all things, holding promise for both the present life and the life to come" 1 Ti 4:7f.

2 / Are We Ashamed of Christ?

"Christ's love compels us" 2 Co 5:14.

"FOR OUT OF THE OVERFLOW of his heart his mouth speaks" Lk. 6:45. Our everyday experience clearly demonstrates the truth of what Jesus said. It is easy to talk about that which fills our hearts. If you think highly of someone, his or her name comes very easily to the tip of your tongue.

But, what about our heart-relationship with the Savior? Many of us find it difficult to talk about Him and matters of the soul are seldom the subject of our conversation. Only with great effort can we talk with one another about that which is most important to us. We avoid asking each other about our spiritual struggle, our prayer life, and our relationship with the Savior. All of this indicates that our salvation is not our highest priority. Our hearts are not filled with the knowledge of Christ.

But, the Lord expects his people to converse about matters of the soul when they encounter one another. He expects us to share news of the inner battle, the continuing fight against sin. He expects us to share with each other Christ's revelations about himself. "Christ's love compels us." If the Lord has become dear to us, it will not be difficult to talk about him.

Sometimes we talk about helping Christians become active. This is a genuine and necessary concern, for we do not need crowds of inactive Christians. No matter what tasks people have, those who know Christ's love have a mutual ministry: talking about matters of salvation with one another. And it is good to bring these matters to the attention of the indifferent, too. It may leave a lasting impression on them that will eventually turn their lives around.

But it is imperative for pilgrims on the spiritual road to share these things with one another, providing much needed support on the narrow road, where spiritual exhaustion and weariness are a constant danger. Many have given up the struggle long before the journey was over.

3 / Prayer Is Not Mere Pious Prattle

"What do you want me to do for you?" Lk 18:41.

IT WAS NOT ENOUGH for the blind beggar alongside the road to Jericho to cry out to Jesus, "Jesus, son of David, have mercy on me!" Jesus wanted him to be more specific, so he asked him, "What do you want me to do for you?"

This happens even today when Jesus stops to help us. In our prayers we rightly seek refuge in God's grace, but it is not enough to acknowledge our need of grace in a general way. The Lord wants to open our eyes to the specific needs that prompt us to call for his help. He asks us to take a closer look at our personal situation and examine ourselves more carefully. He also compels us to check our petitions to see if they are in harmony with God's will. To that end he asks us the significant question, "What do you want me to do for you?"

Now ask yourself what you really are asking from the Lord. Do you really expect him to answer your prayer? Or is your prayer merely an expression of your thoughts and pious feelings?

Jesus talked about people who thought they needed to use a million exquisite words when they prayed and ended up praying for the sake of praying without anything specific in mind. This kind of prayer is empty piety, rather than serious and specific asking, seeking, and knocking.

4 / Christ Is Our Godliness

"Beyond all question, the mystery of godliness is great" 1 Ti 3:16.

WHEN WE MEET a person whose whole being is a powerful testimony to his faith, a person who has the power of godliness and not just the form, we readily assume the godliness hides a mystery, and we look for explanations.

Perhaps the secret is a very active and disciplined prayer life? A godly person is certainly persistent in prayer, spending much time on his knees before the Lord. Walking or working, his thoughts rise to God in prayer.

Or perhaps true godliness is the fruit of intercession? Prayers of intercession have miraculous effect even upon unborn generations. If we expect our children to live true Christian lives, we need to offer plenty of prayers for them.

Again, we may think the mystery of godliness is the cross which a person must bear, both inner and outer crosses. True again! All godly people have a cross to bear. If you desire to live and die in a godly way, be prepared to take up a cross.

But none of these things constitutes the mystery of godliness. The Bible says that Christ is the mystery of godliness. The power of life flows from him, not from us, not from our prayers, not from anything that we are or do. Christ, the Son of God who became man, the Christ who was sacrificed for us on Golgotha, is the mystery of godliness.

And he is a mystery, found only by those who have been awakened. And, in spite of times when it feels that Christ is absent, be assured that you really have found him.

5 / Only God's Will Is Good

"Yet I am always with you; you hold me by my right hand. You guide me with your counsel" Ps 73: 23f.

OUR GOD is a hidden God, whose thoughts are not our thoughts and whose ways are not our ways. That's why we often become impatient and complain when we cannot have our own way.

Misfortunes and troubles are an important part of God's way of teaching us, for they unveil our true goals in life. When we murmur and complain in times of trouble, we show that our own plans are more important to us than God's. In our piety we have been living for ourselves and not for the Lord. Our own interests, prosperity, and will have guided our decisions.

Submitting to God's will is never easy, especially when we sincerely seek the welfare of God's cause but find that the road is blocked. But Paul was able to say that he commends himself as a servant of God "in great endurance, in troubles, hardships and distresses" 2 Co 6:4. He had learned in God's school to surrender his own plans, purposes, and selfish mind, and put his trust in God's guidance. If we believe in God we need not murmur and complain, even in times of trials and tribulations. We can quietly humble ourselves under God's mighty hand, trusting God's will to be done.

God seeks to overrule our sinful will. But God also has our "good will" at heart, to the extent that it is possible to talk about human "good will."

> In misfortune I am bitter,
> In fortune I am proud,
> Unless you guide me, Jesus.

And this will not happen until God breaks our will and takes our entire life into His own hands.

6 / Prayer Presupposes Repentance

"My house will be called a house of prayer, but you are making it a den of robbers" Mt 21:13.

THESE WORDS of Jesus usually bring to mind the commercialism Jesus found in the temple area in Jerusalem. A holy wrath was kindled in our Lord, so that he dumped the tables of the moneychangers and drove out the noisy merchants who were desecrating the holy temple.

Such things never occur in our houses of worship where we observe proper liturgical order! We cannot imagine Jesus visiting our churches with a whip in his hand. When we consider the matter more closely, however, we realize that these words are meant for us, too. This becomes clear when we consider the context of the Old Testament words quoted by Jesus.

Jeremiah spoke these words to people who crowded into the house of the Lord during national catastrophes, practicing their piety with no intention of repenting in their daily life. In doing so they made the temple into a literal "den of robbers," where they attempted to steal God's grace. Disobedient and unclean, guilty of robbery and adultery, they looked for divine help with no intention of changing their way of living.

We must not do this. The house of the Lord is not "a den of robbers," which we can visit once a week only to continue our ungodly ways. The house of the Lord is a place of prayer, where contrite hearts pour out their corruption before the Lord in prayer and experience the forgiving and cleansing power of the blood of Jesus. The House of the Lord is certainly open to the most miserable of sinners, but it must not be made "a den of robbers." It is a place of repentant prayer.

7 / Awakening Comes from Above

"The wind blows wherever it pleases. You hear its sound, but you cannot tell where it comes from or where it is going" Jn 3:8.

WE DO NOT CHOOSE the time of an awakening nor do we direct its course. When times of awakening come, "the wind is blowing from heaven across the earth." But Christians do well to note the signs of the times and to ask about awakenings.

One Christian who lived in the midst of God's works recognized the preconditions of awakening and wrote: An awakening is approaching:

when God sees it necessary;

when the wickedness of sinners begins to sadden, humble, and afflict Christians;

when Christians begin to pray for an awakening;

when ministers and other servants of the Word begin to yearn for an awakening;

when Christians begin to confess their sins to one another; when Christians are ready for the sacrifices which the advancement of God's work asks of them;

when ministers submit to God's using of anyone He pleases in His service; and

when Christians realize that an awakening is absolutely necessary.

Signs such as these are not the product of human activity. They are not decided upon at meetings, nor are they the result of speeches or articles. They are the work of the Holy Spirit. Every Christian who is awake does well to pay attention to them.

Some think it old-fashioned to talk about awakenings today. But there has seldom been a time when awakenings were considered fashionable. Awakenings come from somewhere other than our world, and even today they arrive when "the wind is blowing from heaven across the earth."

8 / Do You Have a Passport?

"Do not be arrogant, but be afraid" Ro 11:20.

A CHILD WHO PLAYS on thin ice in spite of warnings shows the wrong kind of bravery. Many people have faith too weak to carry them across the deep places of life. They daringly set out without a living faith-relationship with the Lord, and venture into the tasks, temptations, and conflicts of the day without Him. They may not run into any serious trouble. But, in the large and small concerns of life they will make wrong decisions, speak wrong words, and think and act in the wrong way, because their faith is superficial. Sins of omission are especially troublesome, resulting from a superficial faith that does not require one to be awake and alert.

Get rid of all false bravery! Let us be more cautious in our faith! Find more time to pause before the holy God! Repent more! Wait and ask more often for the powers of God! Pray for increasing presence of the Holy Spirit!

Reflect on these questions: Will I continue to serve two lords? Will I hang on to a bad conscience in matters about which the Lord has reminded me many times? It is dangerous to live without paying attention to the admonitions of the Holy Spirit. Paul says that all who try to combine a life of faith and a bad conscience will suffer shipwreck in their faith. You will lose everything if you continue recklessly on your way.

In former days devout people said that a Christian must always carry his "passport" with him. By passport they meant the inner witness and assurance of the Holy Spirit. Whoever dares to be without this passport will come to grief. This does not mean that we can carry this passport in our pocket or purse and pull it out on demand. It is something God provides as we strive for it again and again. This passport is the goal of our faith struggle; we need assurance that we are God's children. Do we dare leave home without our passport?

9 / Faith Is Activity

"The work of God is this: to believe in the one he has sent"
Jn 6:29.

AT FIRST these words of Jesus sound strange. How can faith be some kind of work? Is not faith the opposite of work? People have tried to deal with this problem by explaining that Jesus really meant that faith is an accomplishment of God, a work that God performs in a person. However, it still seems that the Biblical context of this word does not justify such an interpretation.

"He who comes to me will never go hungry, and he who believes in me will never be thirsty" Jn 6:35. In this statement two things are set alongside each other: believing in Jesus and coming to Him. Two verses later we have the wonderful promise: "Whoever comes to me I will never drive away" Jn 6:37. This, too, is a matter of believing in Jesus.

In the Gospel of John faith is always spoken of as believing, in other words, as action. Thus, the work involved in believing in Jesus is a movement toward him. Faith is not a state of rest; it is actively coming to Jesus. Yet we must remember that we move toward Jesus only because God draws us. "No one can come to me unless the Father who sent me draws him" Jn 6:44. How the Father draws us is described in the same chapter in the Gospel of John: "Everyone who listens to the Father and learns from Him comes to me" Jn 6:45. Our part in the work of believing involves listening and learning. We are to accept His counsel and follow it. No one comes to faith or lives in faith in a dormant state; faith is movement and activity. There is no other way to believe in Jesus.

10 / Created to Be Loved

"Dear friends, let us love one another, for love comes from God" 1 Jn 4:7.

THE STUDY of human beings has shown that emotions play a decisive role in life. The idea that we are purely rational beings is shallow. A person's fortune and misfortune depend on the healthy development of one's emotional life. For example, many illnesses that seem unrelated to an individual's mental state stem in large measure from our way of dealing with various life-situations, in other words, our emotional life.

This knowledge places special demands on parents and others who deal with little children. The souls of children are like wax, easily impressed by whatever happens in their environment. Impressions received in early years often continue to hurt people the rest of their lives. Perverse and spiritually sick people have often never recovered from childhood wounds to their souls. It is of utmost importance for mothers and fathers to love their children, bring joy and sunshine into their lives, and live intimately with them.

Where can we find the needed patience, tenderness, unselfishness, and love? Only in Jesus Christ who is the fountain of love. Especially today, when the daily struggle drains many parents physically and emotionally, we must find this love. Our hearts must not be taken over by the selfish search for pleasure, lest we become responsible for the suffering of others.

People need to be loved. That is how God has created us. But God also gave His only Son to die on the cross, so that His love might break our selfishness and permeate our world through us.

11 / The Miracle of Peace

"When a man's ways are pleasing to the Lord, he makes even his enemies live at peace with him" Pr 16:7.

TWISTED AND BITTER interpersonal relationships, found even among Christians, are the devil's work. For that reason they can never be repaired by human effort. Even people who pray will be unable to patch them up. No matter how much we ask for forgiveness, reconciliation will not take place. We may be able to live honorably and peacefully on the outside, but our hearts will remain far apart from each other.

What is humanly impossible, however, is possible for God. The Lord is able to make friends out of enemies. How he does it in any one instance is up to him, but there is always mutual humbling. Reconciliation will occur only when hearts break and melt.

When a person has lost his personal dignity and worth, when his own godliness can no longer cover his wicked and vicious nature, when he can no longer see God because of the burden of his sins, then his faith is credited as righteousness. "To the man who does not work but trusts God who justifies the wicked, his faith is credited as righteousness" Ro 4:5. This person, who has lost his own righteousness, is pleasing to God for the sake of Christ's merit. The New Testament tells us that only such a person is pleasing to God, and that He will instill in him a desire for reconciliation.

A person remains unclean, but the righteous God sees Christ in him and he becomes acceptable to Him. Christ's way is pleasing to God and, true to His word, God makes even his enemies live at peace with Him. This miracle is from the Lord.

12 / The Lamb's Way Is the Safe Way

"They follow the Lamb wherever he goes" Rev 14:4.

WE ARE people who live largely in herds. Our political and social views, our understanding of the day's events, our interests and ideals are usually determined by the wind that happens to be blowing. The very possibility of propaganda rests on the fact that people can be manipulated without realizing it. Independent thinkers who form their own opinions and know what they want are few and far between. Independent thinking requires thorough knowledge, freedom from the lust for power, an unprejudiced search for truth, the willingness to suffer, and plenty of reflection.

As Christians we often belong to crowds that are led hither and yon and we are in constant danger of going with the current. The Bible warns that especially in the last times this will have tragic consequences. The worldly spirit of apostasy will gain unprecedented power, and will use that power against everyone unwilling to be an obedient servant. "He also forced everyone, small and great, rich and poor, free and slave, to receive a mark on his right hand or on his forehead, so that no one could buy or sell unless he had the mark, which is the name of the beast or the number of his name" Rev 13:16f.

There is but one way of escape: "They follow the Lamb wherever He goes." We must stay in contact with the crucified and risen Lord, whose way is the true way. Whoever attends the school of this Lord will be freed from the tutelage of others and will learn to discipline himself, deny himself, and willingly accept being a minority of one. Quiet and humble, he dares not take a single step unless the Lord directs him. God's Word is a lamp to his feet, and he will seek to judge all things in its light.

We have been called to follow the Lamb, no matter where He goes. His way is the way of the cross, but it is the way that leads to the dawning of the day of salvation.

13 / True Food for the Soul

"Then Jesus declared, 'I am the bread of life. He who comes to me will never go hungry, and he who believes in me will never be thirsty'" Jn 6:35.

SOME PEOPLE live by what others think of them. All of us are tempted at one time or other to take our turn at such a table. Healthy self-knowledge is important for our spiritual life, and a person who lacks it is unfortunate. "I can't do anything," will be constantly on his lips. Afraid to try anything, he buries the talent God has given him. His self-image becomes distorted by viewing himself repeatedly in the mirror of what others think of him. He is satisfied if he feels they think well of him, but devastated if he senses their disapproval.

A person who lives by what others think of him is easily led into interpersonal difficulties. Numerous conflicts stem from the lust for the glory that comes from other people. Difficulties and disputes among church workers derive from the same source. Under such circumstances people are easily offended and hurt and insist on getting their own way.

This, undoubtedly, is one of the pet sins of Christians. Jesus says, "How can you believe if you accept praise from one another, yet make no effort to obtain the praise that comes from the only God" Jn 5:44. Your effort to believe comes to naught if you feed on your personal glory.

Christ is the life-giving bread. Whoever lives the hidden life in the Lord feasts at a table that makes it unnecessary for him to seek nourishment elsewhere. The more intensely you abide in Him who is the true food of the soul, the more successful will be your striving to overcome the tragic tendency to live by what others think.

14 / Branded by Christ

"... until Christ is formed in you" Ga 4:19.

BEING A CHRISTIAN is neither a matter of ideals nor imitation of the great Lord and Master. Being a Christian is a matter of belonging to Christ and living in union with him. "If we have been united with him like this in his death, we will certainly also be united with him in his resurrection. For we know that our old self was crucified with him so that the body of sin might be done away with, that we should no longer be slaves to sin" Ro 6:5f.

Many Christians wear themselves out trying to achieve some Christian ideal or trying to follow Christ by strictly imitating him. They become victims of the kind of legalism which was practiced by the Pharisees. But, whoever belongs to Christ must live his life with Christ and accept Christ's fate as his own.

The Christian is called to run after Christ, not a Christian ideal. Keep your eyes on Jesus Christ! Find true liberation in being able to run after him! Union with Christ is more than learning his teachings or following his example; it is sharing the same fate. God gives us a cross, making us participants in Christ's death and resurrection. He who carries the cross as he works his way to Christ will receive the mark of Christ. He will be branded with Christ's death and resurrection. Being a Christian means that I, a lost and condemned sinner, belong to Christ. Let Christ be formed in you, so that you will share not only in his death but also in his resurrection!

15 / The Nature of Mercy

"You...delight to show mercy" Mic 7:18.

WE PAY little attention to what total strangers may think about us. We ignore their comments and criticisms. But if someone close to us exposes our faults we are compelled to examine ourselves, especially if our friend appears to suffer because of them. Love that suffers with us softens the blisters of evil and prepares them for lancing.

This is how God works. God's mercy will not overlook our wickedness. Our indifference, half-heartedness, and deliberate sins do not meet with His approval. But, in his mercy He seeks to rescue us from our bondage to sin and Satan, and preserve us from temporal and eternal hell. It would not be an act of mercy were God to pat us on the head and leave us where we are. It is merciful when God frees us from our sins.

"Repentance begins with love," the young Luther was told by his father confessor. We are led to repentance, confession, and the putting away of sin only when we experience God's love. If you only knew how God feels about you, you would want to be freed from your sins, and awakened from the spiritual stupor in which you are still living. "The blood draws one away from sin." Nothing else speaks as powerfully of God's love as the blood of Christ shed on the cross for us.

16 / The Joy Jesus Gives

"Grace and truth came through Jesus Christ" Jn 1:17.

IT MAY BE too much to say that life without Jesus is joyless and gloomy; many an indifferent and worldly person is rather well off and quite happy. But an awakened person, nevertheless, speaks the truth when he says, "Without Jesus I am lost."

Our lives are wastelands without Jesus. Without him we make wrong choices and draw false conclusions, and God's purpose for our lives is not achieved in our homes, at our work places, or among friends--nowhere. Above all, we thwart God's will for eternity. Instead of heaven, hell becomes our home.

We keep trying to be Christians without Jesus, without living in true union with him. Nature and grace, flesh and spirit, fight against each other. Every awakened person still bears in his heart hatred against Jesus. We need to admit that even Christians lack true desire to study the word of God and to do the will of Jesus. In a godly person this is evident in an attempt to manage one's Christianity by oneself through repentance, faith, and striving. In other words, we still live under the law, demanding of ourselves that which the Lord Jesus can and wants to give to sinners. The most unfortunate opposition to Jesus is our unwillingness to be sinners who can live only by grace.

It is really burdensome for an awakened person to try to fight against sin with his own powers. The road of good resolutions, on which a person struggles to gain the upper hand over sin, is a difficult road. On that road we get lost, unless we humble ourselves and turn to the one who calls to himself all who are weary and burdened that he might give them rest (Mt 11:28).

Are you tired of your piety as a way of trying to be a Christian without Christ? Surrender to grace, receive everything as a gift, right now. For in the end you too will be lost without Jesus. In him alone are grace and truth.

17 / What Does Jesus Think of You?

"Jesus would not entrust himself to them, for he knew all men" Jn 2:24.

JOHN TELLS us that while Jesus was in Jerusalem during the Passover festival many believed in his name when they saw the miracles he did; but then adds that Jesus did not entrust himself to them. He knew what was in their hearts. Here, already at the time of the apostles, is a distinction between false faith and true faith. It is not enough to have some kind of faith; only true faith is saving faith.

These Jews apparently admired Jesus as a remarkable man but did not care to become his disciples. They did not really need him, for in their piety they already had a good opinion about themselves. In other words, their imagined goodness, not their wickedness, kept them from true faith in Jesus.

A living faith is born only in a terrified conscience, something that was lacking in these people. For that reason Jesus did not entrust himself to them.

Jesus' true calling is to be the Savior of sinners. He is unwilling to play any lesser or secondary role in our lives. He entrusts himself only to those to whom he has become absolutely necessary. But he offers himself to anyone who turns to him in desperation.

People may look upon you as a believer, but what does Jesus see? Has he entrusted himself to you? Our own opinion, and what others think of us, will not guarantee that our relationship to the Lord is right. The most important thing is what the Lord thinks about our faith.

18 / The Lord's Road the Right Road

"Those who are led by the Spirit of God are sons of God"
Ro 8:14.

THERE IS a big difference between the children of God and the children of the world. The latter think they know everything. They are ready to advise and teach others. They know how to criticize everything and everybody. The children of God, on the other hand, feel helpless. They are childlike. In various ways God has emptied them of their own wisdom and revealed to them their foolishness. Thus He has made room in them for His Holy Spirit. You see, God can fill only empty vessels. All who are led by the Holy Spirit go through many humblings. The more fervently the Lord's people pray for the fullness of the Holy Spirit, the more inept and impoverished they become.

It is not a simple thing to know how to live as one should, to see things in their true light, to make correct observations and to draw the right conclusions, and then to act according to them. We have so little time to be still and to humble ourselves before God, and so we easily fall in step with the world and follow the spirit of the times. Let us not, therefore, depend on people, not even those we most admire. Detached from people; attached to the Lord! The humble and the childlike cling to the Lord, and He guides them. Even today the Lord guides his people. Remember, at any given time only one road is the right road.

19 / Jesus Is My Joy

"You are filled with an inexpressible and glorious joy" 1 P
1:8.

THE BIBLE calls joy the fruit of the Spirit (Ga 5:22). It also says that the kingdom of God is joy in the Holy Spirit (Ro 14:17). The Holy Spirit is the true fountain of Christian joy. The Spirit of the Lord is the Spirit of joy, but not in the sense that the activity of the Holy Spirit always produces joy in the human heart. On the contrary, very often the Spirit of the Lord must make us feel sorry for ourselves and others by revealing to us the reality of sin. But even then the Spirit of the Lord is preparing our hearts for true joy.

Since it is the Spirit of the Lord who brings true joy into our lives, this joy cannot be found where there is conscious opposition to the work of the Holy Spirit or where hidden deceit divides the heart between God and Satan. The Spirit of the Lord is a sensitive Spirit, who withdraws in sorrow because of our disobedience. But where the soul humbly submits to the admonitions of the Holy Spirit, there the way is open for true joy.

In a deeper sense, true joy is joy in the Lord Christ. The task of the Holy Spirit is to reveal Christ. Wherever sin has been unveiled and the sinner has turned to him who is his helper, there is joy in the Lord. It is not joy about myself, joy about who I am or what I have become, but joy in the Lord, who is so wonderful and good he accepts and acknowledges as his own even somone like me. Therefore joy is joy in the Holy Spirit, whose task is to unite us with the living Lord, our helper.

If you desire joy, glorious joy, examine your relationship to your Savior.

Jesus, joy and life,
Lord of grace and friend.

20 / Eyes Fixed on Jesus

"The Lord is able to make him stand" Ro 14:4.

SPIRITUAL WEAKNESS and many interpersonal conflicts stem largely from the false idea that people can do God's work. In our concern for a close friend, wanting him to find the right path for his life, let us not make impossible demands on him. No one can by his own strength or reason believe in Jesus Christ as his Lord or come to Him (Luther, Small Catechism). Some sort of piety is possible, but true faith which can stand up to temptation and produce patient love is something that only the Lord is able to produce. Let us beseech the Lord in behalf of our friends. "The Lord is able to make him stand."

Even in our own situation, only the Lord can sustain us. When we tire in our striving and stumble in the temptations that surround us in our homes, we should not be surprised. However, "those who hope in the Lord will renew their strength"

Is. 40:31. We need a greater willingness to wait; we need to look more often to God, the one who can and will help us!

The Christian who remembers that the Lord alone has power will pray often. Only as we experience our lack of power will we learn to pray. Wherever there is evidence of God's power in human life, there is always much prayer. We can experience God's power only as we receive it from Him. And how can we receive unless we ask? Only the person who prays will experience God's miracles.

Let this be the motto of our lives: "With eyes fixed on Jesus."

21 / The Lord Can Change Us

"Turn my heart toward your statutes" Ps 119:36.

"GIVE YOUR PEOPLE grace to love what you command and desire what you promise." These are the words of an ancient church prayer. "To love what you command." Is that how it is with us? Is not the contrary a truer description of us? We love our own selves, our own comfort, our own well-being, our own interests. We get excited about things other than God's commandments. "Your statutes are my delight; they are my counselors," writes the Psalmist (Ps 119:24). Who can stand with him?

"To desire what you promise." We are far from this, too! We desire many things, but what little interest we show in God's promises!

"Give your people grace to love what you command and desire what you promise." People regularly rebel against God's commandments and reject God promises, but we can ask God to help us turn from our rebellion. Only by grace are we able to love the Lord's statutes.

God's grace is free, given without charge or merit on our part. The Lord is able to make a person who resists his commandments into one who is submissive, who finds his joy in doing the Lord's will.

"I rejoice in following your statutes as one rejoices in great riches. I meditate on your precepts and consider your ways. I delight in your decrees; I will not neglect your word" Ps 119:14-16.   Happy is the person who has received this grace!

22 / Our Weapons Are Useless

"Who serves as a soldier at his own expense?" 1 Co 9:7.

MEMBERS of the early Christian churches were aware that being a Christian meant war. No one was able to remain a neutral bystander. Had not the Lord said, "He who is not with me is against me?" Mt 12:30.

They were also aware that the Lord provided the weapons. "Who serves as a soldier at his own expense?" The Lord does not send anyone into spiritual battles unequipped. The defeats we suffer are usually due to our attempts to get by with our own weapons when only God's weapons will do.

"Put on the full armor of God, so that when the day of evil comes, you may be able to stand your ground, and after you have done everything, to stand" Eph 6:13. We need the full armor of God. Anything less will not be enough.

Let us note that God will freely supply our needs. If we lack spiritual weapons, it is not because they are unavailable. But, we often fail to understand our absolute need for God's weapons, assume that we can get by without them, and suffer the consequences.

We have all been called to fight for and with Christ. And we will be victorious, provided that our weapons are not our own.

23 / Do Not Give Up the Struggle

"Let the wicked forsake his ways and the evil man his thoughts" Is 55:7.

OF COURSE I must rid myself of evil thoughts, but how is this possible? How can I be freed from the complex of thoughts that fill my consciousness? And what about thoughts that erupt now and then from my unconscious, creating seductive and attractive fantasies, evoking feelings of inferiority and jealousy? These frightening and terrifying fantasies can enslave and imprison me. My conscience says that I ought to get rid of them, but I don't know how. Can a person forsake his thoughts, regardless of what they are?

Some of you may be able to guard your thoughts. I write for those of you who, like me, struggle to do so but often fail. Two things have helped me in my struggle. First, the cross of Jesus. "When we were still powerless, Christ died for the ungodly" Ro 5:6. Focus on the cross so that it moves into the center of all your thoughts. The cross is stronger than all other thoughts and will remain unchanged. No matter how miserable I am, how inferior I feel, how enslaved by my thoughts, Jesus has redeemed me.

From my sins I ought to be freed--
The way to the cross is a free-way!
Is this not too much freedom?
The way to the cross is a free-way!

I can receive and enjoy the grace of God just as I am. The cross of Jesus is my "free-way" to salvation. So, I center my thoughts on the cross.

Second, I must continue to struggle and not give up. God has not promised that Christians will live in perpetual sunshine. On the contrary, the one "who perseveres under trial, because when he has stood the test, he will receive the crown of life" Jas 1:12. I must not become depressed by my failures, lay down my weapons, and give up the fight. I must wage the battle until my last breath. The admonition to "avoid every kind of evil" 1 Th 5:22 includes our evil thoughts. We can look to the pastoral care of the church to find relief from the burdens of conscience. But let us not imagine that the struggle will cease before death.

24 / Serve the Lord Wholeheartedly

"'Bring the whole tithe into the storehouse, that there day be food in my house. Test me in this,' says the Lord Almighty" Ml 3:10.

A MEDIEVAL church builders' union had as its motto: "Only the best for God!" This is a suitable motto for all people hired as builders of God's Church, whether the construction takes place in the home, in congregations, or elsewhere. "Only the best for God!" Each of us will likely compromise in this matter. We participate half-heartedly in Christian work. Fathers and mothers, trying to instil the fear of the Lord in their children, are apt to favor things in their own lives which are compromises in the sight of God. With our lives we undermine our work.

The Book of Malachi as a whole offers an illuminating illustration of the fact that participation in the construction of the Lord's temple must be wholehearted. "The whole tithe" must be brought into the Lord's storehouse if one is to receive the Lord's blessing.

In the time of Malachi there was deception in tithing. The tithes were short. Something similar still happens. We compromise and connive as we go about God's business. We do not give our best to God.

When Paul states he had "renounced secret and shameful ways" 2 Co 4:2, as he went about God's work, he is referring to the same thing. It is possible to be about "shameful ways" and yet imagine that we are builders of Christ's Church. For example, we call ourselves Christian and yet hide in our lives things we are ashamed to reveal to others. We favor and foster evil, bitter, and harmful thoughts about our neighbors, our fellow workers, and even other Christians. This must not continue. We must give to God only our best. Secret and shameful ways must be abandoned. Otherwise our work is in vain.

When Christ paid in full our debt of sin on the cross and gained a glorious victory over sin, death, and the devil, he did not intend for those who put their trust in him to continue as helpless victims of their sins. Christ's power is stronger than the power of sin. Let us be sure of this, no matter how serious our situation may seem.

25 / The Road of Self-Denial

"They follow the Lamb wherever he goes" Rev 14:4.

"IF ANYONE would come after me, he must deny himself and take up his cross and follow me" Mt 16:24.

We run after profits and success, but the way of the Savior leads to suffering and death. We exalt ourselves, Christ denies himself. We promote ourselves, his voice is not heard in the streets. We always want to move upward, but his road goes downward. He is different from all of us. No wonder he has so few true followers, even though his admirers are many.

Jesus does not say the road to which he beckons us is easy and enjoyable. Many are afraid to follow him, because the road seems rough and difficult. We assume that self-denial and self-sacrifice will bring misfortune. We think that we will lose our opportunity in life. And so each one tries to pave his own road, paying no attention to the one who calls for self-denial and service. I imagine in my heart that "I was born for something bigger," and turn a deaf ear to the Savior.

Every road eventually comes to an end. Those who have traveled the way of the cross will one day know that the road was not hard. They were simply following their Savior. In the light of eternity everything appears differently.

We need the fresh air of eternity, which is in dangerously short supply. But only as we follow Christ on the road of self denial can we breathe it.

26 / We Cannot Stand Pat

"Let him who does wrong continue to do wrong; let him who is vile continue to be vile; let him who does right continue to do right; and let him who is holy continue to be holy" Rev 22:11.

THERE IS a remarkable law of evolution that makes it impossible for anything to remain as it is. There appear to be times when change or development seems to have been arrested. The wicked person seems to remain relatively respectable; the righteous person seems to have ceased to grow. But evolution does not proceed smoothly.

At times the evolutionary processes seem to become dammed, only to break out again. Then it becomes evident that the direction has remained the same all along, even when there seemed to be no movement. Satan has been active in his own way, and the Lord in his.

During such seemingly inactive periods, the evil doer must not entertain the false hope of not going further in his wickedness. And the righteous person must not despair because of his lack of growth in holiness. Both the good and the bad mature little by little, and all the while the coming of Christ draws near.

This remarkable law of evolution has something else to say to us. During the end times evil doers remain evil doers and doers of righteousness remain in their own group as doers of righteousness. Transfer from one group to the other will no longer possible.

A tragic scene opens before us and we are forced to ask: has the destiny of modern people already been decided? That is what will happen in the end times. Then there will be no more border crossings.

Even if we do not apply this law to others, we must all the more seriously apply it to ourselves. Have I cheapened God's grace so much that I have overlooked the work of His Spirit in my life? Is it no longer possible for me to move from evil deeds to works of righteousness, from that which is vile to that which is holy? Furthermore, do I understand fully that my task is not to complain about the wickedness of the world, much less toy with it, and not to worship the idols of this world, but to keep on struggling ahead on the road of righteousness?

27 / The Great Danger Within

"The heart is deceitful above all things and beyond cure. Who can understand it?" Jr 17:9.

ALL KINDS of bad things happen to us at various times. Among such bad things Paul lists trouble, hardship, persecution, famine, nakedness, danger, and sword. Everyone of us can easily add to the list many things that trouble and threaten us.

We need to note that all these "bad" things do not constitute our greatest misfortune. None of these bad things, you see, can harm those whom Christ loves. They cannot separate us from the love of Christ. We should not, therefore, complain about such things as much as we usually do. We should be more concerned about possessing Christ's love and living by it.

Then we see what the real danger is. Our greatest misfortune is our unbelief, namely, that we do not glorify God, trust His word, and take into account His holy will. Our tragedy is that we have forsaken God, rejected Him and paid no attention to His will. Every day this shows in our lives. Of course we do not often worry about our indifference. Yet that is our real danger and misfortune; about that we should be concerned, that should make us sad, and for that we should seek help.

"My flesh and my heart may fail, but God is the strength of my heart and my portion forever" Ps 73:26. Thus the believer thinks and testifies from experience. Evil overtakes him too and he cannot know what will happen to him. His body and soul may fail in the afflictions that overtake him. But no matter what happens, the striving believer clings to the Lord and His promises. No evil can then overcome him.

Weighed down by the various burdens of life laid upon us, may we see more clearly each day that our unbelieving hearts pose the greatest danger.

28 / God Gives Again and Again

"He who did not spare his own Son, but gave him up for us all--how will he not also, along with him, graciously give us all things?" Ro 8:32.

EVERY religiously-minded person thinks of God as a giving God. That is why people pray to Him, and trust in Him. But when the Holy Spirit works more deeply in the heart, the person sees in more and more instances he is dealing with gifts God has already given.

According to the Gospels Jesus was aware that every step of the way he was dependent upon what the Father gives. The Father's hand dressed the flowers of the field and fed the birds of the air. Beyond nature Jesus saw the gifts of God: the very words he spoke were from the Father; the people who came to him were sent by the Father; the mighty works that he performed were the works of the Father. "The Son can do nothing by himself; he can do only what he sees his Father doing" Jn 5:19. Even his enemies could do only what the Father permitted.

We do well to pause often to reflect on this aspect of the life of the Lord Jesus, lest we begin to assume we are capable of ordering our lives or fall into fear and despair when it appears that our own resources are exhausted. Unbelief can be defined as thinking that you can get by on your own. This is the source of pride, and also of despair.

A person with an awakened conscience wonders how he can withstand the temptations spawned in his corrupt nature on a daily basis. There is good reason to be afraid. But even then it is

true that God is a giver, a giver of help at the right time to all
who seek Him first and His kingdom above all else. If it seems to
you there is no point in trusting the Lord whole-heartedly
because tomorrow the wickedness of your heart will cause you to
fall into the same sin you today tearfully regretted, do not let
this fear keep you from trusting God's grace.

God continues to give; tomorrow He will give you help, when
today you draw near to the Lord Jesus and, just as you are, trust
your problem to him. It is Satan who keeps the awakened soul
from believing in the forgiveness of sins simply because of the
greatness of the corruption. Simply believe in Jesus, do not
worry now about tomorrow, but receive grace and praise God.

You have a God who gives from day to day.

29 / We Need a New Beginning

*"No one can see the kingdom of God unless he is born
again"* Jn 3:3.

IN THE STORY of the Good Samaritan Jesus introduces two
pious men who were able to walk past a suffering neighbor
without helping him, even though they were aware of his plight.
These men, a priest and a Levite, were not ungodly men, but
there had to be some flaw in their piety to enable them to act so
callously. Piety for them had become an end in itself; rather
than a matter of asking about God's will and obeying it. In lieu
of being obedient to God's commandments, they were pious.

We Christians may have the same flaw. We also try to be
pious, at least now and then. In our Christianity we seek the
things that would assure us of our own salvation and at the
same time give others the picture of a pious person. But in doing
so we are seeking that which is of people and not that which is of
God. In other words, our Christianity is ego-centered rather
than God-centered. The self is in the center, not God.

Our old nature cultivates such ego-centered piety. Even
when it performs acts of charity it seeks its own. A real
revolution has to take place for us to be freed from ourselves and
united with God. We are not helped by becoming more pious. We
need a new beginning, a new birth; we need to become
something altogether different.

March

1 / Victory After Battle

"Resist him, standing firm in the faith" 1 P 5:9.

SIN IS always a curse. The unbridled tongue "corrupts the whole person, sets the whole course of his life on fire, and is itself set on fire by hell" Jas 3:6. Immoral thoughts, words, and deeds affect not only the body, they ruin our whole lives. Selfishness, greed, and miserliness scatter their seeds in the "soil" of those who practice them. No matter the sin, the wages is always death.

Sin is a terminal illness. It spoils even the happy moments of our lives and gradually destroys that which is beautiful, tender, and precious. We all know how sin, like a disease, casts a dark and gloomy cloud over our lives.

There is, however, something we can do besides complain and worry. Peter says, "Resist him, standing firm in the faith." He is talking about Satan, whose power accounts for the strong hold sin has over us. But Satan must, and can be, resisted with firm faith.

To fight against the corrupting influence of Satan, we must be "firm in the faith." Satan's power is terrifying, but he has lost his right to accuse us before God. Of course, Satan still says to his victims, "See what sinners you still are; God will not have mercy on you; there's no sense trying to get rid of sin." But remember that Satan is a liar and the father of liars. Satan no longer has the right to accuse us, for Jesus has reconciled us and the whole world with God through his blood. Not only have the sins of the believer been atoned, but the sins of the whole world. "God was reconciling the world to himself in Christ" 2 Co 5:19.

Satan's accusations have lost their power. He is trying to destroy us as well as undermine the atoning work of Christ, thereby frustrating the gracious will of God. We must clearly understand what Satan is up to. Looking at ourselves, we must admit that there is truth in Satan's charges. But as we cling to God's word of reconciliation, which testifies to the power of Jesus' blood, Satan's charges lose their authority. We have but one judge, Jesus Christ, who for us and for our sake has borne the punishment of our sins "once and for all."

Let us not stop with acknowledging and bemoaning how sin has corrupted us, but let us arise to fight against evil. Only he who is victorious will be crowned.

2 / Faithful to the End

"Be faithful, even to the point of death" Rev 2:10.

WHEN OUR BOOKS are audited, we will be asked if we have been faithful. "Be faithful, even to the point of death, and I will give you the crown of life." Our entire life will be wasted and we will lose the crown of life if we are found to have been unfaithful.

The Norwegian revival leader H. N. Hauge confessed at the end of his life, "I have vowed faithfulness to the Holy Spirit of God, and I have not broken my vow." Such a statement challenges us as we think about ourselves and our faith. We must agree that we should not take lightly the promises we make to the Lord. After all, only those who have been faithful will be crowned.

But how could Hauge say he had kept his promise of faithfulness to the Holy Spirit? Was he being honest? Who in the world can keep such a promise?

But, Hauge was not saying he was guiltless before God. The Spirit of God is a Spirit of admonition, through whom the Lord seeks sinners and draws them into the light. Hauge had paid attention to the Spirit's inner warnings, admonitions, and promptings. Having fallen, he did not resist the Spirit but heeded the voice of his conscience and, as a condemned sinner, was drawn into the presence of Jesus. He who is faithful to the Holy Spirit heeds its urgings and deals with his faults in his daily fellowship with the Savior. The only way a sinner finds his way to Jesus is by the call and guidance of the Holy Spirit. Paul says, "Do not grieve the Holy Spirit of God" Eph 4:30. We get nowhere in our striving, unless we heed the gracious workings of the Holy Spirit in our hearts. The time of grace will give way to a time of misery for us, if we have not been faithful to the inner work of the Holy Spirit.

3 / The Wonderful World of Prayer

"I have come that they may have life, and have it to the full" Jn 10:10.

I REMEMBER a conversation I had with fellow soldiers many years ago. The men were physically exhausted from their military maneuvers and the fate of their homeland weighed upon their minds. One of the men pointed out that we were living in a world to which the gates of paradise had been closed. For that reason, he thought, we should not consider it strange that life was what it was. To this one of our comrades replied, "Yes, but the moment will be wonderful when the gates of paradise are opened again. That is what happened to me when I received forgiveness of sins."

This reminds me of Luther's famous saying that the gates of paradise were opened for him when he understood the gospel from the words of Ro 1:17. In a world that has fallen into sin we experience distress and suffering. Life does not take the shape God originally intended. But in the forgiveness of sins the gates of another world are opened for us fallen creatures. "Where there is forgiveness of sins, there is also life and salvation" (Luther, Small Catechism).

Though God is gracious, even we who are Christians live a much more impoverished life than we would need to. For the most part this is due to a weak and neglected prayer life. We do well to recall the words of Baron Paul Nicolay: "Where there is much prayer, there is much blessing; where there is little prayer, there is little blessing; where there is no prayer, there is no blessing."

Johann Arndt called his prayer book "The Garden of Paradise." Our pious forefathers used this book extensively. The title of the book calls attention to the great value of prayer.

Living in a fallen world, prayer gives us the opportunity to move about in the "garden of paradise." If our faith seems pale and flat it is because we are lazy in our prayer life.

4 / With Christ You Will Endure

"Your strength will equal your days" Dt 33:25.

ESPECIALLY mothers have experienced that work can be a heavy burden. Many of them are on the go from early in the morning until late at night. A healthy person may not find the load unbearable, if she is not weighed down by worries. But, the raising of children has its own pressures and concerns, and nerves become strained. A person who was beaming and blooming a few years earlier, shows wrinkles that witness to the wear and tear of her daily tasks.

But "even when work is a heavy burden, God conceals in it a blessing" (Finnish Catechism). The Bible proclaims this "gospel to the weary". It reminds us that it is God who has given us our jobs. No matter how impossible the circumstances, God is Lord over all. We have not been left to the mercy of life's wear and tear, but are in God's hands, even under our heaviest burdens. "Your strength will equal your days."

Therefore, tired friend, lift up your eyes! You have not been forgotten and left alone in your troubles. God knows and understands your burdens, but He also knows your ability to endure. He does not lay a heavier burden on us than we can bear.

What is the divine blessing hidden in work? "Suffering produces perseverance; perseverance, character; and character, hope" Ro 5:3f. We grow inwardly as we endure suffering. We learn to distinguish between little things and big things. As we are tempered by our struggles we acquire strength of character. The wonder is that joy bursts forth in the lives of those who have endured the most. It is among the sufferers that we find the happiest people and the people around them share in their blessings.

Do not lose patience in your weariness, do not give room to bitterness, and do not project your tiredness on others in the form of anger. Who has told you that you have the right to go through life leisurely and playfully? And who has told you life without burdens and suffering is a rich and happy life? On the contrary, burdens enrich life. But heed the voice of the Savior when he calls the weary and burdened (Mt 11:28). With Christ you will be able to endure the burdens of your daily life.

5 / Blessing in Full Measure

"I know that when I come to you, I will come in the full measure of the blessing of Christ" Ro 15:29.

THE NEW TESTAMENT assures us that there is such a thing as "the full measure of the blessing of Christ," even though we may not have experienced it in our own lives. Let us not measure the possibilities of God's grace by our past experiences, but according to the written word of God.

What did "the full measure of the blessing of Christ" mean to Paul? Not unqualified success in his ministry; not the end of temptations; not the elimination of sin. It meant something else. "The full measure of the blessing of Christ" was given to Paul when he realized that he, too, was made right with God through faith in Christ, who at the right time died for the ungodly (Rom. 5:6). Perfection was not Paul's perfection but Christ's. "He is able to save completely those who come to God through him" He 7:25.

Paul had been given not merely the noble example of Christ or his sacred words but Christ himself, the crucified and risen Savior to whom the impossible is possible. In this way, no matter where Paul went he knew that he could possess Christ totally and that his debt of sin had been fully paid on the cross. The riches of Christ were for him unsearchable (Eph 3:8).

The riches of Christ are still unsearchable. "The full measure of the blessing of Christ" has been reserved also for us. Let us not look to Christ simply as a teacher or example, even though he is in a class by himself. For we would be left without the best part, his perfect righeousness, that covers all our sins, as though they were no more. That is "the full measure of the blessing of Christ."

6 / Called to Bear the Cross

*"Anyone who does not carry his cross and follow me
cannot be my disciple"* Lk 14: 27.

THOMAS A'KEMPIS says Christ has many admirers but few
followers. Which are we?

The Lord himself said that no one can be his follower who
does not deny himself on a daily basis. Without self-denial we
are only admirers, not followers.

What do you know about self-denial? In what way are you
willing to go against your own wishes? Have you ever given up
something dear for the sake of Christ? Have you ever rejected
something in favor of Christ?

Modern Christianity is weak because of our failure to obey
the Lord when he calls us to deny ourselves. If we are unwilling
to go against our own feelings the purposes of divine nurture
will not be realized.

But, self-denial is so difficult that there can be no
volunteers, only draftees. So, God has His own ways of drafting
us. He lays a cross upon our backs to expose and break us. As
Jesus says: "If anyone would come after me, he must deny
himself and take up his cross and follow me" Mt 16:24. Only
under a cross can we learn to deny our proud and selfish ego and
submit to Jesus quietly, humbly, and obediently.

If God has laid a cross upon you, and He often makes a cross
out of something that seems very insignificant, accept it from
His hand. Do not argue with Him, for you cannot believe in God
and follow Christ, unless you take up your cross.

7 / Have You Brought Someone to Jesus?

"He brought him to Jesus" Jn 1:42.

WILL THE SAME THING be said of you some day? The best
thing we can do is to bring someone to Jesus. Nothing more is
asked of us, but nothing less either. We are not expected to
convince someone concerning Jesus, for we are unable to do that.
Jesus alone can create faith. He is the beginning or author of
faith. Faith is never a human achievement, but in the company

of Jesus, people are led to faith by the Lord himself. Jesus will reveal himself to them.

We can, of course, bear witness to Jesus, but personal assurance of faith is gained only in the company of Jesus. The greatest thing that we can do for others, therefore, is to bring them to Jesus.

Let us never be satisfied with something less than that. People are not helped by becoming religious. Simply conversing with them does not help. A religious attitude and religious opinions do not satisfy the soul. One must be received into the company of Jesus.

Why is it so difficult to bring another person to Jesus? Andrew had no problem. First of all, he knew Simon very well; they were brothers. They must have talked alot about spiritual matters. Secondly, he loved his brother. Without love we cannot bring anyone to Jesus. And finally, and most importantly, Andrew himself had just been with Jesus and knew him personally. How can we bring anyone to Jesus, unless we ourselves are in his company?

As a disciple Andrew was just a beginner, yet he was able to bring his brother to Jesus. Andrew was not yet ready to be a teacher; in many things he still needed to be taught. But even a beginner can bring others to Jesus.

8 / Waiting in Silence

"My soul waiteth in silence for God only" Ps 62:1 (ASV).

THE WORD OF GOD repeatedly urges us to be silent because, in the presence of the almighty and holy God, insignificant sinful man must be still. "Be still before the Lord, all mankind, because he has roused himself from his holy dwelling" Zec 2:13. There is truth in the saying, "When man speaks, God is silent, but when man is silent, God speaks."

We do not like being forced to be still. For example, if you are justly accused, you cannot defend yourself and must remain quiet. This happens to us in the presence of God. We are forced to shut up, for we have no defense. What bliss to be silent, when God speaks!

But too often we learn to be silent only after God has shut our mouths through various circumstances of life. Job, who had suffered much, tried to explain matters and to defend himself before God, but he finally had to shut his mouth. "I put my hand over my mouth. I spoke once, but I have my answer; twice, but I will say no more" Job 40:4f. Learn to be still in your troubles, so that God will not be forced to lay an even heavier burden on you to silence you!

The silence we learn in the difficult circumstances of life ultimately comes from learning to leave matters in God's hands. We run out of ideas and no longer know what to do, much less how to advise others. We are forced to turn to God for help. "I am like a deaf man, who cannot hear, like a mute, who cannot open his mouth; I have become like a man who does not hear, whose mouth can offer no reply. I wait for you, O Lord; you will answer, O Lord my God" Ps 38:13-15. Happy is the person who waits for help from the Lord in silence and stillness.

9 / Compelled by Christ's Love

"Christ's love compels us" 2 Co 5:14.

THE FOUNTAIN OF LIFE for the apostle Paul was Christ's love. He was able to endure all things and do all things, to deny himself and risk all things, and to serve others, because Christ's love sustained him. He lived by Christ's love.

How comforting it is to know that Christ's love can become the power of life for a frail human being. When other fountains run dry and their toxic effects are exposed, Christ's love remains both inexhaustible and incomprehensible, and this love is available to all. "Whoever comes to me I will never drive away" Jn 6:37.

Christ's love is revealed in his readiness to receive us at any time. When life is hard, do not fret but go to him who calls the weary and the heavy-ladened. Go, no matter how you feel or what you think. He who calls you knows your feelings and understands your thoughts. If sin weighs you down and death frightens you, go to Jesus. He has always had room for such people. The incomprehensible act of his love took place on Golgatha. When we learn in our daily lives what Christ's love is like, it becomes our life-sustaining power.

And Christ's love will even begin to compel us, prompting us to do things that are impossible and overwhelming. Compelled by Christ's love, Paul says, "I can do everything through him who gives me strength" Phil 4:13.

10 / Christ Saves, Not Faith

"Since, then, we know what it is to fear the Lord, we try to persuade men" 2 Co 5:11.

ACCORDING to classical Lutheran teaching, faith has three parts. First, knowledge about the basics of salvation. A sinner needs to know and understand Christ and his atoning death. Knowledge is followed by assent, an inner conviction produced by the Holy Spirit. One knows in a personal way that Christ can and wants to save. The third and decisive part in saving faith is trust in Christ, sinners willfully submitting to Christ for help.

Norwegian pietists used to say that faith is the Holy Spirit drawing a sinner to approach Christ with his sins. This is saving faith, for Jesus said that no one comes to him in vain. But, no one can believe in this way unless he has been compelled to looked deeply into himself and has repented. One must confess before God that he is lost and condemned. Whoever hides his sins and does not submit to God's judgments cannot have saving faith. Without repentance there is no true faith.

A person on his way to the doctor does not ordinarily sing, "On my way rejoicing." Neither does a sinner as he is being drawn to Jesus. Despairing, and barely confident about Christ's ability to help him, he simply casts himself upon him. This is faith-- leaving myself in the hands of the heavenly Physician!

In the moment that we believe, we realize how little we trust in Christ. And so we must say, "Lord, I do believe, help me overcome my unbelief" Mk 9:24. But this is what saving faith is all about. God hides our faith from us, otherwise we might easily begin to believe in our faith as the basis of our salvation, forgetting that Christ, and only Christ can save us.

11 / God's Time Is the Right Time

"My times are in your hands" Ps 31:15.

SOMETIMES seemingly insignificant twists of words in the Bible can refresh the soul. Such is the effect of the possessive pronoun "His" in the statement, "If you humble yourselves under the mighty hand of God, in His good time He will lift you up" 1 P 5:6 (TLB).

Under the mighty hand of God time begins to drag. When troubles come a person becomes impatient and wants to know how long they will last. It begins to feel that the Lord has forgotten and forsaken him. The tempter adds his voice, "You are a sinner; God does not care about you!" And the soul sinks into unbelief, ending up in despair, unless the Lord lets the light of His word shine upon him.

It is for such times in our lives that the Bible contains the small possessive pronoun "His." In "His good time" God will exalt the humble. It is a question of God's time, not man's. God's clock runs differently than our clocks, and His schedule is different.

But, God's time is always the right time. Some English versions of the Bible state directly: "...that he may lift you up in due time." There is no point in arguing against God and finding fault with his sacred plans.

Peter warns his readers about the tempter that "prowls around like a roaring lion looking for someone to devour" 1 P 5:8. When he succeeds in making a person angry at God's plans and God's times, he cuts him off from God and gains a victim. This will happen to us if we forget that God's time, no matter how inconvenient it may seem to us, is always the right time.

Waiting for God's time, we must humble ourselves under the mighty hand of God. We must give up our own wisdom and convenience. Economic difficulties and all kinds of worries and sorrows may follow. Some may experience sickness and suffering, perhaps many years in bed. But in all such suffering God is near, sharing our misfortune. He notices every tear, He hears every sigh. And all the while He bears our load with us or, more accurately, He bears us with our load. In our difficulties we are in the Fatherly embrace of God, even though we may not be aware of it. To the humble God reveals His goodness and saving power at the right time.

12 / Wrong Decisions and Consequences

"Be always on the watch, and pray..." Lk 21:36.

EVERYTHING that happens to us has its prehistory. Actions and thoughts of the past gradually lead to a particular goal, where they assume their final form. This is true in the life of nations, in family life, and in our personal lives.

The inner unity of events and experiences gives daily life a quality of seriousness and accountability. If we have made the wrong decision unfortunate results are to be expected. Even though at this moment things appear under control, if the basic direction of our life is wrong, unexpected harm awaits us.

Many families have been torn apart. These tragedies, however, did not happen suddenly or without warning. They were preceded by a long period of development in the wrong direction in the lives of family members and their relationships. The break-up of the family could have been avoided, if intervention had occurred in time.

There is a saying: "A miserable man, a slave of sin!" When he was a small child he was a darling sitting on his father's knee. But, now he is different. What happened and why? The man changed because he slowly progressed in the wrong direction toward an unfortunate goal.

The Bible speaks about people who have suffered a shipwreck of faith. Think about these people who have fallen from faith and lost their entire inner life in Christ. Why did it happen? Because they followed a slow but constant path in the wrong direction, away from God.

Christians need to take seriously the admonition of Jesus: "Be always on the watch and pray."

13 / The Conflict and the Comfort Continue

"However, do not rejoice that the spirits submit to you, but rejoice that your names are written in heaven" Lk 10:20.

JESUS MUST have been happy when his disciples returned and reported victories of the kingdom of God. After all, unfortunate victims were being freed from the slavery of Satan. Yet, the Lord saw the situation differently than the disciples. "Do not rejoice that the spirits submit to you, but rejoice that your names are written in heaven."

Why did he throw cold water on their enthusiasm? The clue is found in the comment of Jesus, "I saw Satan fall like lightning from heaven" Lk 10:18. We do not know precisely what Jesus meant by this comment, but we do know that Satan has a great deal of power on earth. The disciples are in danger, for their enemy is not on the outside; he is at work in them, in their hearts and lives. They are in every way subject to his attacks and he can hurt them. While the disciples continue to fight for the kingdom of God, they will be exposed to the attacks of Satan. This makes their position precarious.

It is premature for them freely and fully to rejoice that the spirits are subject to them. However, the Lord said that in the midst of temptation they could rejoice that their names also were remembered in heaven. This would give them strength to continue the conflict against the power of evil. They could rely on their Redeemer, no matter how Satan tempted them.

Today the disciples of the Lord can also find strength in the knowledge that their defender is in heaven and that through him they have free access to the Father. Otherwise they could not endure in the conflict into which they are thrown.

14 / Wicked and Deceitful Nature

"The heart is deceitful above all things and beyond cure. Who can understand it?" Jr 17:9.

WE OUGHT to become better acquainted with the deep-rooted wickedness of our hearts. We all know something about our sinfulness. Surely you know the name of your pet sin, for you must have had many heated encounters with it.

But the wickedness of the heart is more than individual evil desires, lusts, and habits, which enslave and control us. Unbelief is the core of the wickedness of the heart. We are indifferent toward God, rebel against Him, find satisfaction in life without Him, and are controlled by selfishness. We have inherited all this from our forefathers. It is evident already in the lives of children.

The educator who ignores this fact makes a serious mistake, as he nurtures the physical and mental growth of the child but neglects to nurture the soul with the word of God. The wicked, unbelieving heart will eventually bear bitter fruit, unless the power of the living Christ, stronger than the power of unbelief, finds room in the life of the child.

The parents of infants do not have the right to neglect the care of souls. Even the hearts of children are evil. The powers of unbelief will grow and spread in our children, unless the power of Christ can overcome them.

Everyone needs a completely new heart. Throughout the Bible we can follow the golden thread of God's recreating and regenerating activity in the world. It is not enough to adopt some Christian customs and ideals. "You must be born again," says Jesus (Jn 3:7).

We must not be satisfied with less. But we must be clear that our wicked, unbelieving hearts resist renewal. Our unbelieving hearts fail to see the gracious work of God and insist on adding to it something of our own. The danger of self-righteousness stalks the struggling Christian every step of the way. We must always be aware and fearful of the wickedness of the heart and our unbelief.

15 / Forgiven Sin Is Sin Removed

"Look, the Lamb of God, who takes away the sin of the world" Jn 1:2.

PEOPLE USED TO hang pictures of the suffering Christ on the walls of their homes. Religious pictures have become less popular in our homes, which is yet another sign of the spread of the secular spirit. What a tremendous opportunity we have to teach our children by imprinting on their souls an early picture of Christ, especially the suffering Christ! "Look, the Lamb of God, who takes away the sin of the world!"

If we delve deeply into this testimony of John the Baptist we find that the phrase "Lamb of God" had become precious to the early Christians as another title for Christ. We see further evidence of this in 1 P 1:19 and Rev 5:6, 12. If we wish to believe as these first Christians believed, the vision of Christ as the Lamb of God must become precious to us and be on our minds.

"The Lamb of God", when describing Christ, does not mean primarily that he has been sacrificed to God but that he is the sacrificial lamb which God has provided. Jesus, the only Son of God, was the true passover lamb who was slaughtered for the sin of the whole world. This phrase speaks about God who has given His only Son for our salvation.

The Lamb of God "takes away the sin of the world." He did not merely take the punishment of the sin of the world upon himself--"the punishment was upon him" Is 53:5. Even more, by carrying the sin of the world he also "takes it away." "You know that he appeared so that he might take away our sins" 1 Jn 3:5. Forgiven sin is sin removed. Overcoming sin and liberation from its power is accomplished by this Lamb of God.

During these weeks of Lent let us take time to consider in a special way "the Lamb of God who takes away the sin of the world."

16 / Fighting Sin by Loving Others

"You, my brothers, were called to be free. But do not use your freedom to indulge the sinful nature; rather, serve one another in love" Ga 5:13.

THE BIBLE offers practical advice to those who want to struggle against sin: "Serve one another in love." This does not mean that by loving and serving others a person can overcome the evil within. Paul does not think that a person is able to get rid of sin by special training. What would then be left for Christ? He is not just our model for service but our Savior from sin. "You are all sons of God through faith in Christ Jesus" Ga 3:26.

Nevertheless, it is a Biblical and an often-experienced truth that a person who seeks to serve is already engaged in the struggle against the power of sin. The watchful Christian is recognized by his service and love.

Whoever serves denies himself. He places the needs of his neighbor ahead of his own interests and conveniences. The saying goes that "idleness is the mother of evil." The Christian is idle if he is not active in service to others. In his idleness he is tempted and wickedness thrives beneath his pious surface.

This is what Paul had in mind when he said, "You were called to be free. But do not use your freedom to indulge the sinful nature; rather, serve one another in love."

Put this word into practice now, beginning at home. Do not wait for others to serve you; serve them. And do not overlook the little ways in which you can serve.

Anyone who occupies himself in such service is fighting against the power of evil.

17 / Joined to Christ, Not to Unbelievers

"Do not be yoked together with unbelievers" 2 Co 6:14.

WE NEED TO pay attention to whom this warning is uttered. Is it meant for unbelievers, newcomers to faith? Not at all! Human reason says we must give up love of the world and our alliance with all forms of sin in order to be acceptable to God. Accordingly, we have sought to overcome, or at least overrule, the sinful desires which have enslaved us. Many serious-minded people have tried to do this. Unsuccessful in their efforts, they have either given up entirely or settled for mediocre accomplishments. As a result they have lost their inner freedom, and remain slaves to sin.

In this "unevangelical" group we undoubtedly will find the larger part of Christendom. Most of us live under the law, with no power to appropriate the good news of God's mercy. As a result we know nothing of the power of the gospel.

"The Lord does not have mercy on me because of my holiness but because of my wickedness," said Paavo Ruotsalainen, the nineteenth-century peasant leader of the spiritual awakening in Finland. A person does not need to try to break the ties of sin to make himself worthy of grace; he may come to God just as he is, for God justifies the wicked (Rom. 4:5). But to sinners who have received mercy, it is said, "Do not be yoked together with unbelievers." With the power God gives them, they must break away from everything that is contrary to God's will, or they will lose the blessing.

18 / We Remain Unworthy

"We are unworthy servants" Lk 17:10.

POSSIBLY the most difficult lesson for a Christian to learn is the one taught by Jesus to his disciples: "So you also, when you have done everything you were told to do, should say, 'We are unworthy servants." The Finnish Bible uses the word which meant "useless" in the language of the New Testament. It is a question of people who are of no use to the employer, who are literally good for nothing, unemployable.

We find it hard to accept such an evaluation of ourselves. Even if we admit, as we must now and then, that we have failed as servants of the Lord, we refuse to see ourselves as useless. Certainly I must be good for something, if only the best in me could come out. So we think. This time I have failed, I did not try my best! But if I really try, I can do something at least! Secretly we add: "Not just something; I was born for big things!"

Christ is not interested in minimizing the work of his disciples. Their work is absolutely necessary. He needs them, and they do not labor in vain. "Your labor in the Lord is not in vain" 1 Co 15:58. His intention is to remove from us all self-righteousness, all self-admiration; in other words, our public and private pride.

We are able to serve the Lord only when we accept the position of a slave. A slave has no right to demand recognition and reward. He belongs to his Master. He exists to serve his Master. The Lord is able to use only those who have been humbled. For that reason he must remind his own of their unworthiness, and do it in such a way that others will recognize them as totally unworthy.

19 / Finding Christ in Moses

*"You are in error because you do not know the Scriptures
or the power of God"* Mt 22:29.

WITHOUT the Old Testament we understand very little about
the New Testament. The former not only helps us to understand
the latter, the two belong together as an organic whole. They
supplement one another as promise and fulfillment. "Christ is
the end of the law," says Paul (Ro 10:4). The "law," meaning the
Old Testament as a whole, points to Christ.

There is an old devotional book by the title *Christ in Moses.*
It expresses a modern scientifically established principle that we
are to look for Christ in the Old Testament. When, for example,
we read 1 Co 10:1-13, we note that the apostles read the Old
Testament through eyes opened by the Holy Spirit and found
Christ. Christ as "the end of the law" is also the beginning of a
new age in the history of divine salvation. For that reason the
Old Testament as such does not apply to the people of the New
Covenant; it must be studied to discover what the passage under
consideration says about Christ.

Paul presents a guideline for the reading of the Old
Testament when he says of the Jews that "when Moses is read, a
veil covers their hearts. But whenever anyone turns to the Lord,
the veil is taken away" 2 Co 3:15f. Whoever turns to the Lord in
true repentance will have his eyes opened to read the Old
Testament so as to find "Christ in Moses." "Christ is the Lord
and King of the Bible" (Martin Luther).

20 / Our Suffering and God's

"In all their distress he too was distressed" Is 63:9.

LENT PORTRAYS the suffering Lord as we follow him to
Gethsemane and Golgatha. However, we are not told to go back
two thousand years, for our God continues to be a suffering God.
Because God is love He continues to suffer. "In all their distress
he too was distressed." That is the kind of God He is.

In all your troubles the Lord, too, is troubled. There is a way
out of your distress. "If by nature you are so weak that you
cannot really think or pray, then Christ is watching beside you

like a mother beside her child, and you do not have to worry about your prayers but can remember that Christ is praying for you. His prayer is more powerful than all your efforts" (Jonas Lagus, one of several ministers who shared leadership in the 19th-century spiritual awakening in Finland).

In yet another way God continues to suffer. A father who has a disobedient son, whom he is forced to spank, suffers more than the child. Because the father loves his child every blow strikes his own heart. God has to punish His disobedient children in many ways: illness, accidents, poverty, conflicts. and various consequences of our sins. The age we live in, which has forgotten and forsaken God, is currently suffering from the blows of the Father. But the Father Himself suffers the most; He continues to be a suffering God.

May this time of Lent direct us to the suffering Lord. Only then will we be able to weep for our sins and repent. Unless our hearts are broken, our lives will not be renewed.

21 / Christ's Way and Our Lifestyle

"I am the way and the truth and the life" Jn 14:6.

THINKING OF CHRIST as the way, we are reminded primarily of his importance as our Savior. He is the way to the Father, the only way to union with God, for he is God's way to us. No one can get to the Father except by way of him.

The Bible, however, speaks of Jesus as the way in yet another sense. He is the way a person must follow to live as he should, to go through life the right way.

In the Acts of the Apostles we come across various phrases that describe Christianity as a "Way" (9:2, 19:9, 19:23, 24:22). Jesus is this way. He is the way in regard to our thoughts. Our thoughts are on the right track when we subject them to Christ, letting him control them; when we seek his opinion, and obey his will. In our relationships to others we do the right thing when we serve them according to the mind of Christ, and do not elevate ourselves above them. "Your attitude should be the same as that of Christ Jesus, who made himself nothing" Phil 2:5-7.

In this sense Christ is the way. Following him we can live our lives as they should be lived. According to the Bible this is how things are because "all things were created by him and for him" Col 1:16. The fundamental laws of life are tied to him. If we forget and deny Christ, we inevitably fall into a false lifestyle. We break the very laws of life. Life lived according to the will of Christ is the only true life.

22 / Doing the Works of Jesus

"Anyone who has faith in me will do what I have been doing. He will do even greater things than these" Jn 14:12.

WE WOULD TRY to forget these words of Jesus, except we know that Jesus never exaggerated. He really meant that his disciples would do his work here on earth.

"Anyone who has faith in me" is the only prerequisite. Human powers are totally inadequate; divine power is needed. And the power of Jesus is unlimited. Such power is available only where there is faith.

We know this, and have often tried to enlarge or enhance our faith, to make it worth displaying before others. We have tried to have faith in our own faith. But Jesus says, "Anyone who has faith in me." He carefully explained the nature of this faith: "Believe in me when I say that I am in the Father and the Father is in me" Jn 14:11.

We can do the works of Jesus here and now to the extent that we can believe as Jesus believed. The Gospels show us the nature of Jesus' faith: total dependence upon the Father. The Father gave him the words he spoke. The Father drew people to him. The Father told him when to go and when to stay put. He received the cup of suffering from the Father's hand. And the Father gave Pilate the power to condemn him to death. Everything was in the Father's hands.

Is this faith extraordinary? No, it is the faith of a child. This is how a child believes. Fathers and mothers, observe your children and let them teach you about childlike faith. To the extent that the Lord can humble us alongside children, take away our great and wise thoughts, eliminate our various theories and teachings, we will be able to do the works of Jesus.

Truly, this world has been given to us as the place where we are to do the works of Jesus. That is why we have a body and soul, a home and work, friends and strangers, unknown neighbors. Under these temporal circumstances we are called daily to do the works of Christ.

23 / In the Flesh but Not of the Flesh

"But we have the mind of Christ" 1 Co 2:16.

WHO DARES to say of himself I have the mind of Christ? Yet, this is what we need more than anything else. We need a new mind; a sober, clear, humble and loving mind. Otherwise, of what use is our faith if our minds are not renewed? You are "to be made new in the attitude of your minds; and to put on the new self, created to be like God in true righteousness and holiness" Eph 4:23f.

The goal is clear, confirmed by the assurance of the apostle: "But we have the mind of Christ." Similarly, he urges: "Your attitude should be the same as that of Christ" Phil 2:5. Let no one lower the ideal.

We have strayed so far from the spirit of the Bible that we have reason to ask whether we would approve of Jesus were he to appear among us. Perhaps we would take him to be a dreamer and a religious fanatic.

"Those who live according to the sinful nature have their minds set on what that nature desires; but those who live in accordance with the Spirit have their minds set on what the Spirit desires" Ro 8:5. This does not mean that sinful nature is dead in those who belong to the Lord; it means they do not "live according to the sinful nature." Paul adds that the "sinful nature" still lives in him, for it "desires what is contrary to the Spirit, and the Spirit what is contrary to the sinful nature" Ga 5:17. Paul was not free from the mind of the flesh; he heard its whispers within himself, but he did not live according to it. This was the reason for his daily struggle.

If we forget that our sinful nature is still very much alive, we live in great danger. But we face equal danger if we forget that we need not live according to the flesh. Paul says, "Live by the Spirit, and you will not gratify the desires of the sinful nature" Ga 5:16.

24 / The Truth Will Come Out

"When words are many, sin is not absent, but he who holds his tongue is wise" Pr 10:19.

THERE ARE all kinds of words: good and bad, friendly and unfriendly, honest and dishonest, straight and crooked. Words reveal who we are, and Jesus says that we are judged by our words. "By your words you will be acquitted, and by your words you will be condemned" Mt 12:37. Words are like the fruit we produce in our lives. "Out of the overflow of the heart the mouth speaks" Mt 12:34.

Words often slip out of our mouths unexpectedly and spontaneously and we rationalize that these are not really representative of who we are. I may utter a little lie now and then, but that does not make me a liar. If I impatiently make some biting remarks to someone, I'm really thinking of what is best for him. And if in good company I spread rumors about my friends, that does not make me a gossip. So we rationalize.

Jesus, who knows our hearts, disagrees. In certain situations we select our words carefully, but these are not a true expression of who we are. The deeper truth about us is revealed in our spontaneous and unpremeditated conversation when we pay no particular attention to what we say. It is then that our heart speaks out of its fullness.

"By your words you will be acquitted, and by your words you will be condemned." It is not by chance that the Bible repeatedly warns against idle talk. Words will not only condemn us but they can corrupt others. "The tongue also is a fire, a world of evil among the parts of the body. It corrupts the whole person, sets the whole course of his life on fire, and is itself set on fire by hell" Jas 3:6.

25 / Doing the Truth in Little Things

"Whoever lives by the truth comes into the light" Jn 3:21.

WE USUALLY assume a person comes to know the truth by thinking. Investigating, weighing arguments for and against, honestly seeking and asking, are the ways in which we discover the truth.

But Jesus says this is not so. Thinking is not enough. The kingdom of truth is more than thoughts; it must involve the whole person. One must enter the kingdom of truth as a whole person. Jesus says that only the person who does the truth will enter into God's light. We cannot just think the truth, we must do it.

How will this look in practice? It means that in the many and diverse decisions of life I am always ready to do the will of God. We may think that in the great moments of life when we face crucial decisions we will be ready to listen to what God wants. But, that is not enough. We must seek to do the truth in the small everyday situations if we want to know God's truth and receive His light.

Above all, we must ask whether we are ready to love and serve one another. Are we willing to deny ourselves to improve the welfare of someone else? Do we speak well of others, interpreting what we know about them so that others may see them in the best possible light? Are we long-suffering and patient with each other? Such things, seemingly insignificant, must be kept in mind as we seek to do the truth.

On this Festival of the Annunciation of our Lord we think of our Lord's mother and all other God-fearing mothers. They are radiant, because they are doers of the truth. Their beauty is not in outward adornment but in the "inner self, the unfading beauty of a gentle and quiet spirit" 1 P 3:4. They exemplify what the Bible says about people who have set apart Christ as Lord in their hearts (1 P 3:15). Such people are found wherever the will of God is done even in little things.

26 / The Battle Continues to Rage

"The battle is not yours, but God's" 2 Ch 20:15.

THERE IS a saying that idleness is the mother of evil. Jesus speaks about the same thing when he relates the story about the wicked servant who, when the return of his absent master is delayed, forgets his responsibility to his master and "begins to beat the menservants and maidservants and to eat and drink and get drunk" Lk 12:45.

We may not have fallen that low, but we may be inwardly idle and for that reason guilty of all kinds of evil. There is such a thing as idle Christianity, which lacks inner movement and striving of the heart. Everything concerning faith becomes familiar and self-evident. Prayer is purely formal, worship merely a habit. Our Christianity goes smoothly and we assume that it is thriving. We no longer feel it necessary to ask for grace; salvation is assured. From the human point of view everything is shipshape.

Some people describe such a life as proper, serene, established and genuine. But the hollowness of this kind of life appears in the idleness which spawns all kinds of evil. Self-exaltation and self-service, criticism and fault-finding grow spontaneously in such people.

Living faith is a matter of waiting for the Lord, asking and striving, continual seeking for the face of Christ who is full of grace and truth, and yearning for the witness of the Spirit. The inner work of faith is a constant battle and hardship. The struggle between the flesh and the Spirit keeps us on the front line, where the battle rages as long as life continues. Each day the fight starts again. Again and again we must ask with fighters of old, "Where are you now, Jesus?" There is no time to get sidetracked in matters that do not concern us. We must seek to remain faithful in the assignments our Lord gives to us.

27 / Turn to the Lord Jesus

"He makes me lie down in green pastures" Ps 23:2.

TODAY WE KNOW how much our vitality and well-being depends on the food we eat. Food that lacks nourishment eventually makes us tired and weak. Lack of proper spiritual nourishment will lead to an anemic faith.

Jesus speaks about this when he says, "I am the gate; whoever enters through me will be saved. He will come in and go out, and find pasture" Jn 10:9. "Find pasture." That's what we need. Food for the soul, food that sustains the Christian life, is found when the Lord Jesus is our daily door through which we "come in and go out."

This is what Christians of old meant by "turning to the Lord" and looking to him in all things. In themselves they were poor and miserable, but they did not rest in their helplessness; in their hunger they turned to the Lord Christ. "We have to go to

Jesus." This was their agenda, which they shared with their equally poor and miserable friends. They reminded each other of their need to go to Jesus and urged each other on, knowing that it was difficult to keep going without the encouragement and support of others. In their poverty they were nourished by their daily discipline of "turning to Jesus." They found good pasture for their souls. Or, as the psalmist says, they were made to lie down "in green pastures."

God's word is the proper nourishment for the soul. Sometimes God's word seems dry and we get nothing out of it. But, that's because we have not entered through the "gate"; we have not made a daily discipline of "turning to the Lord Jesus." Old and familiar Bible passages and hymn verses marvelously come to life, turning green when the Lord Jesus is the gate through which we enter to study God's word.

28 / Refreshed by Remembrance of Jesus

"I have eagerly desired to eat this Passover with you before I suffer" Lk 22:15.

JESUS AND his disciples are at supper in the upper room. Is this not a picture of calm before the storm? Jesus calls us also to experience such calm at the Lord's Table. "Do it in remembrance of me."

We need to remember him, if we are to endure in the many conflicts of life. "Consider him who endured such opposition from sinful men, so that you will not grow weary and lose heart" He 12:3. People easily lose heart in this valley of tears in which we live. Depression weakens us in the face of temptations. But remembering Jesus will encourage the tired heart. He also fell beneath the cross, he also walked to Golgatha, he also swam in his tears.

Let the weary come to the Lord's Table with their tired feelings, even though they have no deep and wonderful thoughts. Those who are tired cannot be expected to be filled with great feelings. The memory of Jesus will refresh their soul.

There is talk today about secularization. Christianity is always in danger of becoming secularized. To battle against the powerful spirit of the world we must remember Jesus much more than we usually do. The sacred memory of our Lord will protect us from all danger. The benediction of the Lord's Table is of crucial importance for our fight of faith. "Whoever claims to live in him must walk as Jesus did" 1 Jn 2:6.

The Lord's Table reminds us primarily of his bitter suffering and death for the sins of the world. This was so vital to Paul that he said, "I resolved to know nothing while I was with you except Jesus Christ and him crucified" 1 Co 2:2.

The time for memories has come again
To remind us, to bring to mind, that
Jesus walked into death for us.

29 / Following in Christ's Steps

"To this you were called, because Christ suffered for you, leaving you an example, that you should follow in his steps" 1 P 2:21.

WHILE WALKING along a narrow snow-packed path I had to be careful. One small step off the path and I would have sunk into the snow. The path was narrow and it was wise to stay in the steps of those who had gone before me.

That is what it is like for the Christian. Christ left an example "that you should follow in his steps." We err if we think that the Christian life has to do primarily with observing certain moral principles. We must follow in the steps of Christ; in other words, we must ask in various life situations how Jesus would act. We must live in his company and ask him what he thinks.

What the Bible tells us about Jesus in specific circumstances show us his steps. Christians of all times must look for his footsteps if they are to stay on the right road. In speaking about Christ's footsteps, Peter pointed to the ones he left among his enemies. "When they hurled their insults at him, he did not retaliate; when he suffered, he made no threats. Instead, he entrusted himself to him who judges justly" 1 P 2:23. How strange! How impossible to imitate! And yet, unless we do likewise, we are not in the steps of Christ and are not following him.

Do you feel misunderstood? Do people oppose you? Are you unable to get your ideas across? Are you hurt? Do tongues speak falsely about you? Do you not get what you want? In the midst of such experiences it will become clear whether or not you are following in the steps of your Savior. You will be able to see if you are walking on the narrow way, the only way that leads home.

30 / Jesus Feeds the Hungry

"I am the bread of life" Jn 6:35.

BREAD IS for the hungry. And Jesus, who is the bread of life, wants to feed those who are hungry for true life. Sometimes our awakened conscience tells us that it is not right to beg from Christ all the time. Since the Lord has given to us so abundantly over the years we ought to have something in reserve. But, when we are hungry and reach out to him, we are not bothering him. Christ knows that a sinner has nothing of his own and no reserves. Christ knows that he was sent to be the bread of life for the hungry. He lives among us to feed us.

Note that Jesus says he is the bread of "life." He wants to give life to us. He offers his help in facing the problems and troubles of real life. When you "eat" him, that is, when you come to him and believe in him, you receive nourishment to continue along your way with renewed strength from him.

As the bread of life, Jesus does not mean he is some vague emotional presence in which we are supposed to live. Christians often dabble with religious ideas and feelings that cannot nourish us. But, Jesus is not inviting us to "swallow air" when he offers himself as the bread of life. "The words I have spoken to you are spirit and they are life" Jn 6:63. We are fed by Jesus' words.

The words of loved ones who have died are precious to us. We feel alive when we remember them. But it is much more important for us that we have Jesus' words in the Bible. The entire Bible is God's word for us; and we live by this word. As we study the words of Jesus in the Bible, we are nourished by the true bread of life.

Jesus also says that his body and blood are true food for us. Jesus gives himself to us in the Lord's Supper. In our hunger let

us go more often to the Lord's Table. In the word and
sacraments Jesus offers himself to all who are hungry.

31 / The Cross Exposes Sin

*"We preach Christ crucified: a stumbling block to Jews
and foolishness to Gentiles"* 1 Co 1:23.

"THE FOOLISHNESS of the cross," Paul points out in Ga 5:11,
was offensive to some people. They could not accept Jesus Christ
portrayed as crucified for them. Why not?

Did the preaching of Christ crucified place demands that
were too great or too high? Not at all! The Pharisees, the very
people who were offended, were accustomed to serious discipline.
They were very serious in matters of faith. Doing God's will was
a sacred duty for them. They were not offended because Paul
demanded too much of them. The offense was that Christ the
crucified one was proclaimed as the only savior. All of their
serious moral and religious striving had no saving value. This
was nonsense to their way of thinking and, therefore, they were
angered by the word of the cross. Their moral and religious
values were threatened.

It is still like that. People are not offended by the demands of
the Christian faith but by its free offer of grace.

We may not think much about our faith, but we try to patch
up its holes. When, for example, we realize that much is lacking
in our prayer life, we still think we are safe. After all, we see in
ourselves many other marks of true faith. What we lack God will
graciously forgive.

This natural piety is offended by the cross of Christ, because
in the light of the cross everything we attempt collapses. The
sins of our hearts are exposed: we do not love God or neighbor,
only ourselves. We realize that we cannot salvage our spiritual
life by patching it up. At the foot of the cross our hearts are
broken and our old nature is buried.

April

1 / In the Beginning Is Grace

"For through him we both have access to the Father by one Spirit" Eph 2:18.

WHAT KIND of freedom is found at the foot of the cross? Is it freedom from sin? Yes, but let us take a closer look. We think of sin as a form of slavery and a heavy burden, but sin is by no means always a burden. There are sinful pleasures, too, and not all sinners want to be freed from the power of sin.

One thing, however, is always burdensome: struggling alone against sin, when one's conscience has been awakened. For this reason we may find our faith to be our heaviest burden.

The cross relieves us of this burden. Someone else has prepared and completed the way for us. "The punishment that brought us peace was upon him" Is 53:5. Did Christ bear this punishment only for the sins that we have confessed and for which we have repented? No, it was for all sins! "When we were still powerless, Christ died for the ungodly" Ro 5:6. Christ was punished for our sins, and the sins of the whole world. We are free, for a sin cannot be punished twice.

We don't need to work on changing ourselves in order to be God's children. "You are all sons of God through faith in Christ Jesus" Ga 3:26. "Through faith," not "because of faith." And what is faith? Faith is going to Jesus with our sins, without first trying to change ourselves or even trying to cover up our sins. Christ gives faith its meaning.

The cross means we are freed from the necessity of trying to please God to gain His favor. Through the blood of Christ we have His favor already.

How wonderful that we do not have to try to be somebody or try to squeeze something out of ourselves! We may rest in the completed work of Christ, and our souls are filled with praise and thanksgiving.

2 / The Blessing of the Cross

"God has poured out his love into our hearts by the Holy Spirit, whom he has given us" Ro 5:5.

AT TIMES we are deeply moved as we contemplate the blessing which is ours through the cross. However, our tears are not the same as the blessing of the cross. What is the blessing? It is the new meaning our lives receive at the foot of the cross!

By nature we are selfish, most glaringly when we assume that our moral and spiritual exercises make us acceptable to God. So many Christians, through the centuries, have languished in selfishness, trying to improve their lives in order to be able to experience God's grace! Sin has the power to torture and imprison a person with this selfishness. Even in our relationship to others we seem to have no choice but always to put ourselves first.

But the cross gives new meaning to our lives. We once tried to please God with our works, but now we can trust in the completed work of Christ. The cross now stands between God and fallen man, and it is the only bridge to grace. Freed from self-made piety, which is nothing but selfishness, our talents are freed for service. We are now ready to give up our life, like the grain of wheat that falls into the ground and dies. We can offer ourselves in service to others. This is what Paul means when he says the love of God has been poured out into our hearts by the Holy Spirit. "Christ's love compels us" 2 Co 5:14. True neighborliness, the desire to lose oneself in the service of others, is the blessing of the cross!

3 / No Need to Defend Ourselves

"...so that every mouth may be silenced and the whole world held accountable to God" Ro 3:19.

AN ELDERLY PASTOR left behind a powerful influence when he died, simply because he had been in the habit of asking forgiveness from his family, friends, and parishioners. He was not a churchman; he was one of those "poorly endowed." Only toward the end of his ministry did he get his own parish in an out of the way place--he was the only candidate! But he made an unusually powerful impact with his humility.

One purpose of God's gracious work is to free us from the need to defend ourselves. We tend to think we are right and others are wrong. We admit with great difficulty that others may understand things better. Even when faced with facts that prove we were wrong we try to defend our own point of view.

This self-righteous attitude shows its true colors when a person argues with God. In the midst of life's difficulties we are often confused and ask why this had to happen to us. We feel we are suffering unfairly. We blame God and become bitter toward Him.

To save us from the temporal and eternal curse of sin, God must first show us our guilt. To do that He puts His hand over our mouth. We are guilty, and can no longer defend ourselves. We are humbled so that God can show His grace.

When we, as condemned sinners with all kinds of faults and failures, cease to defend ourselves before God and submit to being saved by grace for Christ's sake, we will find it unnecessary to defend ourselves before others. On the contrary, we will find reason to ask others to forgive our sins and errors. Through people like this, who walk humbly before God, a sample of the purity and radiance of eternity enters this evil world.

4 / From Disciple to Traitor

"...the man who was called Judas, one of the Twelve, was leading them" Lk 22:47.

HOW SAD! A disciple leading the way for the enemies and captors of Jesus. But the same thing happens today. Disciples forsake the Lord and become leaders of his enemies.

Our hearts are by nature selfish and insensitive. Unless they are broken in the presence of Jesus, unless the inflated and selfish ego is overthrown, unless we learn to fear our hearts more than anything else, we will develop into deceitful disciples. We may admire our Lord and act piously among the pious, but among the worldly we are worldly-minded, behaving, thinking, and acting like the world. In the duplicity of our hearts we are traitors. There is a curse upon us as we become leaders of the enemies of the Lord in the ungodly world.

James says that teachers "will be judged more strictly" Jas 3:1, but this applies to all disciples. Our behavior gives a false picture of the way of salvation to those who do not know the Lord, and they are prevented from finding the narrow way into the company of Jesus.

Some say that people today cannot be reached by sermons calling them to cry over the hardness of their heart and the deep roots of sin in their lives. The Bible, however, clearly states that the way to salvation is always narrow. The tears of the Lord's people will not be wiped away until in glory.

It may be that sermons fail to call sinners to contrition and repentance because the preachers themselves do not yet know how to cry over their selfish and insensitive hearts. We all run the risk of becoming Judas-like traitors who show the way for Jesus' enemies.

Merciful God, open our eyes to see what is required for us to find peace (Lk 19:42).

5 / Righteousness for the Unrighteous

"Deliver me in your righteousness" Ps 31:1.

LUTHER had great difficulty with these words. What happens to sinners if God is true to His righteousness? How can an evil person stand in the presence of the righteous God?

Righteousness, however, does not just mean that God is against sin and evil. God acts righteously when He provides justice to the oppressed and frees the miserable from shame. God's righteousness is saving righteousness.

> From dust He raises the cheap;
> From dirt He rescues the poor.

We see a special quality of righteousness when God gives to those who have nothing. "He has scattered abroad his gifts to the poor, his righteousness endures forever" Ps 112:9. Righteousness has virtually the same meaning as the giving of alms, that is, helping the poor.

In Christ we see the true nature of God's righteousness. The Christ of Gethsemane and Golgatha shows God against all sin and corruption. God does not pretend that the sins of the world are not real. But Christ is the Suffering Servant who reveals that the righteous God does not abandon His people to the power of sin, the devil, and death. In Christ God has made friends of His enemies and He desires to free them.

"Deliver me in your righteousness." Do not leave me in the power of sin, at the mercy of the devil and death. Save me, for you are the Savior of the lost!

6 / Full Salvation in Christ

"I know that my Redeemer lives" Job 19:25.

JESUS LIVES! What does this mean? First of all, it means that your Redeemer lives. He has won the victory over sin, death, and the devil; he has broken your chains. It is finished! God would not have raised him from the dead if even a small part of his work had remained unfinished.

"Therefore he is able to save completely those who come to God through him, because he always lives to intercede for them" He 7:25. Complete salvation has been achieved by Christ, not by you or me. But Jesus gives it to you and me; it becomes ours, not because we have done something but because Jesus is Someone.

We often intercede for people. We are with them in spirit, we think about them, and we pray for them. If our prayers can be like this, what about the prayers of Jesus? "He always lives to intercede for them." He is with us, even today, he is concerned about us, he is sorry for us. Perhaps he even rejoices over us! The living Jesus intercedes for us. Salvation is not something way out there which the sinner must reach for. Jesus comes to sinners and brings them salvation. God raised him from the dead so that now "he always lives to intercede for them" He 7:25.

Can you imagine what "full salvation means?" Luther wrote in his explanation to the seventh petition of the Lord's Prayer: "We pray in this petition, as in a summary, that our Father in heaven may deliver us from all manner of evil, whether it affect our body or soul, property or reputation, and that at last, when the hour of death comes, He may grant us a blessed end and graciously take us from this world of sorrow to Himself in heaven" (Small Catechism).

In the Litany we pray: "From all sin, from all error, from all evil; from the cunning assaults of the devil; from an unprepared and evil death; from war, bloodshed, and violence; from corrupt and unjust government; from sedition and treason; from epidemic, drought, and famine; from fire and flood, earthquake, lightning and storm; and from everlasting death; good Lord, deliver us." This is "full salvation!" Everything that is part of my life is on Jesus' heart, and is included in his prayer.

My Redeemer lives! He is also the Redeemer of the whole world. "I am making everything new.... I am the Alpha and the Omega, the Beginning and the End" Rev 21:5f. This poor, wicked world has already begun to be renewed and the end is also in sight. The living Redeemer is both the beginning and the end.

7 / Experience of Salvation

"Jesus told him, 'Because you have seen me, you have believed; blessed are those who have not seen and yet have believed" Jn 20:29.

BEHIND US are the decisive events of salvation history, the cross of Golgatha and the empty tomb of Easter. They remind us that Christianity has to do with something more than human religious experiences. Our faith rests on a foundation outside of us; it rests on the saving acts of God, on the Lord who died and rose again.

All who are weak in faith and poor in experiences do well to keep this in mind. We need not try to create special experiences for ourselves. Experiences of any kind will not save us. It is the Lord who saves, and he does not depend on us in any way. Experiences are born as we encounter the risen Lord. In the Word and Sacraments he is in our midst. When God gives us His Holy Spirit, so that we believe His holy word, we meet our risen Lord and experience him. This is how experiences are produced, but even then experiences do not save us; the Lord does.

The gospels describe various ways in which the disciples experienced the risen and living Lord. The circumstances of their lives, their personalities, and their struggles were different; therefore, they encountered the Lord differently. John, the first disciple to come to an Easter faith, spent a moment in silence before he entered the empty tomb. Then he "saw and believed" Jn 20:8. If we, too, pause in silent expectation before the saving acts of God, our heart will be prepared to experience a great miracle.

8 / Conflict and the Christian

"You are not a God who takes pleasure in evil; with you the wicked cannot dwell" Ps 5:4.

WE SO EASILY become accustomed to sin. We are able to pray and to love sin at the same time, unaware of any contradiction. Sin has become natural for us. The tension between the holy God and unholy sin has disappeared from our hearts. A spirit of apathy has come over many of us.

When God gives His Holy Spirit the sinner begins to see the outline of a holy God who does not take "pleasure in evil" and with whom "the wicked cannot dwell." Sin becomes a horrible and damning thing. The sinner realizes that with his piety he has created his own God.

What kind of a God do you have? Is He satisfied with your present state? Does He accept you as you are now, without repentance and without rejection of sin? Do not be surprised if Christianity seems unreal to you; you have not yet been interviewed by the God who hates sin. Do not be surprised if you do not know Christ; you are unwilling to accept correction regarding your sins. You escape into your imagined piety as soon as the Holy Spirit begins to draw you into the presence of the living and holy God.

"The sinful nature desires what is contrary to the Spirit, and the Spirit what is contrary to the sinful nature" Ga 5:17. The Holy Spirit works to create conflict between sinful nature and the Spirit. Have you really become angry with yourself and been offended by your sins? Have you regretfully condemned your sins and desired to forsake them? If there is no such conflict in your life, you have not yet really met your holy God.

Yet, at the same time that the Spirit is in conflict with sinful nature, sinful nature is in conflict with the Spirit. In the face of temptations you will see your spiritual laziness and resistance to the gracious work of God. This is how the Holy Spirit works in the awakened Christian. "Conflict identifies the true Christian."

9 / Virtues Are the Fruit of Faith

"Make a tree good and its fruit will be good" Mt 12:33.

THE LIST of Christian virtues includes humility, faithfulness, patience, truthfulness, and freedom. A Christian strives to acquire these virtues. A closer look shows that these virtues are closely related.

A truthful person is free in his relationships with others; he does not need to pretend or feel embarrassed. A humble person does not despise small tasks; he is faithful and patiently accepts whatever comes his way. And truthfulness again is related to humility, for the humble person is willing to be who he is, neither more nor less.

The Christian attitude is not fragmented; it simply has many facets. This is because all virtues grow from the same root: a person's relationship to God. A person who lives in God's presence is humble, for he knows that whatever he has is from God and is undeserved. A person who lives in God's presence feels responsible, so he is faithful even in little things. Living in God's presence, a person is drawn into the eternal light, so he neither pretends nor fabricates. And a person living in God's presence is immune to the criticisms and opinions of others.

Christian virtues are not qualities a person develops on his own; they are the fruit of his life as God's child. Faith in God is the root from which all virtues grow.

10 / Christ's Voice Needs to Be Heard

"If you remain in me and my words remain in you, ask whatever you wish, and it will be given you" Jn 15:7.

WE ARE SICK because our prayer life is anemic. We recognize the illness but the cure is hard to find. The Lord offers help when he says, "If you remain in me and my words remain in you, ask whatever you wish, and it will be given you."

We do not know how to pray because we are not in Christ and his words are not in us. We are fickle, impatient, and unfaithful. We think we can be disciples without seriously deciding for Christ and seriously intending to remain in Him.

Henrik Renqvist, the nineteenth-century Finnish pastor who helped pioneer a spiritual movement that focused on prayer, spoke from experience when he observed that prayer is work we must do "thick and fast," as though rowing up stream. Our problem is that we lack the desire to endure and suffer for Christ.

In the original Greek the word "to remain" means "to abide, dwell, or linger." We are to abide with Christ, dwell in him, linger in his presence. We must do it deliberately, without permitting anything to lure us away from him. Otherwise we will never become people of prayer.

But Christ's words must also remain in us. The Greek text says that it is a matter of Christ's "speech" remaining in us. The Lord speaks to us, with something very personal to say. Unless we pay attention to his speech, and put into practice what God says to us in Christ, we will not know how to pray.

We have all sorts of religious thoughts, but have we allowed Christ to screen them, so that we hear his voice? As you read your Bible, listen for what Christ is saying to you. You will be preparing yourself for prayer. Hearing Christ's voice and remaining in him are the most important requirements for faith.

11 / Suffering for Our Sins

"Woe to us for we have sinned" Lm 5:16.

MANY COMPLAIN about the evil times, unable to talk about anything else. As Christians we should be able to complain and worry about something altogether different--our own wickedness. According to the Bible, when we suffer individually and as a nation, it is because of our sins.

This statement understandably offends a lot of people. We are offended by accusations and admonitions that speak to our consciences, for by nature we can't even begin to understand what God expects of us. Even many Christians have this attitude. Where are people who recognize their guilt? We grumble against God, but who grumbles against himself?

In a grave in Jerusalem ancient urns were found with the inscription: "Woe, woe, woe!" Do we hear such lament today? Consider the writer of Lamentations who, on the ruins of Jerusalem, lamented his personal involvement in the misfortune of his people: "The crown has fallen from our head! Woe to us, for we have sinned" Lm 5:16. Where are the pastors, the fathers and mothers, the teachers and educators, who confess their sins before God?

God's wrath will rest upon us until He is able to bend us to repentance. A frightening future lies before us, unless we humble ourselves under God's mighty hand. We face a miserable future, and a miserable eternity!

12 / Christ Overcomes Fear

*"Therefore do not worry about tomorrow, for tomorrow
will worry about itself"* Mt 6:34.

HOW WILL I manage tomorrow? How will I achieve financial
security? How will I plan for the future? These are the questions
people ask. It takes courage to live today. The economic squeeze
is on.

Fear of tomorrow also includes fear of illness. Such fear is
not always imaginary, especially when illness is a reality and
death is at the door. Who knows how many sleepless nights this
fear has caused.

Nations share a great fear about tomorrow. We move ahead
at jet speed, but no one knows where it will all end. Dark clouds
loom on the horizon; the forecast is not good. No matter how real
this fear of tomorrow may be, it is not the fear that comes from
the Lord. Its vanity is evident in the fact that what we fear
seldom happens. Something else happens, perhaps something
serious, but something else nevertheless. Why then do we
entertain such fear?

A Christian cannot overcome fear by himself; his comfort
and strength lie in the knowledge that God is a living God. "You
guide me with your counsel," says the psalmist (Ps 73:24). And
Paul exclaims, "(Nothing) in all creation will be able to separate
us from the love of God that is in Christ Jesus our Lord" Ro 8:39.
More precious than the presents God gives us is His own
presence.

Fear can be overcome only by union with Christ. There is no
point in fighting fear! Rather, let us fight to get close to Christ
and to remain with him.

13 / Christ Changes Grief into Joy

"I will see you again and you will rejoice" Jn 16:22.

SOME HAVE SAID that Christians comfort one another too
much and that life ought to be lived with rigor and courage. A
person ought to pay the full price for his portion of life, endure it
like a man, and suffer like a hero.

We tend, no doubt, to pity ourselves and complain a lot. We are soft. Nevertheless, God's word, with its abundant comfort, is not irrelevant. "Comfort, comfort my people" says the Lord already in the Old Testament (Is 40:1). In the New Testament Paul praises God as "the God of all comfort, who comforts us in all our troubles, so that we can comfort those in any trouble with the comfort we ourselves have received from God" 2 Co 1:3f.

The Lord does not promise his children life without troubles. "You will grieve." That is still true. "But your grief will turn to joy." That too is still true (Jn 16:20).

How does this happen? Do disciples grow inwardly stronger as they struggle with their troubles? No, Christianity is not a matter of spiritual exercises which strengthen and temper the soul. It is the Lord who brings comfort as he arrives to help us. "I will see you again and you will rejoice" Jn 16:22. We disciples are far too weak to bear the burdens of life alone.

But the strength of the Lord comes alive in our weakness. The Lord changes our grief into joy. The presence of the Lord is the comfort of the soul.

14 / Even a Coward Must Choose

"Make every effort to enter through the narrow door, because many, I tell you, will try to enter and will not be able to" Lk 13:24.

A PERSON has no choice but to choose. The ability to decide brings nobility to human life. When the Bible says man has been created in God's image it means that we are responsible to God for our choices.

On the other hand, our attempt to evade decisions and shirk responsibility gives witness to our fallen state. We hide our cowardice under attractive cover, readily resorting to the excuse that we must not hurry, that the time is not yet ripe. By waiting we try to escape responsibility and avoid decisions.

We talk about constant striving, saying that no one will become complete. We will always remain novices. This is true, but have we ever seriously tried to be responsible? We imagine ourselves as beginners, but have we ever stood at the starting line and made the decision to get going? We cannot be beginners unless we actually start.

Our cowardice also reveals that we view our choices as insignificant. We want something more important to get us going!

But unless you start with little things, you will never make it in bigger things. When you consider something as being too insignificant, you are just concerned about your own skin. You are postponing your decision in order to escape the difficult task of having to choose. Imagining great things about yourself, you are actually motivated by cowardice.

Such is fallen man when it comes to making decisions. But, failure to choose is still a choice. You choose the lifestyle of a divided mind.

15 / To Talk We Need to Listen

"Give ear and come to me; hear me, that your soul may live" Is 55:3.

WE SELDOM ASK why people are deaf-mutes. We often assume that the vocal cords are defective. But, muteness often stems from deafness. If children lose their hearing they often lose their speech, too.

This illustrates a common aspect of spiritual muteness. There is a saying that God has no mute children. Christians need to talk about matters of faith, but we are slow to speak. Our prayer life is often weak and virtually non-existent. How reluctant we are to talk about the Lord with one another! The topics of our conversation cover all areas of life except the spiritual.

The cause of muteness is deafness. We do not pray or converse with others about Christ, because we are deaf to the Lord's voice. Even if we have heard him we have often not bothered to listen. Satan lures us from the discipline of taking time each morning to listen to the Lord.

If you feel that your prayer life needs renewal, start listening to the Lord. Ask him to open your ears. Take time to be still before the Lord and study his word. In addition, listen to what other children of God have to say. Move about among them; let them be your friends. Do not be offended by their faults. No matter what happens, stay in their fellowship.

If you intend to become a talkative child of God, who prays to God and converses with others easily and naturally about spiritual matters, you must do a great deal of listening to God and to His people.

16 / People With God's Wisdom

"He had wisdom from God" 1 K 3:28.

KING SOLOMON had all kinds of advisors. But, he personally took his life and responsibility as king very seriously. He understood that he, more than anyone else, including his many advisors, was expected to know the difference between right and wrong. It was not enough to do what had been done before or what others did. It was necessary to find out what was right and then to do it impartially.

People like this have a positive impact on their surroundings, even though they must often stand alone and withstand bitter attacks. They are people of conscience; but a conscientious person is born and grows only on the road of inner decisions. That was the case with Solomon. The Lord had allowed him to choose what he wanted, and Solomon asked for an obedient heart to distinguish between right and wrong; "for who is able to govern this great people of yours" 1 K 3:9.

Is this how we feel? Or do we dare to express our thoughts and criticisms, dishing out advice and giving directions indiscriminately, without consulting first with the Lord? No wonder we are surrounded by bitter controversy and filled with inner conflict. These are the marks of the worldly wisdom we follow. The wisdom of God, which comes from above, "is first of all pure; then peace-loving, considerate, submissive, full of mercy and good fruit, impartial and sincere" Jas 3:17.

What we need more than anything else is people of whom we can say, "They have God's wisdom." Such people are born and grow in the decisions which are made in the presence of God and not according to one's own mind and will.

17 / Christ Is the Church Door

"I am the gate for the sheep" Jn 10:7.

WHEN the oriental shepherd had gathered his sheep into the sheepfold, he lay down in the entrance and slept there through the night. Thus he stood guard over his flock. When Jesus spoke of himself as the gate of the sheep He had this in mind. He himself is in the opening; no one can enter or leave but through him.

This is Jesus' way of teaching that no one becomes a child of God except through him. He is the only gate, but it is also true that we become members of his flock through him. Believing in him we become members of his Church. There are no individual Christians, only members of the Church. Union with Christ always means membership in his Body.

Once Jesus said of the Jews, "You do not believe because you are not my sheep" Jn 10:26. Unless we belong to Jesus' flock, his Church, we cannot believe in him as Jesus intends. This may offend some who, being very individualistic, despise other Christians and do not fellowship with the Lord. This offense, however, cannot be eliminated, for it belongs to the Gospel. Luther says that God's word does not exist without God's people. Unless we live in communion with God's people we do not have God's word. Jesus is the gate; whoever believes in Him becomes a member of His flock. He is the door of the Church.

But Jesus is the gate also in the sense that only through him can we find entrance into human hearts. There is no use in my trying to get a person to obey God's will, unless I go to him through Jesus, pray to Jesus and believe in him. This pertains especially to teachers, who are responsible for caring for children and youth.

Forget your own efforts! Eliminate all coercion! Do away with depression and despair! Jesus is still the gate, and the gate is open.

18 / One for All, All for One

"...in order that Satan might not outwit us" 2 Co 2:11.

ACCORDING to the Bible a Christian faces danger as long as he is in the world. "Your enemy the devil prowls around like a roaring lion looking for someone to devour" 1 Peter 5:8. But the Christian is not alone. If he were, if he had to fight the enemy alone, his situation would be hopeless. But, as Christians we are members of Christ's Body. We can say, "All for one and one for all."

A member of the church in Corinth had fallen into open sin. Others had noticed it, but for some reason, perhaps politeness, uneasiness, or sympathy, they tolerated him and left the sin unjudged. This gave Paul the occasion for severe admonition and serious action. The poor soul repented from the bottom of his heart, but the others, refusing to forgive him, excluded him from their fellowship. Again the apostle had to intervene: "Now instead, you ought to forgive and comfort him, so that he will not be overwhelmed by excessive sorrow" 2 Co 2:7.

It is moving to see how Paul cares for this individual who had caused him such great sorrow. It shows what "one for all and all for one" really means in practice. We need both strong words of admonition and healing words of forgiveness in our Christian relationships. Satan will get his way unless this happens.

Let us not imitate the world by spending our time in idle talk, or looking away from unfortunate incidents. Let us not join the crowd in judging the judged, or beating the beaten. We must be alert lest Satan outwit us. One for all and all for one.

19 / "Although" Faith

"Although our sins testify against us, O Lord, do something for the sake of your name" Jr 14:7.

WHEN A PERSON is awakened, he realizes he is in the Lord's hands, but also discovers that he is a poor and condemned sinner. He can no longer doubt that the Lord is at work in him, but he recognizes his failure to cooperate with him in this saving work. He understands that the Lord wants to help him, but only if he lives wholeheartedly for the Lord. But when experience reveals deceit in the depths of his heart, and dishonest intentions, doubt begins to undermine his confidence and he loses the courage to ask the Lord's assistance. He can believe that the Lord does his work in others, but not in him.

Such must have been the struggle of the man of God who prayed: "Although our sins testify against us, O Lord, do something for the sake of your name." My sins testify that, because of my own will, I have fallen into sin and found pleasure in it. Still, I must ask the Lord to do something for me, too. This prayer reveals an "although" faith.

But how long can anyone continue to utter such a prayer? Not long, if not for the Lord's work which he accomplished once and for all on Golgatha. The cross shows us the kind of God we have and how precious our salvation is to him. Only those who, defeated by sin, turn their eyes upon the Christ of the cross are able to pray: "Although our sins testify against us, O Lord, do something for the sake of your name."

20 / Jesus Is Our Friend

"I have told you this so that my joy may be in you and that your joy may be complete" Jn 15:11.

THE GOSPEL is good news, joyful news. The people who heard the Lord Jesus preach the gospel in person were caught up in such joy that he compared them to wedding guests. "I have told you this so that my joy may be in you and that your joy may be complete."

In John 15 Jesus calls his disciples his friends. True friendship always sparks joy, as well as longing and loneliness. One is lonely when the friend is gone; longing fills the heart. Friends of Jesus will experience such longing and loneliness. The closer their friendship with Jesus the greater their loneliness when they no longer sense his presence. They long for Jesus; it is him they await; nothing can take his place. This is the mark by which the true friends of Jesus are known.

Many people are happy when they have no troubles and life moves according to plan. If they are pious, they find joy in their piety and religious experiences. With head knowledge they assure themselves and others that they are very happy. The true friends of Jesus, however, are not satisfied with anything but him. They do not trust their knowledge about spiritual things, nor their experiences. When Jesus is among them, their hearts are filled with joy and they know they are among the wedding guests.

Longing is neither merit nor a condition of salvation for the friends of Jesus; it is, however, an indication of whose friends they are.

21 / Jesus Opens Heaven for Us

"I tell you the truth, you shall see heaven open, and the angels of God ascending and descending on the Son of Man" Jn 1:51.

THIS STATEMENT declares, first of all, that in the company of Jesus we are beneath an open heaven. That's what happened to the disciples on the Mount of Transfiguration. It happened on other occasions, too, when the Lord revealed his great power in the midst of human misery and poverty; as he freed the victims of Satan and forgave sins. In many ways the disciples witnessed the powers of an open heaven.

Today the followers of Jesus experience something similar. Our wishes and aspirations do not open heaven; the presence of Jesus does.

The promise of Jesus reminds us of Jacob's experience in Bethel. In a dream he saw heaven open and God's angels ascending and descending on a ladder. These angels were God's servants, sent to the guilty Jacob to tend to God's business. Strange that a man whose life was such a mess received such grace! Today the affairs of many whom God has chosen and called are also a mess. But the Lord does not leave them in their sins; he remembers them, comes to them and takes them back into his fellowship.

Notice that the Lord says his disciples will see angels ascending and descending. The order is important. The angels first carry the prayers of frail, fallen creatures to the throne of God and then return with his answers. Often we feel that our prayers are too weak to rise to God. But God sends his angels to handle the delivery of the petitions of the poor pilgrims.

No matter how things are with us, when the Lord calls us to join him, we do well to heed his call without delay. Otherwise heaven will remain closed; both now, while we are on the road, as well as when we reach our destination, and eternity begins.

22 / God Works in Us

"He who began a good work in you will carry it on to completion until the day of Christ Jesus" Phil 1:6.

GOD'S SAVING ACTS in our lives are often such that only afterwards are we aware of having been in His hands. God has difficulty making us callous and cold creatures aware of and sorry for our sins. The only way He can do it is by laying a heavy hand on us. He must work repentance and faith in us by Himself. Even when God's hand is heavy upon us, everything He is doing is part of His good and gracious work.

Who wouldn't want to be saved with an unrepentant and unbroken heart? However, Christianity without sorrow over sin and tears of repentance has no power for new life. It is only surface glitter. Whoever sorrowfully admits the corruption in his heart knows that he is the object of God's good work. Let him humble himself under God's mighty hand, and not make it necessary for God to increase the pressure.

There are Christians who go about the work of confessing their sins, believing in Christ, and living the Christian life as though it were a personal project. They tell others many things about their "experiences" with complete sincerity.

Then there are others who do not know how to confess their sins, who fear that their confessions are imperfect, who do not know how to believe as they should. They are unable to continue the struggle and give up.

Christians must depend entirely upon what God does in them. Whether we are saints or sinners, we must continue to work our way toward the Lord, so that he might save us. With people like us in mind the Bible says, "He who began a good work in you will carry it to completion until the day of Christ Jesus."

23 / Awareness of Sin and Guilt

*"Each one is tempted when, by his own evil desire, he is
dragged away and enticed"* Jas 1:14.

EVIL DESIRES tempt all of us. The Bible says that even the
best of us is tempted by his own evil desires. We are all enticed
by the promise of gratification and happiness. Christians are no
exception to this powerful influence.

The old nature is the dwelling place of evil. In the words of a
hymn:

> In your flesh the tempter dwells,
> Deep in your heart the power of sin.

If we concentrate on the evil desires of others we may
become oblivious to our own. Fully aware of another's evil
desires, even wishing to do penance for them, we must not
ignore the evil desires in our own heart.

God's Spirit will show us our own evil desires and we will
learn to call them by their true name. Greed, vanity, ambition,
lust: our personal evil desires have many names.

When we clearly see that we have deliberately yielded to
these sinful desires, we become aware of our guilt before God.
We have fallen in love with evil when we ought to have resisted
and rejected it.

But, awareness of our weakness to temptation is not enough.
Knowledge of sin is also consciousness of guilt, the shameful
awareness that we have deliberately followed our evil desires.
Until this happens, and consciousness of guilt deepens into a
personal guilty conscience in the presence of God, the need for
grace will not become real in our hearts.

24 / Words of Spirit and Life

*"The words I have spoken to you are spirit and they are
life"* Jn 6:63.

SPIRIT AND LIFE; we need both. If the Spirit is missing, life is
also missing. Jesus says that "the words I have spoken to you

are spirit and they are life." Only the words of Jesus can give spirit and life.

We do not need to have wonderful experiences. We do not need to force something significant out of ourselves. Paul asks, "Did you receive the Spirit by observing the law, or by believing what you heard?" Ga 3:2. The Spirit is not received by doing something but by believing in Someone. And this belief comes through the Word.

The words of Jesus are still spirit and life for us, preserved for us in the gospels. They have special significance precisely because they are spirit and life.

When we thirst for spirit and life let us remember Jesus' own words, and let them speak to us. Our faithfulness toward the Bible needs to be renewed. To be able to read the very words that Jesus once uttered is an incredible joy. These words are a priceless treasure, for they are spirit and life for us.

25 / Baptism Signifies Daily Repentance

"Whoever believes and is baptized will be saved" Mk 16:16.

FOR MANY people baptism means giving a name to a child and entering it in the parish register. According to the New Testament, however, baptism is something quite different. Paul says, "Don't you know that all of us who were baptized into Christ Jesus were baptized into his death? We were therefore buried with him through baptism into death in order that just as Christ was raised from the dead through the glory of the Father, we too may live a new life" Ro 6:3f. Baptism unites us with Christ, with his death and resurrection.

Do you understand what baptism means to you? Are you living by the grace of God given to you in baptism? Throughout his life Luther could say, "I have been baptized, I shall be saved!" Besieged by temptations and troubles, Luther appealed to the fact that in baptism God had received him as His child, and that Satan had no claim on him. Even today, a troubled person may find that at times his only refuge is his baptism. Against the accusations of Satan we can only appeal to the grace of baptism, to the fact that in baptism God's grace has become mine, too. "I have been baptized; I shall be saved."

Living in the grace of my baptism does not just mean that I may appeal to the promises given in baptism for the strengthening of my faith. In baptism, in addition to being assured of God's grace, I have also been grafted into Christ. Just as a gardener improves the trees by grafting branches from one tree to another, so God in baptism grafts us into Christ that we might bear good fruit. We are united with the powers of redemption that erupted into this world through Christ's death and resurrection. We have been improved, and our old nature no longer has any claim on us. "Our old self was crucified with him so that the body of sin might be done away with, so that we should no longer be slaves to sin" Ro 6:6. Paul implies that baptism has done away with this body of sin.

Living in baptismal grace means that each day we experience the death of the old nature and the rising to life of the new. In other words, we live in daily repentance. By the grace of God, and through the death and resurrection of Christ, we have been given the power to live a new life.

26 / Heaven Is My Home

"My Father's house..." Jn 14:2.

SOME PEOPLE criticize Christians when they talk about yearning for heaven. "Things of the afterlife are not our business," they say. "We need to deal with the things entrusted to us in this life." However, Jesus does not reproach those who are homesick for heaven. On the contrary, we get the impression from the writings of his apostles that they often talked about the Father's house and encouraged believers to keep heaven in mind. If we follow the teachings of the New Testament, we not only have permission to look forward to our homecoming, but the command to do so.

The genuineness of our Christianity is in direct proportion to the attention we give to heaven. But, this longing for heaven does not imply that we live in a fantasy world. It is natural for a child who is away to remember his home and long for it, but he also keeps in mind what that home means to him. He lives in the spirit of his family wherever he may be. A Christian who longs for heaven seeks to live and move about in the spirit of heaven. He loves the spirit of his heavenly home and seeks to live out God's will in that spirit. He feels like a stranger in this world, which is dominated by a foreign spirit, for his mind is on heavenly things. As the apostle says, "Set your minds on things above, not on earthly things" Col 3:2.

Of course we do not think of heaven unless we know it to be our true home. We can live in hope, in the spirit of heaven, only if we have been reborn as God's children. Heaven is the Father's house, and only his children long for home.

27 / Power to Put Off the Old Self

"You were taught to put off your old self...and to put on the new self" Eph 4:22, 24.

THERE IS the story of the wind and the sun arguing about who was stronger. An elderly woman happened to be going by, and the two decided that the one who could get the coat off the woman would be the stronger. The wind blew as hard as it could, but the woman simply wrapped her coat more tightly around herself. Then the sun tried its power. It did not take long before the woman opened her coat and then removed it. The sun had won.

Paul talks about the old self and compares it and its deceitful desires to a tattered coat that should be removed. What power can make us do that? Will we follow the stern commands of the law? Hardly! The law is like the cold wind. Many hearts are freezing, aware of their evil nature, weighed down by sin, ashamed of their filthy thoughts, cruel words, and undisciplined behavior. But under the demands of the law they shiver inwardly and are unable to put off the old self; they only wrap themselves in it more tightly and continue their sad journey.

But when the warm sun of God's grace begins to shine on a poor miserable creature, his heart begins to open up. The gracious word of God, shining upon us in Christ, begins to warm the cold heart. The sinner begins to understand that God loves him, that Christ has made him a friend of God, and that he is one of the ungodly who are justified for Christ's sake. Not until God's abundant grace shines upon the sinner will he be able to put off the old self and to put on the new.

There are many Christians who are depressed because of their sins but are unable to get rid of them. The only power that can do that comes from the warm rays of God's grace.

28 / Power Comes from God

"The kingdom of God is not a matter of talk but of power"
1 Co 4:20.

WE ARE FED UP with words, even pious words. How often have sermons and devotional talks bored us to death? We do not need words, we want power.

According to one way of thinking, we need reliable information if we are to live right. If I have the right words, all I have to do is implement them. But, our problem is not that we don't have the right words; it is our failure to implement the divine truths we have learned. This is what Paul means when he says "the kingdom of God is not a matter of talk but of power."

The power Paul has in mind has nothing to do with our ability or inability to carry out the necessary action. God Himself is the active and effective power in His kingdom. Jesus said the same thing: "If I drive out demons by the finger of God, then the kingdom of God has come to you" Lk 11:20.

Can this have any practical significance for our lives? Yes, if we remember, first of all, that the power is God's. We do not need to generate this power in ourselves. Power is not found in our spiritual enthusiasm or will power; it is always found in God. The less we trust our own power, the more we will experience God's power. If we experience so little of God's power it is because we have tried to live by our own.

We also must not despair, even though until now we have received only words. We may feel deeply disappointed because we have not yet experienced God's power. But, the resources of God's kingdom are still available. We have great things ahead of us. True Christians long for the fulfillment of great expectations. "Expect great things from God!"

29 / Obey Your Conscience

"When Herod heard John, he was greatly puzzled, yet he liked to listen to him" Mk 6:20

WHEN HEROD listened to John the Baptist, he was greatly puzzled because the word touched a sensitive spot. He had not yet been awakened to awareness of sin, but the word aroused questions and made him uncomfortable. However, he paid no attention to the word. Then, in a critical moment, he gave in to Satan and rushed headlong into temporal and eternal destruction.

Has this ever happened to you? Listening to the word you found yourself puzzled. Reflecting on things that had happened in your life, you began to ask whether certain things were sins. Has your relationship to that person been an honorable one? Do you behave responsibly at all times? In money matters, do you put your own interest ahead of others? Are you irresponsible in your work?

These and many similar questions come to mind as a person listens to God. Take heed of the word that has made you restless, otherwise you will face what Herod faced. The puzzling word is meant to save you. If you do not heed it, nothing can keep you from becoming Satan's next victim.

In the depths of your soul there may be a word that once made you restless but which you still have not obeyed. Your day of salvation will never dawn, unless you obey that voice of your conscience.

30 / We Need Not Be Everywhere

"Paul, a servant of Christ Jesus, called to be an apostle and set apart for the gospel of God" Ro 1:1.

GOD CHOSE Paul as His servant and gave him a special assignment. Aware of this calling, Paul describes himself as every Christian can describe himself. We have all been called to be people who are apart, people who have only one interest. We are to be people who do not scatter our efforts but focus them and plow a deep furrow.

There are many reasons for such scattered efforts. Sometimes for lack of help the same person must assume too many responsibilities. But, most of the time this is not the reason. People are usually driven by lust for power and glory. We keep ourselves in the limelight, make ourselves important, and think we are indispensable. Related closely to lust for power and glory is lust for money. We run wherever there is money to be made.

In short, a fragmented life results from trying to make it on our own without seeking God's will.

In order to center his life in Christ, Paul had to consider as rubbish things that in themselves were precious. "Whatever was to my profit I now consider loss for the sake of Christ" Phil 3:7. He paid a heavy price to remain faithful to his heavenly vision.

It will not be by magic that we are set apart and become people able to concentrate on being obedient to God's will. Through faith we will not take a single step in any direction without the Lord's permission. We need not be everywhere; but, we do need the Lord wherever we are.

May

1 / The Power of Persistent Prayer

"The prayer of a righteous man is powerful and effective"
Jas 5:16.

CHRISTIAN LIFE becomes impotent largely because of our continuing neglect of prayer. We turn deaf ears to the Bible as it speaks to us about the possibilities of prayer. One of the often ignored references to prayer is Jesus' exhortation to his own to pray for their enemies. "But I tell you: Love your enemies and pray for those who persecute you" Mt 5:44. Jesus is talking about enemies who systematically and knowingly, not accidentally or incidentally, harass and persecute his disciples. These enemies represent the united forces of Satan, who has available for his use all the skills and talents of the human spirit. In our day we need not think of the executioner's block or prison cells, used by Satan in the past to express his hatred toward Christ. We know that evil words, ungodly propaganda, and similar weapons employed against Christ and his Church are just as powerful.

How does Christ want us to defend ourselves against the attacks of our enemies? By prayer! "Pray for those who persecute you." Jesus knew that prayer is a weapon Satan fears. Satan is not afraid of big words, but he cannot stand prayer.

This throws new light on the possibilities of prayer in general. Jesus urges us to resort to prayer when oppressed and persecuted. The power of prayer is greater than the power of darkness, and prayer has practical value in all sorts of life situations. Perhaps you are especially perplexed by a particular problem and have agonized a great deal about it. In your restlessness and impatience perhaps you have even troubled your neighbors. Why don't you pray? If you do, you will discover the hidden power of persistent prayer.

2 / Faith as Response to God

"Now faith is being sure of what we hope for and certain of what we do not see" He 11:1.

IF WE HAVE no faith, we have nothing at all. Faith contains everything, for only through faith does God become real for us. Without faith all we have is some inner religious stirrings or moral strivings. In faith we can see God active in and behind everything, working for our salvation. Faith is not a human achievement; no one can decide to begin to believe. Faith is born when God works within a person. Faith is our human response to a divine summons. Faith, as a human response, includes a specific element of personal activity. It does not come about in a mechanical way. It is born, maintained, and nurtured in the process of decision-making on the path of obedience.

Some people try to believe without repentance. They are willing to claim God's grace, but they have not submitted to what God requires of them. They are Christians with minds untransformed, revealing their lack of basic trust in God.

Some of us have been Christians for many years. When we were first awakened, God's will was so holy we could not evade it. We were caught up in repentance, but with time we have become inwardly calloused, no longer feeling the need for repentance. Such faith has ceased to be living faith; and God has ceased to be a living reality.

Faith without repentance cannot see the works of God nor can it rejoice over God's gracious activity in our lives. "Now faith is being sure of what we hope for and certain of what we do not see." Without faith to bring certain knowledge of God's active love, we will also lack the hope that is born of faith.

3 / Certainty in the Midst of Uncertainty

"Against all hope, Abraham in hope believed.... He did not waver through unbelief regarding the promise of God, but was strengthened in his faith and gave glory to God" Ro 4:18,20.

LIVING FAITH is both hopelessness and hope; a state of tension similar to that experienced by the father who said to Jesus, "I do believe; help me overcome my unbelief' Mk 9:24. Some judge such faith as weak, assuming that God's wold and His help are always clear and certain to the eye of faith, and that belief eliminates all panic and hopelessness.

This is not why Paul sets Abraham up as the model for Christians. Abraham looked squarely at the fact that he and Sarah were far beyond the normal age to bear children, yet he did not waver in his faith despite the hopelessness of his situation. Sometimes we imagine that faith turns our eyes away from raw reality to the hills from whence God will help us. We think God will find some way to keep His people from hopeless situations and let them live in unbroken awareness of His marvelous power.

Paul says otherwise. He had personally experienced times of utter despair (2 Co 1:8). Faith means hoping when there is no hope, something that is possible only when we cling to the promises of God. That is what Abraham did and what all believers have done. Were faith a matter of certainty without despair, there would be very few who could be called believers. If we are even slightly conscious of the corruption of our hearts, and have even glimpsed the deceptive cunning of Satan that leads us into hopeless situations, we would be driven even farther from certainty.

But we hopeless creatures, who know the raw reality of despair and hoplessness, may cling to God's promises, just as we are. Above all, we cling to the promise that God justifies the ungodly for the sake of Jesus Christ.

No matter the situation, no matter how hopeless the cold facts may seem, we may believe. Especially in times of despair, faith clings to the Good News of God's promise.

4 / Life and Deeds of Faith

"The righteous will live by faith" Ro 1:17.

WE SHOULD be living Christians. The Lord expects us to be available for his service and to do his works. We should function according to God's will no matter what the circumstances. This means serving and loving our neighbors, denying ourselves and living for others.

How shall we become such living, active Christians? Paul answers: "The righteous will live by faith." People often separate faith and works, insisting that in addition to faith, good works are required for us to be true Christians. Nothing is farther from Paul's view of faith. Only one who has been justified by faith can live and work; and when God Himself is at work in us we will certainly be quite active. We will be turned from the power of Satan to the power of God's beloved Son (Ac 26:18), where Christ's love compels us. New life and new Christian deeds are always born from faith.

Paul clearly restates this truth when he says that God's righteousness is revealed "by faith from first to last" Ro 1:17. Faith from first to last! Faith is the starting point, to which God brings the unbeliever; but faith is also the goal. In this life we never get beyond faith. Only in heaven will faith become sight. For now, in our spiritual lives, we can help one another only as believers.

It is said of the men who carried their paralyzed friend to Jesus for healing that "Jesus saw their faith" Mk 2:5. In their own eyes they were not believers, but Jesus saw their faith in their efforts to help their friend. We, too, can only do the works of God in this world as believers. "The righteous will live by faith." He who is justified by faith will live and be involved in the things of God.

5 / Blessed to Be a Blessing

"I will bless you..., and you will be a blessing" Gn 12:2.

WE ARE ALWAYS under the influence of other people. We know individuals in whose company our souls suffer. They impress us negatively, stirring the murky and muddy waters within us. Our tongues begin to sing forbidden tunes, impure thoughts awaken in our souls, a selfish and deceitful spirit takes over. God's Spirit withdraws and our relationship to the Lord is disturbed.

Then there are people in whose presence we experience the opposite. In their company we cease to speak evil about others. When they are near, unclean and deceitful thoughts stay far from us. Their very being has the effect of checking the powers of darkness within us and we feel cleansed in their company. When they are present it is easier to pray, and the Word comes alive! These friends bless us without uttering a word, for God's Spirit is active in them. The blessing does not come from them but from the Lord, whose presence sanctifies them.

What is your impact on your environment? Do your stumblings and defeats become stumblings and defeats to your friends; or are your strivings and victories strivings and victories for them? Your influence on other people does not depend on what you say but on who you are. And the Lord wants to have something to say about that. He wants to make you his own, his child. You can be a blessing to others only if you have first received a blessing from the Lord.

6 / Salvation Must Have Top Priority

"But our citizenship is in heaven" Phil 3:20.

CHRISTIANITY is criticized for its preoccupation with the hereafter and neglect of the here and now. Christians supposedly think too much about heaven and forget earth. The message of Christian faith, it is argued, should aim at temporal things, while contemplation of eternal things is useless if not dangerous.

These arguments contain kernels of truth, but there is no greater mistake than to think of Jesus as some kind of apologist for temporal things. This life, this temporary existence, was most certainly not the core of his message. He did not come to tell people how to live this present life most conveniently and purposefully. Heaven was his home.

In Jesus' view the great human tragedy was lack of contact with heaven. Rather than being God's children, citizens of heaven, people had fallen into sin, become victimized by Satan and death, and were imprisoned in darkness. He came to give

them the right to become God's children. He came to save them
and destroy the works of Satan. Heaven would become their
home.

 We are true to the teachings of Jesus when our faith is
centered on questions such as: Am I saved? Will I get to heaven
where all things are new? These questions are not a false
spiritualizing of Christianity, which would weaken its influence
on things in this world. The matter of salvation must be of
utmost importance to us, for we need to be transferred from the
power of sin and Satan into the kingdom of God's beloved Son.
This takes place in personal repentance and faith. As Augustine
says, "Hasten, hasten to eternal joys!"

7 / As a Cripple to Heaven

*"The Lord comforts his people and will have compassion
on his afflicted ones"* Is 49:13.

MANY YEARS ago a book came out with the title *As a Cripple to
Heaven*. This combination of words illustrates an important
truth of Christian life: God takes His own as "cripples to
heaven." Someone who is physically crippled, missing an arm or
a leg, can be mentally heroic and strong, tenaciously able to take
care of himself. A spiritual cripple, however, is helpless in the
very core of his being. Even his faith, his prayers, and the rest of
his Christian striving are flawed. Nevertheless, he may be on his
way to heaven. As a prisoner of Herod, John the Baptist was
inwardly crippled. In the solitude of prison, dark thoughts
overwhelmed him, so that he no longer recognized the Lamb of
God, which takes away the sin of the world. Some interpreters
feel that this could not have happened to John, so they suggest
that John himself had no doubts but sent his questions to Jesus
because of his disciples, who were in danger of taking offense in
Christ. Such an assumption, however, will not hold water. If
that were the case it would be difficult to grasp why Jesus told
the messengers to return to John with the news of what was
taking place. John himself had become inwardly crippled and
needed light in his darkness.

 Perhaps you are such a cripple, having reached the point
where you can no longer believe in Christ. For that reason you
have neglected prayer, and you find it difficult to think of

yourself as being on the road to eternal life. God's work is covered by layers of your personal flaws and failures, so that even your friends find it difficult to see you as a friend of the Lord. Take notice of John in the dark prison cell. It may be divine providence that has put you in a similar place.

God is in process of humbling you by destroying your illusions about yourself and your Christianity. The Lord wants to take you to heaven, but he cannot do it, unless you have become inwardly a cripple.

8 / Faith Comes from Hearing

"Consequently, faith comes from hearing the message, and the message is heard through the word of Christ" Ro 10:17.

ACCORDING to the Bible, it is proper to say to a troubled person: "Believe in the Lord God, He will take care of you!" But certain things must be kept in mind. When we are encouraged to believe in God, we may feel warmth and relief, as if a burden is lifted from us. But soon we realize that our feet are not on solid ground and we become depressed. This reveals that our faith had only to do with our own thoughts and opinions and was not a living Christian faith.

A person cannot just start believing. Our own efforts can only lead us deeper into the quagmire of unbelief. But God never intended for us to believe on our own. During the Old Covenant God spoke to people "many times and in various ways" He 1:1. This divine speech created living faith in His people, so that they could say, "We give thanks to you, O God, we give thanks, for your Name is near; men tell of your wonderful deeds" Ps 75:1.

We are now living in the New Covenant and God speaks to us in His Son. Above all, He has spoken to us in the Christ of Golgatha. We cannot find living Christian faith unless we have heard God speaking to us from the cross. When God speaks in the Christ of Golgatha, we are led to see the reality of sin and grace.

In light of the cross we see that we have no right to live on our own, that no sin has the right to live in us, that our sinful nature must be crucified. But there we also see that the promissory note has been cancelled, our debt has been paid. The guilty conscience has found a place where it can be cleansed, for there is now a fountain flowing with grace and forgiveness.

Luther calls God's kingdom a "kingdom of hearing." He meant that only where the voice of Christ from Golgatha is heard can people believe.

9 / God Hears Prayers for His Sake

"I am the Lord their God and I will answer them" Zec 10:6.

THE SPIRIT of devotion is a divine gift given to enable people to pour their hearts before the Lord in solitude. If you have tasted this grace, be grateful and remember it is a gift God can also take away. Yet, we are mistaken if we pray only when the spirit of devotion fills our souls. After all, God does not hear us because we know how to pray in a devout and quiet spirit. When He hears us it is always solely for His name's sake, for Christ's sake. Do not make your devoutness a condition for God's hearing your prayers. We have special reason to reflect on this, for our minds are often restless and confused with no room for devoutness. As we pray it seems our requests barely reach the ceiling of the room where we kneel in prayer, much less the throne of God on high. But you do not have to pray with the idea of launching your petitions into the realm above the clouds. God indeed "lives in a high and holy place, but also with him who is contrite and lowly in spirit" Is 57:15. He hears the poor petitions that rise out of your confused and restless soul. You may not feel it, but afterwards you will see that God heard you when you cried out to Him. He heard you for His own sake, for Christ's sake.

"But do I have the right to pray when my mind is dead and cold, and nothing in particular bothers me?" you ask. "Does that not make me a hypocrite and my prayers an abomination to the Lord?" In his Large Catechism, Luther advises such people to pray to God because God commands them to pray. Do not wait until in your own mind you have become qualified to pray. Continue to pray in spite of your sense of unworthiness and do it often and regularly, but especially when the Holy Spirit urges you. Remember, God hears even the prayers that rise from cold hearts (O. Hallesby).

10 / Christ Is a Qualified Helper

*"The point of what we are saying is this: We do have such
a high priest, who sat down at the right hand of the
throne of the Majesty in heaven"* He 8:1.

ON ASCENSION DAY Jesus took his place "at the right hand of
the throne of the Majesty in heaven." Before he himself had
taken his proper place he could not send the Holy Spirit upon
his disciples. For this reason the writer of the Letter to the
Hebrews, a man struggling with numerous afflictions, speaks of
Christ's being seated at the right hand of the Father as the
cardinal truth of Christianity.

It doesn't matter what we are, but where Christ is. We
cannot withstand temptations and trials by our own piety, nor
even on divine mercies of yesterday. The secret of our strength is
the exalted Christ.

Look to heaven, you who are weak and weary. Look even
though the cloud into which Christ disappeared from his
disciples on Ascension Day continues to hide him from you.
Christ has been exalted; that's what is important. Our cause is
Christ's. Whatever the reason for our despair, it is the concern of
this exalted Lord. We need no longer consider what is possible
for us, for we can look at what is possibile for Christ. We need to
consider his qualifications.

No matter where we are or what our struggles, we belong in
Christ's sphere of influence and his realm of power. Christ's
place is on the right side of the throne. But before he can give
you his Holy Spirit, you, too, must be in your right place. You
must be on your knees before the throne, the place of a beggar.

11 / The Source of Comfort and Strength

"Be joyful always" 1 Th 5:16.

JESUS HAS Christian joy in mind when he says to his disciples,
"If you obey my commands, you will remain in my love, just as I
have obeyed my Father's commands and remain in his love. I
have told you this so that my joy may be in you and that your joy

may be complete" Jn 15:10f. Only the person who obeys Christ's commandments will find true Christian joy.

Living according to human opinions, following the thoughts of others, doing what others do, making decisions without asking what God says in His word, we will never find true joy. Our joy will be artificial and superficial, unstable and easily disturbed unless we give God's will top billing in our whole lives.

God's will is repulsive to human nature; we prefer to follow our own. But whoever submits to God's will, no matter how difficult it may be, will find true joy.

Jesus points to the source of true joy when he says: "If you obey my commands, you will remain in my love" Jn 15:10. That's where it is. In His marvelous mercy God loves everyone. However, it is one thing to be the object of this love that seeks us, and another to "remain in my love," as Jesus puts it. He who submits to God's word experiences inwardly the wonder of God's love.

A sense of God's presence sustains him on the path of obedience. The Christian has to carry his cross as he walks this path, but even the sorrows that weigh him down cannot deprive him of joy, for he knows they cannot separate him from Christ's love. This is the secret source of his comfort and strength.

12 / Pentecost Comes with Prayer

"They all joined together constantly in prayer" Acts 1:14.

THE LAST THING the disciples saw as they watched their Lord ascend into heaven was his hands lifted up in blessing. The Bible says that "a cloud hid him from their sight" Ac 1:9. Into that cloud disappeared also the hands lifted in blessing. Still, these hands remained real to them and have remained real to every disciple of Jesus to this very day. Those who belong to the Lord have nothing to worry about, as long as the hands lifted up in blessing are also over them.

But, the cloud still hides the Lord and his hands. Only in faith can we talk about our Lord; we cannot see him. This gives rise to many problems. On Ascension Day the disciples returned to the upper room where it was their custom to gather, and there they joined in prayer as they waited for the outpouring of the Spirit. Likewise, when we do not see the Lord or even his hands lifted up in blessing, we must get down on our knees and join other helpless friends of Jesus in prayer. We must remember that Pentecost first arrived and continues to arrive to people who pray. God gives nothing to the lazy.

Pentecost is the answer to the common prayers of the Lord's people. As we wait for Pentecost we need to pray that preachers of the word may speak about the Lord with the power of the Lord's Spirit. We must pray that in our churches we might hear the living word from these tired, tempted and disheartened servants of the word as they draw with joy from the spring of salvation for themselves and for their hearers.

13 / Christianity Is Life

"For with you is the fountain of life" Ps 36:9.

CHRISTIANITY is life; it is personal union with the living Lord. Jesus said, "If you knew the gift of God and who it is that asks you for a drink, you would have asked him and he would have given you living water" Jn 4:10. In the Psalms we read: "With you is the fountain of life." As Christians we live at the fountain of life itself.

When it is genuine, Christian life is characterized by freshness, immediacy and naturalness. Unless we draw from the fountain of life we will have little of this true life. We draw from this fountain through prayer. Is prayer part of life for us, or just something that we associate with Christianity? Are we empowered by our prayers? Do we rise from our knees refreshed? Does prayer transform our thoughts and hopes? Is our prayer transformed into realities of life?

In the light of such pointed questions it becomes clear why our Christianity is often so lifeless. We should not be surprised that what we think is Christianity is not always union with the risen Lord but only a preoccupation with certain religious thoughts and opinions we have picked up here and there. We defend, and even fight for, these ideas, but personal union and fellowship with the Lord is often missing.

Religious ideas do not produce prayers. Only when prayer becomes conversation in the company of the living Lord will we grow into people of prayer. When we are no longer satisfied with religious opinions but seek him who died for us and was raised from the dead, we will begin to draw from the fountain of life.

14 / Water for the Thirsty

"If anyone is thirsty, let him come to me and drink" Jn 7:37.

DURING their wanderings in the wilderness, the children of Israel murmured against the Lord because they had no water to drink. The Lord commanded Moses to strike a rock with his staff, and refreshing water gushed forth. Paul comments that "they drank from the spiritual rock that accompanied them, and that rock was Christ" 1 Co 10:4. Marvelous! In the wilderness you come across a hard rock that cracks open to provide water for you.

This is the life of faith. Not until we find ourselves in a wilderness do we care for the water that gushes from the Christ-Rock. And we have to stand before a hard rock which yields nothing to our efforts before we understand that we need the Holy Spirit.

In the Bible, water is a symbol of the Holy Spirit (Jn 7:39). When the Holy Spirit intercedes, living water begins to bubble forth for the thirsty soul. The Holy Spirit is never given to self-sufficient people full of self-made piety. The Holy Spirit is the heavenly Comforter of thirsty, empty and impoverished souls.

When at the Feast that commemorated the wilderness wanderings of Israel, Jesus called out to the crowd, "If anyone is thirsty, let him come to me and drink," he proclaimed himself as the rock that would crack and provide the water of the Holy Spirit for thirsty souls. Do you believe in the power of the Holy Spirit? Water has flowed out of a rock before; it can happen again for all who are thirsty.

15 / Fear Takes Away, Grief Gives

"Weeping may remain for a night, but rejoicing comes in the morning" Ps 30:5.

"FEAR MAKES a man poor, but sorrow makes him rich." It is worth our while to reflect on this saying.

Fear makes us poor. If we are afraid, a heavy weight enters our hearts. Fear robs us of taste for work, joy and strength. Fear depresses, fostering all sorts of fantasies and prompting desperate action. Fearful, we run away from tasks we would otherwise tackle eagerly. A fearful person trembles like a leaf in the slightest breeze. The Bible speaks of people who for fear of death "were held in slavery" He 1:15. Every form of fear enslaves; a fearful person has the mind of a slave. It is with good reason that doctors and counselors work to free their patients from fears that truly make people poor.

Grief is different, although it is also a heavy burden. But grief somehow clears the air. We know what has happened and can make use of available means of help. The unknown agent that caused fear has left. A starting point for action has been provided. A grieving person is able to gather his resources and take action. In this way grief turns into riches.

Consider the good that grief has accomplished especially for others! At times, grief can immobilize a person, but it doesn't need to. Evil can turn to good when a grieving person begins to take action.

Lord, take away my fears! Add your blessing to my grief and let it enrich my life.

16 / Words That Reach the Heart

"Each one heard them speaking in his own language" Ac 2:6.

EXPERIENCE shows that our words do not always reach the people to whom they are addressed. This is especially well known by those involved in spiritual ministry. It is, sadly, also true in the home: our advice, encouragement, commands and prohibitions do not reach our children. Our words lack power.

It was different on Pentecost. The most marvelous thing in the narrative in Acts is not that tongues of fire came to rest upon the disciples, but that each person present heard and understood the disciples' message. "Each one heard them speaking in his own language." The apostles were on the same wave length as their hearers and their words were effective. The people had no choice but to listen; their lives were clearly the subject of the message. But take note that this happened on Pentecost as a result of the Holy Spirit's activity. Only the Holy Spirit is capable of a miracle like this. How can we give words of advice, commands and prohibitions to our children so that they hear them? Shall we raise our voices, reprimand them or become violent? Hardly! Empty barrels make the most noise! Unless the Holy Spirit is allowed to renew our family life parents' words will not have the power that compels their children to listen.

Let us observe Pentecost by approaching the Lord in prayer and supplication. The dew settles on the lowest spots, and the dew of the Holy Spirit will come to those who are low, humbled by their many failures. This is how we will learn to speak words that reach the heart.

17 / Does Christ Show in Your Life?

"I have been crucified with Christ and I no longer live, but Christ lives in me. The life I live in the body, I live by faith in the Son of God" Ga 2:20.

PAUL'S WORDS, illuminating the Christian life, are incomprehensible during the early stages of a Christian's journey. They start to make sense only as we struggle toward wholeness.

But this much should be clear: being a Christian is something other than the growth of one's ego, or the development of one's personality. In fact, Paul says that he himself no longer lives. It is Christ who lives in him. In this sense Christ is the new self; Christ is the control center of one's life. Christ is the heart of everything in the life of a Christian.

Life in Christ does not consist of special behavior that I can display for others; it is a matter of having Christ in control of my entire life. Christ wants to put his stamp on everything. One cannot be a part-time Christian--it's all or nothing!

The Christian continues to live "in the body," but we are also to live "by faith in the Son of God." Our faith is not limited to worship services or devotional meetings; we are ordained to live by faith in our vocations. In the various affairs of everyday life, the Christian lives in Christ.

In the life of faith the cross of Golgatha occupies a prominent place. "The life I live in the body, I live by faith in the Son of God, who loved me and gave himself for me," says Paul. A Christian's struggle continues throughout life.

The tension between the old self and the new self, "Christ in me", must be faced daily in repentance. Both selves pull at us, each demanding loyalty. We cannot succeed in our struggle without believing in Christ's mercy on the cross, his gift of himself for us. As our faith grows, Christ's hold on us grows stronger, and his love reaches others through our lives.

Galatians 4:19 speaks of how Christ is formed in a person. Life in Christ is not confined to the inner realm. If Christ lives in me, he will certainly be revealed in my life. We need to be concerned that so little of Christ shows in our lives!

18 / Summer Follows Spring

"Now learn this lesson from the fig tree: As soon as its twigs get tender and its leaves come out, you know that summer is near" Mt 24:32.

WE ALL ADMIRE the signs of spring. We get into a festive mood as we watch the new buds on trees and shrubs. New life is ready to burst forth; spring has come.

But imagine if everything stopped with spring and there was no summer at all! How tragic if, after planting and sowing, we could not harvest! What would spring mean if summer did not follow?

In God's kingdom there are also signs of spring. There are stirrings in the spiritual lives of people; God's work is taking place in human hearts. Though often hidden and seemingly insignificant, the signs of the Spirit's activity are evident to those who have eyes to see. Every person convicted in his conscience, every soul hungering for God's word, and every heart reaching toward the Lord--no matter how insignificant these may seem--are signs of the Lord's work. The same is true of children who promise faithfulness to the Lord as they receive the sacrament at the Lord's Table for the first time. This, too, is a sign of spring in God's kingdom.

But let us not be satisfied with these signs; let us look for summer. For it is summer which we await in God's kingdom, the fulfillment of God's promises. The Lord himself tells us that the swollen buds indicate that summer is near. Let us expect the summer of God's kingdom, and work as we wait for its arrival. We may expect great things when summer comes to the Kingdom of God!

19 / Burn Your Bridges Behind You

"Brace yourself like a man" Job 38:3.

NO GREAT CAUSE prospers unless there are people who are willing to invest themselves in the cause. Neither will Christ's cause prosper in this world unless people get involved. Faith is undermined and witness negated when, for reasons of personal safety, we calculate personal risks before following Christ. We maintain emergency exits, hanging on to possibilities other than the one Christ offers. We try to conserve and rationalize instead of following the way of the cross. Unless we burn our bridges behind us, we will have dared nothing, and sacrificed nothing. The Christian is a person with but one cause. We must make our choice and burn our bridges.

The wholehearted servant of the Lord, dedicated to one cause, will also be willing to protest against the world's sinful ways even when it is not personally convenient. Even within Christian groups, attempts to conceal improprieties or flatter one another insincerely will certainly destroy spiritual life. An inner voice compels us to protest whenever and wherever the Christian conscience is violated. Protest is not optional, it is essential.

Jesus expects his friends to be people of good conscience, intent on following the call of God, for only a person with a good conscience can heed his word: "Do not be afraid of those who kill the body and after that can do no more" Lk 12:4. With good reason Jesus said that being ashamed of him, and not following

God's will, is so serious that it leads to not being acknowleged in heaven.

These three, risking oneself, willingness to protest, and good conscience, are the hallmarks of Jesus' friends. Their group has never been large, but whenever God has given new life to His church, He has done so by pouring His Spirit upon small groups of sincere people.

20 / You Must Be Born Again

"Neither circumcision nor uncircumcision means anything; what counts is a new creation" Ga 6:15.

NORMALLY the Christian life is fragmented. We struggle against our own pet sins; we try to help others on special occasions, now and then we read a verse or two of the Bible, and we participate in various Christian activities. Our Christianity is thus a series of large or small acts and exercises, which we attend to at specific times.

The Bible gives a different picture of the Christian life. Being a Christian is not a matter of the various acts and exercises we do, but it is a matter of new life in the Lord. Adorning ourselves in various ways will not help; it will only produce Pharisaical Christianity. New birth is necessary; we must become new people from within to be God's children. "If anyone is in Christ, he is a new creation" 2 Co 5:17.

This biblical truth is in harmony with the modern psychological view of man. Each person is an indivisible whole. His behavior in various situations is determined from within, by the core of his being. Today even physicians are concerned not just with parts of persons, the human organs, but whole persons, human beings.

May this biblical truth, which we ought to understand more deeply in the light of modern psychology, sensitize our consciences to the truth of God's word, "You must be born again." Patching will not help; everything needs to be made over again. The glory of it all is that everything is made over again when Christ makes a person his own. Christ makes all things new.

21 / God Will Take Care of You

"He cares for you" 1 P 5:7.

THE BIBLE often urges us to leave all our cares with the Lord. "Commit your way to the Lord, trust in him and he will do this" Ps 37:5. "Do not be anxious about anything, but in everything, by prayer and petition, with thanksgiving, present your requests to God" Phil 4:6. "Cast your cares on the Lord and he will sustain you" Ps 55:22.

These words contain the secret of peace; they have the renewing power, spirit, and life of God's word. They are seminal words, gently guiding us in the patient art of being a Christian. We all know that seed must be sown into the ground before it can yield a harvest. But we also know that the ground must be plowed and harrowed, fertilized and watered for the seed to germinate and grow. It is the same with God's word.

God's words of blessing cannot germinate, much less produce a harvest, unless our hearts have been cultivated and cared for. This work God Himself wisely performs in us.

Often God must plow deep to get rid of the weeds and break the clods in our hearts. If you are unable to turn your affairs over to the Lord, as His word directs, you can at least be still in His presence. Do not hide in your own activities or try to decide for yourself where the Holy Spirit wants to lead you. Let God work in you. Keep one thing in mind: in order to trust the Lord in our hearts we must be friends of our heavenly Father.

When an anxious sinner believes that he has a friendly Father, and the Holy Spirit keeps his mind focused on this fatherly love, then the promises of God are sweeter than honey, and he is able to trust his cares to God. Only in hearts that are cultivated and cared for can God's word bear fruit.

22 / We Are Not Our Own

"At harvest time he sent a servant to the tenants to collect from them some of the fruit of the vineyard" Mk 12:2.

THE PARABLE of the wicked tenants describes the relationship of people to God. God has the right to everything we have and produce. We are tenants with whom God has shared His possessions. All that we have--money, home, children, friends, occupations, body, and spiritual gifts--is divine property entrusted to us. We are all stewards, accountable to God.

When Paul tells believers to serve God wholeheartedly, "as if you were serving the Lord, not men" Eph 6:7, he is describing the right attitude toward the tasks God has assigned us. We have no right to keep anything for ourselves, for it all belongs to the Lord. But we are like the wicked tenants of the parable, living for ourselves and unwilling to turn over to the Lord what belongs to Him.

We use our time, our goods, everything we have, as though it were our own and not something God has entrusted to us. Like the owner of the vineyard, God sends servants to remind us that everything belongs to Him. Particular circumstances of our lives can act as God's servants in this matter. Especially sickness and death remind us of God's right of ownership. We must finally let go of everything; why not voluntarily turn over to Him what really belongs to Him!

God also uses people as His servants to guide us to repentance. One seldom finds his way to the Lord without someone functioning as God's servant to direct him to the path of repentance. Most importantly, however, God sent His own Son to ask for His portion of the harvest. Christ has been given to us that we might no longer live for ourselves but for God. His sufferings and death are God's most powerful statement that we have no right to live for ourselves.

There may be things in your life that you have not given to God for His use. How do you respond when God's servants point to the need for a radical change in your life? How do you relate to suffering, sickness, and death? To God's people who call you to repentance? To Christ who continues to wait to save you?

23 / To Love Is to Know

"He who loves me will be loved by my Father, and I too will love him and show myself to him" Jn 14:2.

JESUS SAYS he will reveal himself to us. When that happens he will no longer be someone far away, a teacher who lived once upon a time. When Christ has revealed himself, God is more than something we have heard others talk about. God is near us, talks to us, makes Himself known to us and stays with us. As Jesus says, "We will come to him and make our home with him" Jn 14:23.

To whom is this wonderful promise given? Jesus answers, "Whoever hears my commands and obeys them, he is the one who loves me" Jn 14:21. We do not need to have exceptionally remarkable feelings of grace and experiences of salvation to love Jesus. Jesus says we simply must keep his commands. This means exactly what it says. You know in your conscience what he now commands you. Perhaps you think it is so insignificant that it is hardly worth your attention. You look for something bigger and more important to do. But Jesus has given a command, and it must be taken seriously and obeyed. There is no other path to knowing him. Peter says that God has given the Holy Spirit to those who obey Him (Ac 5:32).

"And this is his command: to believe in the name of his Son, Jesus Christ, and to love one another as he commanded us" 1 Jn 3:23. The first and the greatest commandment is this: "Believe in the Lord Jesus!"

24 / The Soul Thirsts for God

"Whoever drinks the water I give him will never thirst"
Jn 4:14.

DOESN'T THIS conflict with certain other Bible verses? Doesn't Jesus call people blessed who hunger and thirst for righteousness? And in Revelation it is said of the blessed that even in glory they will draw the water of life to quench their thirst (Rev 22:17).

Jesus creates a thirst for eternal life in our souls, but he also satisfies it. These Bible verses tell us how Jesus creates that thirst, which continues, and even increases, in his company. We struggle to get close to Jesus, to have an even more real experience of the refreshing power of the Holy Spirit.

But Jesus also tells about the satisfaction he provides. We might argue whether the satisfaction found in religious experiences is really from God. There is certainly much false pleasure to be found in our spiritual life. Consider the Bible verse, "Whoever wants to save his life [soul] will lose it" Mt 16:25.

Nevertheless, Jesus does quench the thirst of the soul as he promises in Jn 4:14. When Jesus quenches the thirst of our soul we find ourselves more completely in his hands and we want to continue in his company. We find our joy in Jesus. Temporal goals lose their power of enchantment when Jesus satisfies the soul. Even the heavy burdens of life become bearable and we can say, "Whom have I in heaven but you? And earth has nothing I desire besides you" Ps 73:25.

25 / God Judges to Save

"Deliver me in your righteousness" Ps 31:1.

THE WOMAN caught in adultery was dragged before Jesus to be tried and condemned. But the tables were turned and her accusers were put on trial. When Jesus said to them, "If any one of you is without sin, let him be the first to throw a stone at her" Jn 8:7, their consciences declared them guilty and they "began to go away one at a time" Jh 8:9. The difference between the woman and her accusers was that while she continued to stand condemned before Jesus, the others left him. But then the woman heard the liberating word which released her from her sin. Jesus said to her, "Neither do I condemn you. Go now and leave your life of sin" Jn 8:11. Her accusers, however, remained in their sins, for they had fled from Jesus.

God's judgments humble us and cause us pain. We realize that others do not know the whole truth about our wickedness. If they could see through us, their judgments would be far more severe. Faced with God's judgments we are defenseless; we are forced into silence.

But God's judgments are expressions of His grace, the way God seeks to free us from our sins. If in your conscience you have faced God's judgment, do not flee from Him but stay put. Remain as a condemned creature before Jesus. Be still and let the Lord do His work. When His time arrives you will hear from His mouth the word of absolution, and you will experience the power of that word.

26 / Blessing Upon Blessing

"From the fullness of his grace we have all received one blessing after another" Jn 1:16.

IS IT POSSIBLE to accumulate grace? Hardly, for grace cannot be pickled. How then will we receive "one blessing after another"? Grace is provided for the specific situations and tasks we face, not as some kind of consumer good, but as God's way of dealing with people who have fallen into sin.

What is "one blessing after another"? It is God's being gracious on a continuing basis, each day and each moment renewing His grace. We lose and waste His grace, but He does not get tired, become frustrated, or give up. God is willing to be gracious again as though for the first time. For example, it is by God's grace that we get something out of His word. Our hearts are such that we cannot grasp a single one of His words unless He shows us His marvelous grace.

But look what happens! Our hearts are like cemeteries where we bury the innumerable fragments of truth that have been revealed to us by the Word. We ought to have put them into practice, but in our laziness and indifference we have not progressed beyond hearing to obedience. Consider the many gracious words from God that we have buried in our unbelieving hearts! But now God shows His grace by giving us "one blessing after another." In other words, He does not leave us in our state of death, but in His marvelous mercy He once again lays His word upon our hearts. And so He gives "one blessing after another." Where would we be, if we did not have such a God?

27 / Light Is Stronger Than Darkness

"The light shines in the darkness, but the darkness has not understood it" Jn 1:5.

WHAT A TRAGIC picture of the world! "Darkness" in this connection does not mean sickness, suffering, misfortune or the other things that darken our life. The word has a deeper meaning. "Darkness" means a world without God, a world that has fallen away from Him and rebelled against Him. "Darkness has not understood it." Time after time people reject Christ. As you read this do not think of the darkness that is all around you. Your own heart is in darkness. The spirit of enmity against God has a dwelling place there. You yourself are a part of this darkness.

"The light shines in the darkness." Christ is seeking you. Time and again he has approached you, called you, and enlightened you with his grace. Stay awake, be alert! Now the light shines in the darkness. Do not look for the light anywhere but in the gospel of Christ. You will never find it in your own heart.

According to the original language of the Bible this verse could be translated differently, as many interpreters have done. The word "understand" in the Greek can also mean "to overcome." "The darkness has not overcome it" is another possible translation. If it is comforting to hear that the light is still shining in the darkness, it is also comforting to hear that darkness has not overcome it. Let us approach the matter personally once more. The darkness of your heart has not overcome the light which continues to radiate from Christ. Christ has been the stronger one.

Are you one of those who must admit that all of this is true in your life? Can you say, "In my case, too, Christ has been the stronger one. I have fought against him. I have been his enemy. I still argue and rebel. But 'darkness has not overcome it.'"

28 / Christ Provides the Cleansing

"How much more, then, will the blood of Christ cleanse our consciences from acts that lead to death, so that we may serve the living God" He 9:14.

RITES OF PURIFICATION of many kinds played a role in Jewish religious life. We are told that at the wedding in Cana, to which Jesus and his disciples had been invited, there were large stone jars, "the kind used by the Jews for ceremonial washing" Jn. 2:6. The washing of hands, feet, dishes, and other utensils were parables of the inner cleansing needed by the true servant of God. Many no longer thought of anything but the outward cleansing, but pious Jews knew that the Lord must be served with clean hands and clean hearts, as David says, "Create in me a pure heart, O God" Ps 51:10.

The people of the New Covenant should learn from these Jews what it means to be conscious of God's holiness. "Wash your hands, you sinners, and purify your hearts, you double-minded" Jas 4:8. And Peter writes, "Now that you have purified yourselves by obeying the truth so that you have sincere love for your brothers, love one another deeply, from the heart" 1 P 1:22. The need for purification is still very real.

At the wedding in Cana, Jesus demonstrated by changing water into wine that the former methods of purification were ineffective and that he, the Lord Jesus Christ, is the one and only Purifier. The "new wine" tasted better than the "old wine" in the opinion of the master of the banquet; proclaiming Christ as the superior source of purification from sin and corruption. He is the "Lamb of God, who takes away the sin of the world" Jh 1:29. That is his glory.

Do we give the glory to Christ by allowing him to cleanse us of our corruption? In other words, can he do to us what he came to do, or do we try to be Christians without cleansing? Let us not claim to believe in him, if we don't allow him to cleanse our hearts as well as our lives.

29 / Old and New Natures

"Watch and pray so that you will not fall into temptation. The spirit is willing, but the body is weak" Mt 26:41.

A FINNISH hymn describes the "reluctance of nature" which "digs a grave for the soul." Pilgrims traveling "toward the Fatherland" along "the narrow way" are accompanied by this dangerous enemy. We sinful people are in every respect enemies of God. In an unconverted state we are rebels, uninterested in God's will. Even our practice of religion is nothing but opposition to God. We use God's great gifts for our own purposes according to our selfish, corrupt mind. Even after conversion we have within us the old nature which is always against God. This old nature "digs a grave for the soul," which is the new nature born of God. The conflict between the flesh and the Spirit continues without interruption in all people whom God has saved and will save.

The "reluctance of nature" has to do with the reading of God's word and prayer. We all know the many obstacles that rise in the way of Bible-reading and prayer. This reluctance translates into unwillingness to consider what God's will might be in a given situation and neglect in following the revealed course of action. This reluctance finally develops into a pattern of dissatisfaction, dissension and rebellion with regard to God's guidance. Our whole life becomes contaminated.

This reluctance "digs a grave for the soul," meaning that if we surrender to our former nature and fulfill its desires, we grieve God's Spirit and our relationship to God is broken.

If we want to reach the goal of our salvation, we must watch and struggle. But let us not lose heart. All who have traveled the road of life have had to put up with this "reluctance" as a traveling companion.

30 / Healing for the Nations

"Blessed are the peacemakers, for they will be called sons of God" Mt 5:9.

IN WARS between nations the victors dictate the terms of peace. If they truly desire peace they will act justly. An unjust peace is seed for new conflict.

But the responsibility for peace rests not on the leaders of nations, not even the victorious nations, but on every one of us. We are called to create an atmosphere in which injustice, dissension, and conflict will not thrive. The renewal of nations begins with the renewal of individuals and families.

There are people who have no peace themselves and deprive others of peace. Then there are those who have peace and seek to spread it to others. They are the peacemakers, the ones called blessed. That is how they will be remembered.

But the Savior says even more about them. "Blessed are the peacemakers, for they will be called sons of God." They are blessed as children of God. We need to note that they are not children of God because they are peacemakers; on the contrary, they are peacemakers because they are children of God. They are peacemakers because the powers of heaven are at work in them. God's grace has broken and crushed them, so they do not seek their own interests or hide their faults and failures, nor are they too proud to ask for forgiveness and be reconciled with their enemies

These are the people the world needs. Through their efforts they create the atmosphere that brings healing even to international relationships.

31 / There Are No Hopeless Cases

"I am the way and the truth and the life" Jn 14:6.

JESUS IS the way to the Father's home. When we know the truth about God and about ourselves we are on our way home. This way is unique, for to travel it a person does not need to be particularly strong, for Jesus, who is the truth, is also the life which we need in order to reach the Father's home. The apostle says, "I no longer live, but Christ lives in me" Ga 2:20.

This is a wonderful way. The Bible speaks of the "living way" Jesus has opened for us through his death (He 10:20). On our own we get nowhere; but Jesus lifts us up, carries us, and takes us home. If our salvation depended on our ability to travel the way to heaven, we would never make it. As it is, we can rejoice over the salvation we have in Jesus, the way that "carries" as it "leads" us. "He is able to save completely" He 7:25.

A person's situation may be hopeless, from our point of view; but for Jesus there are no hopeless cases. "He is able to save completely," for he is the living way. Do not despair, even though there seems to be no hope! We repeat, there are no hopeless cases. Let the fallen sinner see the heart of Jesus! If it cannot be done with words, it can be done with sacrificial, self-effacing love.

Love believes all things and hopes all things. This is what the Lord Jesus himself has done and continues to do, and this is what he calls us to do.

June

1 / The Small Things of Life

"You have been faithful in managing small amounts" Mt
25:21 (TEV).

IN EARLY JUNE people in Finland leave the city to spend the
summer in the country. Loading their cars or pickups, they have
no trouble with the larger items. It is the smaller things that can
be a headache. When everything is ready, all it takes is for one
of the smaller items to become dislodged and the whole load is in
jeopardy.

Life is like that. There are important matters and
demanding tasks that bring sweat to our brow and force us to
turn to God. But there are also "small amounts", duties at home
and in the neighborhood, which call for tact, friendliness, self-
control and quietness. Consider our routine tasks, alongside of
which other matters loom large and important. In their
performance we easily get careless and sloppy. But, in the long
run, everything may depend on them. Jesus teaches us to be
faithful managers of "small amounts."

For a child of God nothing is too small. He knows that in
every moment of life we deal with the Lord and serve Him. God
meets us in the little things which occupy us on a daily basis.
Pay attention, therefore, to small amounts!

Especially dangerous are the "small sins." A small stone in
the shoe forces even a strong man to stop to remove it. Do not be
careless in regard to small sins. They can hurt you! The loads of

people on the move from time to eternity will collapse because of small unconfessed and unforgiven sins.

2 / Faith and Love Go Together

"In the same way, faith by itself, if it is not accompanied by action, is dead" Jas 2:17.

WITHOUT the gospel and faith, works will become misplaced in our lives. We think that to please God we must do something or be someone special. We do all kinds of things to court God's favor. Lutheran Christians no longer do good works with the same frame of mind as did the medieval monks, but we are much like them when we look upon our spirituality and piety as having merit before God.

Natural piety is thought to be a good work done for God, and it can serve to make us feel special and better than other people. Such piety causes us secretly to fondle our devilish self-love, with the result that we neglect the works God expects of us. In this false piety we serve God according to our own plans for good works, and ignore God's plan.

But, the gospel reveals that between fallen man and holy God there is room for only one work. And it is Christ who has done everything in our behalf: "It is finished." Whoever tries, with prayers and other spiritual exercises, to add to what Christ has done, dishonors Christ's completed work.

The gospel frees us from the false belief that we must do something to become God's friends. It does not free us from works, but it is no longer a question of works done for God but works done for our neighbor.

In short, faith belongs between the condemned sinner and the holy God, while works belong between the forgiven sinner and his neighbor. True Christianity includes both. There is no true faith without love, but neither is there true love without living faith.

3 / Innocent on All Counts

"It is finished" Jn 19:30.

THESE THREE WORDS, "It is finished," mark the spot where we are to cast our anchor in the midst of life's storms. All else may change, "mountains may be shaken and the hills be removed" Is 54:10, before one dot will be erased from these words: "It is finished!" When our inner life is easily thrown out of kilter by the storms of life we must learn the truth of these words. It attests to a fact which we can set against the bloody facts of sin and Satan and death.

"It is finished." Someone else has done what I, in my unbelief, have tried to do. Satan does not want me, in my weakness, to rely on this finished work. The Lord, nevertheless, goes ahead and prepares "a table before me in the presence of my enemies" Ps 23:5. Neither enemies within me nor outside of me can upset God's table of grace. We may be dogged by all kinds of evil spirits, tearing at our souls, depriving us of restful sleep, making us skittish, and wearing out our already frazzled nerves. We must hasten to God's table of grace. The enemies of our souls and bodies cannot touch a single crumb on, or even under, that table. "It is finished."

Jesus has already suffered the punishment of my sins. I am free; two cannot be punished for the same crime. Because he stood before God in my stead and in my behalf, cursed for my sins, my unbelief, my death, the verdict in my case is "innocent on all counts."

> On rock most solid
> I build my hope,
> On Jesus' death
> I build my life.
> No violent storm,
> Satan or world
> Can topple the Lord.

"Give an account of your management" Lk 16:2.

IN OUR BEST moments we feel sad that we have so often misused and wasted God's gifts. I performed the task entrusted to me carelessly and reluctantly, and yet that task was God's gift. I grudgingly bore the trouble associated with the task, forgetting that work is a gift. I was given years of health, but I squandered them. And what about friends who are also God's gifts? How little I have cared for these gifts, forgetting that friendships must be cultivated and nurtured.

There are other gifts of God, more precious than the above. Every movement of my heart toward God, every longing thought for His fellowship, every moment I have yearned to get closer to Him, these have all been gifts of God. The Lord gave me thirst for the living God (Ps 42:2). With these gifts God wanted to give Himself to me, His own presence, a new and richer experience of His holiness and love.

But what happened? I squandered and lost them in worldly pursuits and my own shallowness. I did not take advantage of those moments; I did not permit God to plow a deeper furrow in my heart. I was offered grace, but I chose glitter. What infinite responsibility will rest on me when I stand before God and give an account of His gifts to me. What will I say when He asks me why I did not make use of what He gave me? Many times God spoke to me in my heart but I paid no attention. Lord, help me to start from scratch!

5 / Cultivating Community

*"But you are a chosen people, a royal priesthood, a holy
nation, a people belonging to God, that you may declare
the praises of him who called you out of darkness into his
wonderful light"* 1 P 2:9.

THE IMPOTENCE of our spiritual life is often caused by false
individualism which prompts us to neglect fellowship with the
Lord's people. God's people do not always appear attractive, for,
as long as this life continues, we all have our faults and failures.
What the Bible says about the Jesus is also true of God's people:
"He had no beauty or majesty to attract us to him, nothing in his
appearance that we should desire him. He was despised and
rejected by men, a man of sorrows, and familiar with suffering.
Like one from whom men hide their faces he was despised, and
we esteemed him not" Is 53:2f. There is every reason to be
offended by God's people.

But wherever the gospel is heard and received in repentance
and faith, we will find God's people, and there the Christian
finds a home. The Lord's people are not a collective of like-
minded people, an association organized by those who have
similar thoughts and work toward similar goals. God Himself
calls into being and maintains His people through the gospel. In
all Christian fellowship and friendship the central concern is the
hearing and the receiving of the Word. This is indeed a matter of
the gospel, for the law is not able to unite us with one another.
Legalistic Christians want to be important and invariably erect
fences to separate themselves from both weaker and stronger
believers. But wherever people live from the gospel all
distinctions disappear. We are all equally guilty, we share
equally in the grace of Christ's blood and we have all become
God's friends through the free gift of Christ received by faith.

6 / Christlike Charity

*"Whatever you did not do for one of the least of these, you
did not do for me"* Mt 25:45.

WE USUALLY NOTICE people who are important. We show
charity and friendship to those whom we respect and who

respect our services. We are charitable to people who have prestige, influence and money. But Jesus talked about being charitable "for one of the least of these."

These people very likely do not know how to value the attention we give them. Instead, they may often create problems for us as we try to help them. They are rude and take advantage of our good will. But, Jesus says this must not keep us from noticing and serving them. They are the "least" of his relatives, lacking the human courtesy to recognize the value of the good things they have been given and show gratitude toward the givers.

Jesus wants to free us from the need to ask about the worth of the people around us. "For one of the least of them." Note that Jesus says, "for one." The Lord does not ask you to serve the needs of the whole world. You are not freed of your responsibilities by participating in a general fund-raising campaign or putting your gift in the offering plate. Jesus wants you to recognize individuals as you encounter them. Just as he gave himself totally to every individual who came to him, he expects us also to notice individuals and to help them in their physical and spiritual needs.

7 / Shun the Ways of the World

"Get rid of all bitterness, rage and anger, brawling and slander, along with every form of malice" Eph 4:31.

THE WORLD is filled with bitterness, rage and anger, brawling and slander. These already powerful forces are constantly fueled and fanned, and much is accomplished in the world through them. We might easily begin to assume that this is how things should be done. Instead, we need to guard against such methods. We cannot help that the world is full of all kinds of evil, but we can keep our distance. A righteous cause need not be promoted by anger and brawling and slander.

In the end, the crucified always wins, the crucifiers always lose. History shows this to be true. A righteous and true cause can be nailed to a cross, but in the end it will triumph, and the crucifiers will be brought to shame. But promoters of truth must be willing to travel the road of suffering. They cannot seek their own interests. Self-discipline and faith in the ultimate triumph of the forces of good will be required in order to disown bitterness, rage and anger, brawling and slander. We learn self-discipline and faith in the company of Jesus, who was "gentle and humble in heart" Mt 11:29, and who "entrusted himself to him who judges justly" 1 P 2:23. Let us not make the mistake of fighting the world's wickedness with the world's weapons. "Be kind and compassionate to one another, forgiving each other, just as in Christ God forgave you" Eph 4:32.

8 / Illness as a Servant of God

"Just say the word, and my servant will be healed" Mt 8:8.

THE CENTURION of Capernaum was convinced that the Lord had the power to heal his paralyzed servant with a single word. He believed that illness was under the command of the Lord. "For I myself am a man under authority, with soldiers under me. I tell this one 'Go,' and he goes, and that one, 'Come,' and he comes. I say to my servant, 'Do this,' and he does it" Mt 8:9. The centurion thought that Jesus could command the illness, as he himself commanded his servants. He implies that illness is God's servant.

What a thought! Illness is a servant of God! Illness then is not an enemy, for it has a God-given assignment. A patient who had suffered greatly related that he experienced his illness not as a punishment from God but as a trust that God had shown toward him. The Bible urges us to humble ourselves in this way under God's mighty hand.

Let us not be anxious and difficult when God sends His servant to us, even in the form of illness. It may appear that illness keeps us from fulfilling our tasks. But perhaps only when illness takes over are we able to perform tasks that have eternal value and are a true blessing to others. We are right to trust that even illness is under God's command, fall down before Jesus as the centurion did, and seek friendship with God. The main purpose of illness is to present us to the Lord.

9 / Peace Follows Faith

"Therefore, since we have been justified through faith, we have peace with God" Ro 5:1.

PAUL STATES that a person justified through faith has peace with God. This means that peace is the result of faith. Faith first, then peace. This truth quickly became clouded among Christians, with the result that already in ancient manuscripts of the Bible this verse, Ro 5:1, reads: "Because we have been justified by faith, let us keep peace with God." Early Christians apparently thought that the Christian himself must maintain peace with God. This made peace no longer the result of faith but a distinct human achievement.

How can we say that a person justified by faith has peace? When God justifies He does not do it on the basis of what He finds in the person. Not even a person's faith provides the basis for justification. Justification happens when something is added to a person from the outside; namely, Jesus Christ, who is our righteousness. Our only God-pleasing righteousness is from outside of us; it is "alien righteousness."

In faith we hold on to this righteousness. God has placed a great treasure into our empty hands--his own hand. When we have been justified through faith in this way, we have peace with God. Peace is not an inner emotional state but the experience of God's favor toward us. We have been moved from wrath to grace. A person's life may be filled with bitter conflict and great restlessness, yet he will continue to be in the Lord's gracious care. This is our peace.

10 / Friends Are From God

"Do not forsake your friend and the friend of your father" Pr 27:10.

FRIENDS are precious gifts from God. The Finnish word for friend stands for a special kind of warmth. To a Finn a friend is a very special kind of person. In the spiritual folk movements friends have played an important role. Many people have experienced the truth of the ancient hymn:

When weariness overcomes,
Friends take over,
When the poor creature
Cries out in despair.

In this wicked world it is difficult to hang on to God's gifts. This is true also of the gift of friendship. We must fight, often hard and long, to keep our friends, struggling to be faithful, honest, and unselfish. To be faithful we must be dependable, not permitting our feelings of the moment to change our mind and scatter our interests. It also means we look upon friends as God's gifts, feeling an inward constraint to be faithful toward them. It takes poets to describe the beauty of enduring faithfulness between friends. But, we must be faithful and view our friends as God's gifts to us.

Unless we are honest and open we will not be able keep our friends. Hypocrisy is a poor foundation for friendship. People from whom we must conceal things, with whom we cannot be our true selves, with whom we must pretend to be someone we are not, cannot be our true friends. If friendship cannot endure frank talk and total honesty, it is not genuine.

Our most precious friends are those who tell us the truth about us. Friendship calls also for unselfishness. Friends are not always pleasant. They may disturb us in our work, their habits annoy us, they may unwittingly hurt us. To nurture a friendship requires that we become unselfish and patient. The thing we need to fear the most is that we on our part may become a burden to our friends by our inconsiderate, selfish, and indifferent attitude toward their needs. Whoever wants to cultivate and nurture friendship, let him walk humbly in his Lord's footsteps.

11 / The Beauty of the Gospel

"The boundary lines have fallen for me in pleasant places; surely I have a delightful inheritance" Ps 16:6.

LUTHER relates that when the gospel dawned for him and he was able to believe that God justifies the ungodly, the gates of paradise were flung wide open. During these early weeks of summer we admire the beauty of nature coming alive again. Our tired bodies and minds relax as we gaze upon the newness in God's creation.

The gates of paradise, however, remain closed. Nature is an admirable and refreshing gift of God, but it will not help us out of our despair.

We have been created for union with God. We were meant to live in this world as His faithful and obedient children. We live as we ought to live only when we live in union with Him. But the fall into sin has deprived us of the possibility of this happening. Where the fall occurred, salvation must now occur. We must be restored to God, which is something nature with all its beauty cannot accomplish. No one can find his way back to God by relaxing his tired body and mind in God's creation. Only grace, the grace that appeared in Jesus Christ, can do that. The gates of paradise are swung open when the good news about Jesus Christ dawns upon the fallen sinner. What sin has broken, grace restores.

More beautiful than the beauty of summer is the glory that radiates from the Beautiful Savior. More than the beauty of nature is the beauty of the gospel. Psalm 23 tells us about the Good Shepherd, who "makes me lie down in green pastures and leads me beside quiet waters" Ps 23:2: God's gospel is the soul's true resting place and true refreshment.

Why be satisfied with temporal things when the eternal are available?

12 / The Giver Comes With the Gift

"Ask and it will be given to you; seek and you will find; knock and the door will be opened to you" Mt 7:7.

PRAYER is heart talk with God. It is not wrong for us to sit down at the feet of our Savior and rest a spell. But we miss the true blessing of prayer if we fail to remember the many promises of the Savior, by which he entices us to ask and seek in a serious way. He looks for us to lay all our concerns before him in prayer, believing that he will answer. "Ask and it will be given to you." The Savior encourages us to ask for his gifts. Whatever your needs, tell him, who controls all things.

But let us not stop with the gifts and forget the Giver. "Seek and you will find." The Savior is waiting for us to seek him in prayer. He is more than his gifts. He promises that the seeking soul will find him. What a blessed moment when the sinner meets his helper.

But a mere meeting is not enough. We need a permanent union with him, so that we can say, "In him we live and have our being." And so we are told, "Knock and the door will be opened to you." To him who knocks Christ opens the door, and so the sinner finds himself in the company of the Lord. Paul says that he strives that he might be found in Christ (Phil 3:9). That is the secret of Christian life; it is life in Christ. To him who knocks, the door to this hidden life will be opened. You say, "Many times I have asked and have not received. Doesn't God hear my prayers?" He does hear; do not despair as you wait for an answer. The answer may show you that you have not asked according to God's will, that in your life there are things which deprive you of His blessing and that you must take to the road of repentance.

God gives the Holy Spirit to all who ask. And the Holy Spirit teaches us to abide in God's word in obedience to Him. In this obedience we then learn to pray according to God' will.

13 / God Will Take Care of You

"Commit your way to the Lord; trust in him and he will do it" Ps 37:5.

IN EXPLAINING the sixth petition of the Lord's Prayer, Luther lists the evil deeds of the devil, the world, and our own flesh. At the top of the list he places unbelief and despair, ahead of what are usually considered gross sins. Drunkenness, adultery, selfishness and other vices are obvious sources of corruption, but the worst thing that can happen to us is to fall into unbelief and despair.

In line with his own experience Luther concludes the explanation: "but that, although we may be so tempted, we may finally prevail and gain the victory" (Small Catechism.) It is of great comfort to know that God's saints have been tempted and have gained the victory. Don't be surprised when you encounter temptations; but, find comfort in knowing that the Lord Jesus himself was tempted in all things. In full awareness of temptations, therefore, "Commit your way to the Lord."

Caught in the temptation of unbelief the chosen people of Israel once cried out, "My way is hidden from the Lord; my cause is disregarded by my God" Is 40:27. But the prophet comforted them by reminding them that the Lord "will not grow tired or weary; and his understanding no one can fathom" Is 40:28. He concluded by saying: "He gives strength to the weary and increases the power of the weak" Is 40:29. All who wait for the Lord while facing temptations will receive new strength to continue their journey. If, despite our fear, we trust in God and commit our way to Him, we will some day praise God for His wonders. "For the power of the wicked will be broken, but the Lord upholds the righteous" Ps 37:17. It is of utmost importance that with repentant hearts we truly forsake our own ways and trust our entire lives unconditionally to the Lord, for with Him there is abundant forgiveness.

14 / The Wholesome Fear of God

"Serve the Lord with fear" Ps 2:11.

FEAR OF THE LORD is essential if faith is to be alive. A Christian's conscience is sensitive in the presence of God and His word. He works out his salvation "with fear and trembling" Phil 2:12. While other people encourage one another to trust in the future, the Christian finds courage and hope in the living God, viewing temporal events in the light of divine judgment. Aware of the tremendous power of sin in the world and in himself, a Christian has to deal with the reality of judgment.

The Christian, therefore, trembles when he realizes that true repentance is lacking and people carelessly console one another with "Peace, peace!" when the very prerequisites for peace are missing. Christians must truly fear God. It then becomes more difficult to slip into false peace on the rim of a live volcano about to erupt. It is to be feared that unbelievers will some day accuse us Christians for not disturbing their false peace. By our silence we give them the impression we agree with their illusions. The Finnish poet and hymn writer, Lauri Stenback, described his own situation, and ours:

The Lord's judgments cover the land,
In full view of its poor inhabitants,
Who have no inkling of what's going on
In the midst of changing times.

Conscious of the living God, the Christian also fears death, for he knows that death will usher him into the divine judgment hall. This makes the difference in the manner in which Christians prepare for death. A Christian has other fears too. Having personally experienced the terrible power of sin, he has a wholesome fear of it and avoids occasions that arouse his lusts. He is also afraid of people who lure him away from God. There are fears a Christian has because of God. "I will inspire them to fear me," says the Lord (Jr 32:40). For good reason the Book of Proverbs states, "He who fears the Lord has a secure fortress," and again, "The fear of the Lord is a fountain of life" Pr 14:26f.

15 / The Rich and the Fearful

"God did not give us a spirit of timidity" 2 Ti 1:7.

TRUE FEAR of God does not make us timid. The same Spirit who creates true fear dispels timidity. Whoever truly fears God need fear nothing else, not people nor circumstances nor death. John says, "Perfect love drives out fear" 1 Jn 4:18. Through faith in Christ we experience God's perfect love and lose all sense of timidity. As we struggle with the many fears that surround us we find a living and ever new witness to God's love in the Gospel of Jesus Christ. The cross becomes a secure haven for us in the storms of life.
Our material possessions are often the real reason for our timidity. We refuse to give them up at any price. If we had nothing to lose we would be much freer and braver. When the apostle says "God did not give us a spirit of timidity," he was speaking as one who had inwardly renounced everything we normally consider precious. In his prison cell Paul was awaiting a martyr's death, but gave the following admonition: "From now on those who have wives should live as if they had none; those who mourn, as if they did not, those who are happy, as if they were not; those who buy something, as if it were not theirs to

keep; those who use the things of the world, as if not engrossed in them" 1 Co 7:29-31.

When time seems in short supply, and "this world in its present form is passing away" 1 Co 7:31, a gnawing fear and anxiety grows within those who are prisoners of their temporal possessions. This spirit of timidity is not from God. Instead, God calls us to struggle against our fears and seek refuge at the foot of the cross, where perfect love casts out fear.

Let us examine our inner relationship to our temporal possessions. Jesus said, "Do not worry about tomorrow, for tomorrow will worry about itself" Mt 6:34. The spirit of timidity will not flee until we expel the false gods, regardless of what they may be. Happy is he who gives his heart into the hands of the Lord, who surrenders to His will, satisfied His will is done.

16 / More Than Meets the Eye

"That which we have heard, which we have seen with our eyes, which we have looked at and our hands have touched, this we proclaim concerning the Word of life" 1 Jn 1:1.

ANYONE paging through the New Testament must remember that the writers were men who had personally experienced the reality of God. Within them they had the knowledge that God is real. "Anyone who believes in the Son of God has this testimony in his heart" 1 Jn 4:10. Because they lived in Christ they could say, "In Him we live and move and have our being" Ac 17:28.

The lives of many Christians today are spiritually impoverished. Now and then we hear His voice as from a distance, and in our best moments a sense of the presence of Christ satisfies our deepest yearning. But, for the most part, God's world is a foreign land to us, and we are usually satisfied with things that meet our temporal needs. We hear virtually nothing about longing for the living God. This cannot be God's will.

Faith is not born in full bloom, it must develop and change. The gruesome reality of sin continues to contaminate our lives. But, Christians live in continual hope that God has reserved for us much greater blessings than we have yet received. This does not mean some extraordinary experience of grace, but simply a deeper and more certain awareness of God's presence. In this way God will give direction to our lives, and we will walk in full view of God.

The Bible offers no other way to know God and experience His power than the gospel. "It is the power of God for the salvation of everyone who believes" Ro 1:16. The gospel calls us to life, but it calls to us from the cross. How well does the cross suit us? God's free gift of salvation is difficult to accept, for we are too proud to accept something for nothing. We want to feel important. And that is the real reason we lack the inner testimony of the Spirit, God's presence with us. God is unable to bless us in this way as long as we continue to live with illusions about ourselves.

17 / Now and Not Yet

"We know that the whole creation has been groaning as in the pains of child birth right up to the present time" Ro 8:22.

THE HOLY SPIRIT causes a person to groan inwardly by creating a painful awareness of the tension between what he is and what he ought to be. Others know reasonably well how to pray, but he who has the Holy Spirit does not (Ro 8:26). Others commit themselves wholeheartedly to the Lord, but he who has the Holy Spirit must continue to complain about the deceitfulness of his heart. While others courageously trust the Lord, he also casts his cares upon the Lord, at the same time sighing inwardly, fearful that his courage might be false security.

Mothers and fathers who have received the down payment of the Spirit raise their children with groanings, for they are afraid the Lord will punish their children for the parents' deceitfulness and indifference. People who have received the gift of the Holy Spirit are people who groan inwardly. Such "groaners" need to hear: "You have the down payment of the Holy Spirit. You are in God's hands; He is working in you. You are already children, and you can look forward to becoming who you are. Do not lose courage." An elderly Christian once remarked that he will not lose hope as long as the Holy Spirit admonishes him of sin at least once a day. Every Christian needs such an attitude as he occupies his small place before God and other people.

18 / The Lord Is Not Deaf

"The Lord has heard my weeping. The Lord has heard my cry for mercy; the Lord accepts my prayer" Ps 6:8f.

WE FULLY expect God to hear the prayers of those who live in faith and pray with heartfelt confidence. Of course God wants to hear those who pray fervently; He will be merciful to His children. The Bible urges those who pray to do so with confidence.

But there are those whose troubles are so heavy and whose strength is so weak that they find no comfort in knowing that their prayers are heard. They hear nothing but accusations in their consciences and they often eat the words they utter to God and others, break their promises, and squander God's grace. When they are pressured, such as during extended periods of illness or in the midst of family financial crises, they view these trials as the righteous judgments of God. They are receiving what they deserve; God has hidden Himself; there is no one to help them. Prayer becomes pointless as their spirits succumb to these struggles. Joy, strength, childlike confidence and trust that the Father hears them all vanish. But, the Bible remarkably has something to say to such people.

In Psalm 6 we hear a man grown faint, whose bones ache under God's wrath. "I am worn out from groaning; all night long I flood my bed with weeping and drench my couch with tears" Ps 6:6. Enough trouble for one time! Still, this weary soul is sure of one thing: "The Lord has heard my weeping. The Lord has heard my cry for mercy; the Lord accepts my prayers." Jesus says, "Blessed are those who mourn, for they will be comforted" Mt 5:4. They will know that God heard them when they tossed about and cried out in anguish to the Lord, even though the Lord seemed so far away at the time.

When tears and weariness overwhelm you, don't let anything keep you from crying to the Lord for help. He hears your cries of despair and involves Himself in your struggles. The problems we anguish over in life are necessary so that our deceitful hearts might be exposed, our hardened hearts broken, and that we might acknowledge the ways of the Lord.

19 / Faith Does Not Save, Christ Does

"You are all sons of God through faith in Christ Jesus"
Ga 3:26.

PAUL TELLS us how we become God's children: "Through faith." This faith is not a human idea or fantasy, but the work of the Holy Spirit in the heart. Notice that Paul says "through faith", not "because of faith." The difference is important, and we must understand it. If we are God's children "because of faith," our faith is a prerequisite of grace. Faith is then our own achievement, giving God the reason to receive us into His kingdom. We often think this way, with the result that, to secure our position with God, we try to improve and strengthen our faith as much as possible.

But nothing is more foreign to the Bible. If we seek to be something in God's sight "because" of our faith we are still under the law, no matter how much we talk about faith. Faith does not save, Christ does. Faith was not crucified for us, Christ was. The foundation of our salvation is found entirely outside of us. Thus, Paul says we are God's children "through faith," with faith being the empty hand into which God places His gift.

If you live in continuous awareness of the weakness of your faith and of the power of sin, you need to remember that God gives you faith as He saves you. Otherwise you will think that a radical change has to take place in your life in order to be a believer and a child of God. If so, you will end up in a hopeless struggle against sin with an awakened conscience, afraid to approach Christ until you have improved yourself and overcome sin. The Bible states that God justifies the ungodly and that true faith looks to Christ even when it feels it has no right to do so.

He who lives as a child of God, let him do what Jonas Lagus, a nineteenth-century Finnish revival preacher, urged: "Storms without, storms within, look for Christ!"

20 / Prayer and Times of Distress

*"Call upon me in the day of trouble, I will deliver you;
and you will honor me"* Ps 50:15.

THE DOOR through which God's recreative power enters the
world is the prayer of the distressed soul. This means, first of
all, that times of distress and prayer go together. Some think a
person's faith is still immature if they continue to experience
times of distress. Besides, should not a person pray even when
he is not in distress?

The truth of the matter, however, is that according to Jesus
distress and prayer go together. Even the Lord's Prayer, which
he taught, is a prayer of distress. As long as we live in this
world, distress remains and a Christian has more than his
share. He who teaches otherwise is unrealistic.

Through the prayer of the distressed soul God's recreative
power invades our world. The person who prays has received an
important assignment from God. "Call upon me in the day of
trouble, I will deliver you; and you will honor me." When God
helps us He creates something new in this temporal world. This
happens even in little things, for example, in the events in our
homes. We easily assume God's help is limited to the spiritual
and the significant. God helps with such things, but much more
often He helps with things we do not associate with Him at all.

As long as we are capable of handling things on our own,
God cannot work among us. Therefore, God's power has to wait
for times of distress.

21 / Christ Wants Friends

"You are my friends if you do what I command" Jn 15:14.

ACQUAINTANCES are people we meet occasionally, whom we
visit now and then, whom we greet on the streets, to whom we
perhaps show a smile. But that is all they mean to us. We
seldom think about them; their opinions and hopes are not
important to us.

Christ has many acquaintances among us. We cannot deny
we have met him on occasion. We know something about him. In
certain situations we greet him politely, acknowledging that we

know him. But then we hasten along and in our weekday world we seldom think about him. He is not especially important to us. Christ wants more; he wants to make us his friends. He wants us to think of him always, not just now and then. He wants to take charge of our lives, to become a part of us. He also wants us to listen to him, to view the world through his eyes, and to be about his business. He wants to confide in his friends and commit to them the task of warning, admonishing, and comforting others.   We must examine ourselves and evaluate our behavior, lest we remain Christ's acquaintances and never become His friends. We do not become his friend by obeying the law and doing something well enough to please him. "You are my friends if you do what I command," Christ says. Our faith will come alive if we are obedient to Christ's command to follow him and love others.

22 / The Father Suffers for His Children

"You, O Lord, are our Father, our Redeemer from of old is your name" Is 63:16.

MOTHERS and fathers who know the difficult art of raising children refrain from constant fault finding and prohibitions. Their hearts are filled with sorrow over their children's disobedience, but they hide their tears. This adds weight to their words and effectiveness to their discipline, for children sense what is genuine and what is not.

Our heavenly Father is such a parent. He grieves over His children, but He does not constantly find fault and clamp down on us. At times He speaks in a sharp reprimanding voice; at times He even resorts to the rod to discipline the disobedient. But more often than not He draws us to repentance with His goodness. God alone knows how much of His goodness we have experienced in the course of our lives!

We all have caused our heavenly Father great sorrow. As the hymn writer says:

> Every pet sin of mine I fail to put away
> Is like a fresh new thorn in the crown of my Lord.

God suffers, but He hides His suffering from us. Of course you see the suffering God on the cross of Golgatha, but even there you can grasp only a small part of His agony. God did not stage His unfathomable suffering on the cross for spectators. His suffering is real and necessary. In His love for us He spared nothing, not even His only Son, to save us miserable creatures. That is the measure of God's love.

"While he was still a long way off, his father saw him and was filled with compassion for him" Lk 15:20. This is the kind of father we prodigal children have. The suffering God waits patiently for His prodigal children to return. He sees even those who are still far away, for love has sharpened His vision. Beneath the rags He spots the features of His child.

"How great is the love the Father has lavished on us, that we should be called children of God! And that is what we are!" 1 Jn 3:1.

23 / How Do You Feel About Jesus?

"I am a rose of Sharon, a lily of the valleys" Sgs 2:1.

JESUS WAS visiting in the home of his friends in Bethany. Mary, one of the sisters, took a jar of very expensive perfume and poured it on Jesus' feet and wiped them with her hair (Jn 12:3). John adds that "the house was filled with the fragrance of the perfume." Mary's heart was filled to overflowing with love, but already there were those who could not comprehend such an act of love. But Jesus understood and came to Mary's defense. "I tell you the truth, wherever this gospel is preached throughout the world, what she has done will also be told, in memory of her" Mt 26:13. So great is the love of a heart enraptured in the presence of Jesus.   Today we emphasize common sense and practicality; there are not many enraptured souls like Mary's. We are like the disciples who asked: "Why this waste?" Why do we understand so little? Why are we unable to get ecstatic about Jesus.

There is much ecstasy, to be sure, but it is the kind in which a person seeks only himself and his own happiness. We cannot become happy by wanting to be happy. But in the company of Jesus our souls find their supreme joy. Sin keeps us from experiencing the presence of Jesus. It covers us like a morning fog and hides from our view the glory of Christ. Living with a divided heart, we never become ecstatic about the Lord.

There have never been very many "fools of God," enraptured souls who give their best to the Lord. If they ever become extinct, the Lord's people will have lost a treasure. Perhaps you do not have a bottle of expensive perfume to waste, but surely there is something you can do to show how you feel about Jesus!

24 / Life Is for the Glory of God

"The heavens declare the glory of God; the skies proclaim the work of his hands. Day after day they pour forth speech, night after night they display knowledge.... The sun is like a bridegroom coming forth from his pavilion, like a champion rejoicing to run his course" Ps 19:1-2, 5.

DURING early summer we begin to see signs of God working to restore and recreate nature. No matter which way we turn we see reason to rejoice over the beauty and perfection of God's works. The wonders of God's creation are not limited to the beauty and brightness of Finland's relatively short summer. All life is His handiwork. In a special way He has enlisted human beings as co- workers in his project of continuing creation. The farmer is in a good position to understand this, for through his efforts he promotes the growth of the fields and gardens. But God has created every person to be His co-worker. For that purpose He has given each of us our vocation.

Consider mothers and fathers as they care for their children. They certainly are involved in promoting God's purposes for generations to come. Similarly, every factory worker, public servant, and businessman is called to work in harmony with God's purposes for His creation. How differently we would feel about our work, if we shared this Biblical attitude toward secular vocations. Our work would then take on some of the beauty and innocence we so admire in nature.

God is love. He intends for each of us in his own vocation to promote the cause of love in this world by serving our neighbor and seeking his welfare. But our sinful selfishness diverts our efforts. Is it any wonder then that work has lost its appeal and life has so much that is ugly? Gaze upon God's works of creation and your heart will be filled with pure joy. "The heavens declare the glory of God; the skies proclaim the work of his hands. Day after day they pour forth speech; night after night they display knowledge.... The sun is like a bridegroom coming forth from his pavilion, like a champion rejoicing to run his course."

Human life, too, in its various vocations is intended for the praise of His glory. When Christ frees a person by cleansing him with his precious blood, his life begins to declare the glory of God, the glory which will fill eternity with its radiance.

25 / God Does Answer Prayer

"Your prayer has been heard" Lk 1:13.

HOW FORTUNATE Zechariah was to be greeted with these words from the Lord. For many years this God-fearing priest and his wife had carried on a prayer struggle for an heir. From the human point of view there was no hope. Prayers seemed hopeless, but they did not quit, nor did they blame the Lord for delaying His answer. And so the day came when they were told of the coming birth of John the Baptist. "Your prayer has been heard."

It still happens when people pray sincerely. The Lord is still eager to hear our prayers, even the prayers He cannot answer literally and those He must answer strangely. But He expects all who pray to be sincere, praying not merely with their mouth and lips but with their whole being. It is said of Zechariah and his wife Elizabeth that they "were upright in the sight of God, observing all the Lord's commandments and regulations blamelessly" Lk 1:6. In other words, they sought with their whole lives to please the Lord to whom they prayed.

Is this what you do? Do you pray only with your lips, or with your whole life? People who pray sincerely will not become disappointed with the Lord or begin to complain when the answers are delayed. They will not yield to the temptation of unbelief. Instead, they will blame themselves and become dissatisfied with themselves. They will notice the depth of the corruption of their hearts. They know they are unworthy of all they already possess, acknowledging as God's gift what others take for granted. They do not approach God with demands but pray in humility and honesty. All in all, they trust in the Lord's

mercy, clinging to His promise: "Your prayer has been heard."
Can this be said of you, too?

26 / Two Commandments of Love

*"Love the Lord your God with all your heart and with all
your soul and with all your strength and with all your
mind'; and, 'Love your neighbor as yourself"* Lk 10:27.

THERE ARE two commandments of love: "Love the Lord your
God, and your neighbor as yourself." Make no mistake, these are
indeed two commandments; we must not collapse them into one.
Some consider it enough to think about and serve their neighbor,
with no need to give separate service to God. This is an
unfortunate error.

In fact, Jesus did not come primarily to teach us how to love
our neighbor, but to make it possible to do so. He came to give us
the power to love by giving us access to the heavenly source of
that power through forgiveness of our sins. "The great love she
has shown proves that her many sins have been forgiven" Lk
7:47 (TEV).

By the same token, we must remember that love of neighbor
is not to be replaced by the claim that we love God. Love of
neighbor is the touchstone of true Christianity. If we do not love
our neighbor, we cannot love God. Love of God does not take
place outside daily life; we cannot love God simply with our
hearts, our prayers and words. On the contrary, the Bible states:
"Religion that God our Father accepts as pure and faultless is
this: to look after orphans and widows in their distress and to
keep oneself from being polluted by the world" Jas 1:27.

The words of Jesus, "Dear woman, here is your son," and
"Here is your mother" Jn 19:26f., are a powerful sermon about
loving one's neighbors. On Good Friday the beloved disciple
discovered that love of neighbor meant giving food and shelter to
another person. In that way "he who had leaned against him at
the supper" (Jn 21:23) was to love his Master. We learn love at
the foot of the cross.

The commandments of love are two. Neither negates the
other; neither substitutes for the other. Genuine love stems only
from a true relationship to God.

27 / The Secret of Spiritual Renewal

"And we, who with unveiled faces all reflect the Lord's glory, are being transformed into his likeness with ever-increasing glory, which comes from the Lord, who is the Spirit" 2 Co 3:18.

EVEN IN far northern latitudes summer is a time of change and renewal. Tanned faces and bodies are just one piece of evidence. The Bible often speaks of change, using the phrase "with unveiled faces" to describe it.

Reading and hearing of the Word do not benefit us, if our "faces" are "veiled." Something prevents us from receiving positive influences from the Word. If we think of how little Christ has been "formed" in us, how little of him is seen in the lives of modern Christians, how little true renewal there is in our lives, we can only conclude that we have looked upon Christ with "veiled faces."

Paul points to the reason when he says: "Whenever anyone turns to the Lord, the veil is taken away" 2 Co 3:16. Are we Christians who have not turned? God has sought us with His grace, awakening in us concern about our sins, making us dissatisfied with our state of affairs, and sometimes leading us to peak experiences. But because we have not turned to the Lord, the veil has not been removed. Sometimes we try to remove the veil that hinders renewal; but as Paul says, "the veil is taken away." A condemned and helpless person can be changed if he will turn to Christ as his Helper. By clinging to the gracious promises of the Word, without relying on human reason, he is drawn into the light and his life is changed.

Do not make excuses for your faults and weaknesses on the basis of general human corruption. Such excuses are the death of all true piety. Do not be your own judge and dismiss your evil thoughts and words, your feelings of lust and greed, and the wrong movements of your will. Such self-help accounts for the lack of renewal among Christians. Turn to Christ with your sins whenever the Holy Spirit convicts you. That is the secret of renewal.

28 / God Draws the Boundaries

"He will separate the people one from another as a
shepherd separates the sheep from the goats" Mt 25:32.

SEPARATION often causes sorrow and pain. When a child leaves home, both the child and his parents experience the pain of separation. The separation of death is excruciating. One cannot imagine the anguish of those who will find themselves on the wrong side in the final judgment.

One ought to reflect on the length of eternity! God's management of the world includes separation, and He establishes boundaries already in the course of this life. The last day will simply expose the boundaries that have been in existence all along. "I was hungry and you gave me nothing to eat, I was thirsty and you gave me nothing to drink, I was a stranger and you did not invite me in, I needed clothes and you did not clothe me, I was sick and in prison and you did not look after me" Mt 25:42f. Every decision we make, every act and every failure to act, means taking our position on one side of the boundary or the other. Natural man does not want to know about such boundaries, thinking it unnecessary to separate good and evil, truth and error.

We do not want to hear about repentance, preferring to think about God's overflowing love. But God's love is holy love; He cannot love sin in any form. His Spirit teaches us to see sin as sin and to turn from sin in repentance. Those whom God has chosen must separate evil from good, lies from truth, first in their own lives, but then also in the lives of others. In this way God points to the boundaries which exist already in this life, even though they will not be fully exposed until the final judgment.

29 / Right With God by Faith

"To the man who does not work but trusts God who
justifies the wicked, his faith is credited as righteousness"
Ro 4:5.

DEPRESSED by troubles in his ministry, a Finnish pastor found himself in a spiritual wilderness. A friend urged him to pray more, for he diagnosed that lack of prayer was the reason the Lord had hidden Himself. "Ask and you will receive." Another counselor told him to believe. "Believe, and you will be saved." But no matter how much the poor pastor tried to believe, things did not clear up. A third explained that his problem was the lack of the Holy Spirit. "Be filled with the Holy Spirit." Whoever heeds this admonition will find light, it was said. But no help came.

Sitting with his troubles in a cottage meeting one day, the depressed man listened as a layman, Juho Malkamaki, talked about justification of sinners. Malkamaki had no knowledge of the pastor's problems, but the Lord used his message to provide the needed solution. "It is no miracle," Malkamaki said, "if God justifies him who prays. Even the fact that God justifies the believer is not a miracle. And of course God justifies him who has the Holy Spirit. The miracle is that God justifies the wicked." Here was the answer that freed the soul of the pastor and unlocked the door of grace. "God justifies the wicked."

Malkamaki's message stated clearly the paradox of the Christian faith, namely, that God is truly "God of the impossible." Very often we try to offer God something of our own, afraid to trust in Christ unless we feel we are making some progress in holiness. We resolve to overcome sin, to pray more fervently and to believe more wholeheartedly. Our conscience, however, insists that our own righteousness is a filthy rag. We are only trying to squeeze out of ourselves what is already ours by grace, unwittingly turning our backs to Christ. Our situation will not improve unless we surrender to the God who justifies the wicked.

God's regenerative power finds room to work only where people acknowledge how wicked they are, but believe in Christ anyway. Christ is our true and only righteousness.

30 / Do Not Lose Your First Love

"Your love is like the morning mist, like the early dew that disappears" Ho 6:4.

HAVE YOU ever walked barefoot in grass that is wet with the morning dew? You knew you could look forward to a bright sunny day. The writer of Hosea felt this way, but his thoughts turned quickly to other things. He gives voice not only to his own thoughts but also to the thoughts of the Lord: "What can I do with you, Ephraim? What can I do with you, Judah? Your love is like the morning mist, like the early dew that disappears."

How beautiful the love of the soul for God when God graciously shares the riches of heaven. This is how a newly converted soul feels about his relationship to God. It brings joy to the heart of God, too.

But "your love is like the morning mist, like the early dew that disappears." The "first love" (Rev 2:4) grows cold all too soon. The end of the honeymoon comes and real Christian life begins. Many have turned God's gracious love for them into a pillow for their heads and slipped into the slumber of indifference.

But, love must not disappear like the early dew. The Lord speaks through His prophet: "I desire mercy, not sacrifice, and acknowledgment of God rather than burnt offerings" Ho 6:6. Love for the Lord will not endure the heat of day unless it is changed into loving service toward our neighbor. Worship of God in the form of purely spiritual exercises is only boring, lifeless ritual, unless it is transformed into the mercy of simple service to others.

When we no longer love our neighbors, God's work in us is lost "like the morning mist."

July

1 / Beggars Need a Rich God

"God, who is rich in mercy, made us alive in Christ" Eph 2:4.

UNLESS GOD reveals Himself nobody knows Him. But, God reveals Himself to us in various ways: the works of creation, our conscience, the events of our lives, and the fortunes of nations. To learn what kind of God we have, we must take time to pay attention to all that fills our lives.

You may marvel at God's good and beautiful works in nature during these summer months, finding yourself in silent meditation and prayer. By lifting your eyes and looking around you see the works of your Creator and find strength for your struggles. Jesus took note of the flowers of the field and the birds of the air and wants us to do the same. We will also be strengthened in our faith.

However, we find God's true self-revelation in the Bible and, most clearly, in His only Son Jesus Christ. It is the Bible--not just nature--that we need to study to discover that God is rich in mercy. If we measure God's grace by our own thoughts and experiences we will never know Him properly. Rather, we must measure our thoughts and experiences with the Bible. If you want to know God spend time with His Word, meditating during the day on a word or phrase from the Bible. Only our own laziness is to blame for our poor knowledge of the riches of God's grace.

Above all, however, God has revealed Himself in Jesus Christ, who is the key that unlocks the Bible. We cannot explain how Christ "dwells" in the Bible, but we can experience him as the living Lord who is still available for all who seek him in prayer. Through fellowship with our Lord we can know that we have a God who is rich in mercy.

We do not receive true spiritual riches because we are something special; we receive them from a God who is rich in mercy. We are and will continue to be beggars.

2 / The Earth Belongs to God

"This is what the Lord says, 'Heaven is my throne, and the earth is my footstool" Is 66:1.

A CHRISTIAN is one who is on his way to heaven. Heaven becomes very real when we think of loved ones who died in faith, recalling that heaven is our Father's house with many rooms (Jn 14:2).

But the Christian does not forget that the earth also belongs to the Lord. "The earth is the Lord's, and everything in it" Ps 24:1. Or do we forget? Do we really understand that the Lord has the right of ownership to everything? When we deal with people, we are dealing with the Lord's possessions. As we tend to our everyday tasks, we are in the Lord's workshop. Everything is His.   If we remembered that the earth also belongs to God, we would surely act more responsibly, genuinely, considerately, and humbly. We would be more careful, more diligent, and more merciful in our treatment of others. We would not dare to elevate ourselves the way we do.

We often neglect the task at hand, because it appears to be insignificant. We don't give a second thought to words we utter; we do not listen to one another. For all this we blame our lack of time and our weariness. But the real reason is that we do not understand that the earth and all that is in it belongs to the Lord. We do not live with the awareness that even in our daily duties we are dealing with the Lord. Our busyness and tiredness often result from assuming assignments the Lord wants to give to others.

We must live with greater awareness of the living God, the God to whom heaven and earth belong.

3 / Are You a Friend of God?

"Abraham was called God's friend" Jas 3:7.

IT IS SAID of some of the people of the Old Testament that "the Lord went with them." They were God's friends. Can you think of anything more beautiful than being God's friend, a part of the Lord's company? Such biblical statements are not merely statements that people made about themselves or that others made about them. God says that they were His friends.

When we listen to God's word about His friends, we are told: "Who may ascend the hill of the Lord? Who may stand in his holy place? He who has clean hands and a pure heart, who does not lift up his soul to an idol or swear by what is false. He will receive blessing from the Lord and vindication from God his Savior" Ps 24:3-5. If your hands are not clean and your heart is not pure, if you lift up your soul to an idol, do not think that you are God's friend.

But, God takes as His friend every ungodly person who, despairing over sin, puts his trust in God's grace. God stands ready to justify sinners. The father's arms continue to be wide open to welcome the prodigal son. But keep in mind that the prodigal son was sorry for his sins. The robe and the ring were not brought to the prodigal son in the distant country; he had to return home. That means confession and rejection of sin. Only at the end of the journey back home can the boy sit down once again at the father's table. Only when we have made a radical break with sin and heeded the voice of our conscience can we enter into friendship with God.

Who today will be immediately recognized as God's friends? By calling us into His kingdom the Lord intended to make all of us His friends. Because of our disobedience and lack of repentance we have remained friends of the world. Before we say that we are God's friends, let us examine our hearts and hands, our thoughts, words, and deeds, in order that we might turn our backs on wickedness and evil. Access to the Lord's hill, life in His presence, is denied to all that is unclean and impure. But God will welcome His friends.

4 / Always on the Alert

"Narrow is the road that leads to life" Mt 7:14.

RIDING a bicycle on a busy highway is an object lesson in Christian watchfulness. If concentration is lost, something bad may happen.

Likewise, we are not sufficiently alert on our Christian journey. We travel along as though there were no danger. We are aware of pitfalls on life's highways, but we are in far greater peril from our own sins--carnal thoughts and fantasies, improper words and insensitive criticism, envy, laziness--than the temptations of the world. If you intend to reach your destination, look ahead and pay attention.

When riding a bicycle, you must often avoid an accident by taking a narrow path, perhaps the shoulder of the road, between the traffic and the ditch. And you cannot lose control even for a moment if you want to make it without serious injury.

A Christian is apt to breathe a sigh of relief when temptation has passed, but often we face the greatest dangers just when, by God's grace, we have overcome temptation. Be careful that you do not lose concentration and fall. Be careful that you do not lose what God has given you by falling soon after you have resisted and overcome temptation.

Wake up, watch, be on the alert!

5 / To Whom Do You Belong?

*"Choose for yourselves this day whom you will serve....
But as for me and my household, we will serve the Lord"*
Js 24:15.

THESE WORDS of Joshua, the godly leader of the people of Israel, call attention to the responsibility of every Christian mother and father. We cannot force anyone to serve the Lord, not even our own children. Our responsibility is to make known the importance of this matter, to underline the implicit demand for decision, and then to serve as a model.

Everyone must make his own decision, but is it really within our power to choose whom we serve? Today a servant or employee can choose whom he wants to serve. But servanthood was different in the world of the Bible. It was different when servants were slaves, the property of their master. As long as the master-slave relationship was in force, the servant was obligated to serve the master to whom he belonged. This is the background for the biblical thinking about serving the Lord.

We cannot serve the Lord at times and places of our own choosing. We cannot observe His holy laws and His holy will in certain instances but otherwise live as we please. The Lord is to be served wholeheartedly, with all we have. But this assumes that we truly are the Lord's possession, His servants.

Are we the Lord's servants? Do we belong to Him? If Christ's death involves us personally, we must certainly be aware that we do not belong to ourselves nor to anyone else. He is mine and I am His! It is precisely to those people who are redeemed and made righteous by faith that the summons is issued: Serve the Lord! We must choose; and we can!

6 / Religion the Enemy of Faith

"But the natural man does not receive the things of the Spirit of God" 1 Co 2:14 (KJ).

ON OUR SPIRITUAL journey we must guard against mixing our natural religious feelings and the life of faith. Everyone is by nature religious, in one sense or another. Living in a Christian society, we assimilate certain elements of Christianity into our behavior, so that it begins to look like the true life of faith. But there is a decisive difference between the two: in our natural piety we build our own structure of self-righteousness in order to find acceptance with God and other people, while true Christianity rests on God's unmerited grace in Jesus Christ. The life of faith is always the work of the Holy Spirit, not ours.

With our natural piety we lack the freedom of God's children. We become self-centered, always striving to become pleasing to God. We become victims of self-pity, and what we think is sin is in reality an inferiority complex. The fact of the matter is that the part of us which is naturally religious continues to dwell in us even when we truly believe. Every traveler on the road of life must contend every day with the natural religiosity of his old nature.

It is said that the "old man" is always trying to snatch the sack lunch of the "new man." When God offers nourishment for our new nature, the old nature pilfers it and deprives us of the gospel, which is God's power for the salvation of everyone who believes (Ro 1:16). The old nature keeps us from believing that God justifies the ungodly. The old nature simply refuses to accept that a sinner may believe in free grace and live in the spirit as a free child of God.

7 / Put Your Heart in Your Work

"Whatever you do, work at it with all your heart, as working for the Lord, not for men" Col 3:23.

IN THE COURSE of everyday life it becomes evident how inwardly broken and restless we really are. We run around, dabbling here and there, lacking purpose in our activities. We do many things and others look upon us as people who contribute to society. But, in fact, we do not know how to give ourselves completely to our work. We play at it. Inwardly, we know that nothing worthwhile is accomplished and we grow more frustrated.

The attitude toward life implied in Scripture is very different. The apostle Paul faced the pressure of his concern for the churches every day (2 Co 11:28), but he did not resort to shortcuts. He invested his heart in his work. "Whatever you do, work at it with all your heart." Whoever does that gives himself to his work, not complaining if the work seems heavy and difficult, dull and boring.

We should not worry about results, nor wish to be doing something else. We are to invest our hearts in what we are doing in the present moment. When we meet other people, we share our hearts with them. It sometimes happens that, in the company of other people, we are not truly present with them. Our hearts are somewhere else and our behavior is superficial and cold. Our worship can be like that, too. We sing, we listen, we talk, but our hearts are absent.

Paul's words point to the reason for our problem: "...as for the Lord, and not for men." If we really understood that this particular task, this person, this moment of prayer, was from God, wouldn't we put our hearts into it? We would see our lives as opportunities to serve the Lord in worthwhile ways, not as burdens and obligations.

"You serve the Lord Christ." In this very situation in which I find myself I serve the Lord and am in His presence. Right now He is asking for my heart; right now He wants to bless me.

8 / God's Business Is Your Business

"If anyone would come after me, he must deny himself and take up his cross and follow me" Mk 8:34.

SELF-DENIAL, demanded here by Jesus of his followers, does not mean giving up things generally labeled as sin. Such self-denial is a matter of one's own choice. I choose one thing, you choose something else, but in each case the choice is personal. Ordinarily we follow the line of least resistance in our choices. But no matter how well or poorly we do in giving something up, we retain our independence. We do not deny ourselves; we merely deny something.

While practicing this kind of self-denial we are actually practicing self-preservation. We can easily remain inwardly hard and cold toward others and admire only ourselves. This was the self-denial practiced by the Pharisees of Jesus' day; the pious of every age have followed suit.

When Jesus demands that his followers deny themselves, his point is not to produce good, exemplary disciples. He has in mind that God might have in these people instruments for the doing of His work. Christ's followers are called to follow the example of their Master as they go about God's business. It means that they are not to be about their own business; they have no right to live for themselves. They must live for the Lord.

Whenever someone begins to do God's will, he runs into irresolvable conflict with the world and his own self. This is the cross which we must take up. We will find ourselves in war against sin, the world, and our own flesh, all of which work against our obedience to God's will. The struggle to do God's business leads us to deny ourselves and to take up our cross.

9 / Obedience in Little Things

"Train yourself to be godly" 1 Ti 4:7.

THE KEY WORD in the Christian growth process is obedience. Obedience certainly will not acquire special status for us before God. As the Bible says, "The righteous will live by faith" Ro 1:17. But unless we are willing to obey God, we shut ourselves off from God's gracious work and lose even that which we have already received. This is what Paul had in mind when he warned his friends not to grieve the Holy Spirit by their disobedience (Eph 4:30).

We can easily understand that our obedience is at stake in the momentous decisions of life, such as choice of vocation and spouse. But we cannot overlook the decisions we face on a daily basis, the small tasks in our homes, our conversations with each other, what we buy, and so on. Yet our obedience to the Holy Spirit which speaks in our consciences ought to begin with these little things.

Do you want to grow in the knowledge of Christ? Pay attention to little things. Begin with them, no matter how unwilling you may feel about doing God's will. Do not let anything keep you from being obedient in whatever the Lord sets before you.

10 / Discipleship is Listening

"He wakens me morning by morning, wakens my ear to listen like one being taught" Is 50:4.

DISCIPLESHIP means listening to the words and instructions of the teacher. The disciple who lacks knowledge must pay close attention to the teacher who has knowledge. In Christian life such listening is of primary importance. One must heed the inner admonitions of the Lord's Spirit, paying attention to what the Lord wants to say in His word.

In reading the Bible and listening to the word, the Christian disciple prays silently and sighs inwardly; anticipating the morsels the Lord Himself will break for him from His word. We do not possess this art of listening naturally. Our natural tendency is to clarify matters with our own mind. But that leads us astray, for human reason is blind in spiritual matters. On our own we cannot correctly comprehend the word. The Lord must open our ears, if we are to listen and learn.

We need to pay attention to the words "morning by morning." It is a wonder of wonders that the Lord awakens His disciples each and every day to listen properly. He does not become discouraged with our hearing problem; He is willing to go to a great deal of trouble as He works to draw His own to the place of the disciple.   Since the disciple himself does not know, he is totally dependent on his teacher. He continues to pester his Lord with questions and requests. When he runs into things he cannot understand, even then he humbly accepts what he is given, confident in the faith that it is for his best.

11 / The Living Stream of the Spirit

"The streams of God are filled with water" Ps 65:9.

"A POWERFUL stream, making its own waves, flows through the ocean." This saying was inspired by mighty ocean currents, such as the Gulf Stream which affects the climate of Scandinavia. It describes a kind of spiritual independence which is needed to avoid being carried away by the circumstances and turmoils of the world.   Christians could use such a motto, for there is great danger of being swamped by the world so that we fail to reach the shores of our homeland. We must know which stream will be able to carry us through the ocean--the stream of God's Holy Spirit. Nothing else will carry us through our struggle. Not congregational loyalty or support of some spiritual movement. Not our own fervent spirit, or the fervent spirit of others. Not our will power. Only the power of the Holy Spirit will do.

The struggle is so difficult that human powers are of no help; divine power is needed. We need the stream of the Holy Spirit, a stream filled with water, a stream that is strong and powerful. It is the only stream that makes its own waves through the ocean of humanity; the only one that can carry us to the shores of eternity.

Are you in this stream? Has the Holy Spirit picked you up or are you drifting aimlessly along? Are you still trying to make your own way through the seas of life, or have you learned to trust yourself completely to the Lord? We feel utterly powerless to help this miserable world. But let us not forget that the Lord's stream is filled with water, water that can revive the dry desert, quench our thirst, and carry us to our destination. The Spirit is filled with water also for this new day and new age.

12 / The Glory of the Cross

"We have seen his glory" Jn 1:14.

THE LORD reveals His glory and power in the death of Christ. Concerning the burnt offering of the Old Covenant, the Lord said, "There I will meet with the Israelites, and the place will be consecrated by my glory" Ex 29:43. Christ, facing death on the cross, prayed, "Father, glorify your name!" And the answer came, "I have glorified it, and will glorify it again" Jn 12:28.

We will not learn to know Christ aright unless we see him in his suffering and death. We do not see his power and holiness displayed anywhere as clearly as on the cross. He is the Lamb of God whose obedience put an end to all other offerings once and for all. "But now he has appeared once for all at the end of the ages to do away with sin by the sacrifice of himself" He 9:26. Nothing else must come between the holy God and fallen man. Only the once-and-for-all offering of Christ on Golgatha belongs there.

The glory of Christ's death is visible in its universality. In the light of the cross we do not see godly and ungodly people as separate groups, for all are ungodly and guilty. There is no difference. God-fearing Nicodemus and the Samaritan woman are in the same boat. We divide people into various groups, but all boundaries disappear when we stand beneath the cross. The cross declares everyone guilty. Christ is the one "who takes away the sin of the world" Jn 1:29. The words "takes away" mean to remove by carrying away. As the Lamb of God, Christ carried away the guilt and punishment of our sins, thereby removing them. Look at Christ on the cross and the repentant thief beside him. You will see the glory of Christ; it will brighten your life, too.

13/ Dying to Live

"For our light and momentary troubles are achieving for us an eternal glory that far outweighs them all" 2 Co 4:17.

ACCORDING to the natural order, life comes first and then death. Our instinct of self-preservation makes us fear and flee from not only death but everything that points to death, such as suffering, pain, and the cross. But, despite the best efforts of doctors, we cannot avoid suffering and affliction nor escape death. Our lives are always under a dark, gloomy cloud.

It is no surprise that ancient classical poetry both bubbled with the joy of life and moaned the melancholy melodies of cypress trees and cemeteries. This is in perfect harmony with the viewpoint of human nature.

The Christian conviction of faith, however, is the reverse. "You died, and your life is now hidden with Christ in God" Col 3:3. First death, then life. "We always carry around in our body the death of Jesus, so that the life of Jesus may also be revealed in our body. For we who are alive are always being given over to death for Jesus' sake, so that his life may be revealed in our mortal body. So then, death is at work in us, but life is at work in you" 2 Co 4:10-12. In baptism you were buried with Christ into death, so that like Christ and with Christ, you might die to the corruption of this world.

The road to life is the way of the cross. Faith does not know the cemetery mood of ancient poets, for the way of the cross leads to life. As Good Friday was followed by Easter, the crucifixion by the resurrection, so the Christian finds life after he has emptied the cup of death.

Christians can anticipate this joy in a mysterious way while still on the road of suffering. This is what prompted Paul to utter the otherwise enigmatic words, "Sorrowful, yet always rejoicing; poor, yet making many rich; having nothing, and yet possessing everything" 2 Co 6:10. The Christian finds joy even in trials and tribulations, for he knows that he has been given over to death for Jesus' sake, so that he might enter also into his life. First death, and only then, life. First sorrow, then joy. But already on the road of sorrow we taste the hidden joy.

14 / The Blessing of Hard Times

"Observe the commands of the Lord your God, walking in his ways and revering him" Dt 8:6.

WE ARE ALWAYS uncertain about what lies ahead, but we need not be ignorant concerning God's will for us. In the Bible, God lays out a plain path for us. "The way of the righteous is made plain" Pr 15:19 (KJ). It is liberating to know, in the midst of our afflictions, that God is revealing the way we are to go. Let us not stand idly by, gazing anxiously about; let us travel the road of obedience in faith. "Observe the commands of the Lord your God, walking in his ways and revering him."

Let us be on guard, obeying the Lord wherever we are, being faithful in the little things of everyday life. If we walk this plain path of obedience, we will reach our destination, no matter what storms rage around us. Along the way, in the afflictions we face, something of God's purposes will be revealed to us. In our struggles, God will humble us, test us, and let us look into our hearts. In tight situations we will discover what our hearts really cling to, what our hopes and desires really are. We will see how little faith and trust we have, in spite of our piety. We can learn how totally dependent we are on God. This is the blessing of hard times. "As a man disciplines his son, so the Lord your God disciplines you" Dt 8:5. We can confidently leave the worries of tomorrow with God and concentrate on obeying the Lord's commandments, walking in His ways, and fearing Him.

15 / Answers Are Given

"As soon as you began to pray, an answer was given, which I have come to tell you" Dn 9:23.

LUTHERAN Christians think of themselves as people who find life in God's word. As heirs of the Reformation they have learned that on the journey of faith they are absolutely dependent on the Word.

We may all know and accept this teaching in theory, but in the practical affairs of life we often discover how weak, and even non-existent, our reliance on the Word really is. The Word does not appeal to us. Weeks and months may pass without our opening the Bible. Other books and the messages of respected preachers leave our souls untouched. This should not be considered normal for the Christian life. These are signs that all is not well.

Like an earthly father, God is interested in conversing with His children. But when children have been disobedient, the father closes the door and lets his children wait and knock. God's silence is a judgment on our neglect of His word. God keeps His children waiting behind the door in order to humble them and to teach them.

The words of the Lord's messenger apply to all who stand behind the Lord's door: "As soon as you began to pray, an answer was given, which I have come to tell you." All who struggle in vain to find something in the Word, who discover that they are standing behind a closed door, who feel that God has become a stranger to them, may rest assured that for them, too, "an answer was given." It has been on the way from the moment when they were humbled and knocked on the door of grace in the prayers of a contrite heart. "As soon as you began to pray, an answer was given." That's how God works.

16 / Baptism as God's Beginning

"God saved us, not because of righteous things we had done, but because of His mercy. He saved us through the washing of rebirth and renewal by the Holy Spirit" Titus 3:5.

THERE ARE primarily two ways of thinking about baptism. According to the first, baptism is a rite of confession. A person confesses his faith in Jesus and receives baptism as a sign of his faith. Baptism is thus a kind of vow by which the person decisively acknowledges that he belongs to Christ. No one can claim that they are able, by their own efforts, to surrender fully to the Lord. Without God's grace they would be unable to make their confession.

The second view of baptism is found in churches that practice infant baptism. Here, baptism is seen as the gracious work of God in an individual which has nothing to do with human merit or worthiness. God makes us His own, regardless of what we are or how far His gracious work has progressed in

us. When infants are baptized it becomes crystal clear that God
gives His grace to one who has done nothing.

Only one of these ways of thinking about baptism enables us
to talk about baptismal grace. If baptism is looked upon as a rite
of confession, with only adult believers qualified for baptism, it
is not possible to talk about God's grace in connection with
baptism. But, in infant baptism God's grace is given to sinful
human beings, and shines forth in all its glory.

All who struggle to understand baptism should ponder this
difference. In teaching and practicing infant baptism, the church
proclaims God's unmerited grace toward sinners. If we are to
have any hope of salvation, it must rest totally on the grace of
God.

17 / Travel Has Its Dangers

*"I have swept away your offenses like a cloud, your sins
like the morning mist"* Is 44:22.

IT IS DANGEROUS for ships, and unpleasant for travelers, to
be caught in a fog. You cannot see where you are going. Danger
can overtake any moment. We talk about the "mist [fog] of sin,"
which is described in a hymn as "covering the soul." The Bible
sees sin as a darkness that "fills the soul." Visibility is zero, and
an error in judgment can have tragic consequences.

Many are careless as they travel blind in the fog of sin.
Unaware of what they are doing or where they are going, and
oblivious to possible dangers ahead, they assume they are safe
and secure. Surrounded by people who are similarly blind, their
false security is confirmed, although destruction lies ahead.

Stop! Do you see where you are going? If you are struggling
toward wholeness, study the map and the road!

Fog covers the swamps even during summer. Our hearts are
like swamps from which the fog of sin rises, blinding and
eventually destroying us. Out of the heart come evil thoughts,
evil desires and lusts (Mt. 15:19). We cannot blame others for
the fog. We ourselves are to blame.

As we travel along God's way we must always deal with the
wickedness of our hearts, which spue forth all kinds of
dangerous poisons. But, the Lord Jesus Christ can sweep away
this dangerous fog. Faith is, from beginning to end, a series of

transactions between the sinner and the Lord Jesus Christ. If these inner transactions cease, the soul will remain in a fog. We must constantly seek him, call for his help, and seek to live with him.

18 / We Need to Learn Contentment

"I have learned to be content whatever the circumstances"
Phil 4:11

PAUL DID NOT have an easy life. Yet, he was able to say: "I have learned to be content whatever the circumstances." One can only imagine the life events referred to in this observation, knowing only that he had attended the school of contentment and had learned well.

People who have learned to be content have been in the company of one who is "gentle and humble in heart" Mt 11:29, and are able to be a blessing to others. Note the words, "humble in heart." Sometimes we try to be content with discontented hearts. But, our discontent eventually expresses itself in words and deeds.

True Christian contentment is something other than cold acceptance of fate. Rather, it arises from the confidence that our Father knows at all times what is best for us. This faith is often like a flickering candle, for temptations are many and God seems to be far away. But the flickering candle is not snuffed out. God counts our wounds and our tears. He takes the vexed and dissatisfied heart into His care, sometimes using strong medicine to teach us to accept His will. It is these wounds and tears, however, which reveal to us the corruption of our hearts and our unbelief. They help us to learn to be contented and submissive friends of the Lord.

Christian contentment comes from knowing Jesus, our most precious treasure and greatest joy. We are satisfied with whatever God wants to give us.

19 / The Lord Provides Friends

"You are fellow citizens with God's people and members of God's household" Eph 2:19.

GOD DOES NOT intend for anyone to walk the Christian way without friends. He has not created solitary Christians. By belonging to Christ, we are made members of his body and family. One of the early church fathers remarked, "Whoever has God as Father has the Church as Mother."

More and more Christians are beginning to see the great value of this basic biblical truth. The spread of the ecumenical movement among Christian churches is the result of Christian unity seeking expression also in the everyday affairs of individual Christians.

We cannot make it as Christians if we are alone. We need one another, not simply to make life happier and richer, but to make it Christian. We need people who will admonish us and challenge us to repentance, but who will also proclaim to us the good news of Christ, who has redeemed us with his blood from the curse and condemnation of sin. Luther actually suggested that we ought to be Christs to one another, taking care of one another as Christ has taken care of us.

In this day and age, when the battle is intense and signs point to the imminence of Christ's return, Christians need mutual support more than ever. But how is such unity achieved? There are many ways, such as the one offered by the hymn writer:

If Jesus you love truly,
Friends you will have surely.

If Jesus is so dear to us that we gladly speak of him as we converse with one another, even with strangers, friendly relationships will be established. If we can talk about the Lord of Life, then even among total strangers we will find friends.

20 / All We Need Is Jesus

"When they looked up, they saw no one except Jesus" Mt
17:8.

THE STORY of the Transfiguration concludes with the comment
that the disciples "saw no one except Jesus." Someone may
conclude that this was an unfortunate situation, that having
only Jesus was not enough. On the Mount of Transfiguration it
dawned on the disciples that they needed no one but Jesus. They
needed only the Lord.

Soon after this experience, these men were entrusted with
the task of taking the gospel to the ends of the earth. They were
to face powerful world rulers, philosophical traditions with long
histories, seductive forms of vice with enticements many of us
know nothing about, as well as a rich variety of religious
movements. They needed a banner for these battles. "Jesus
only!" became this banner. After the Mount of Transfiguration
they saw the truth more brightly in their souls: It's the Lord's
battle! Only Jesus' glory matters; Jesus alone will advance his
cause.

This is the motto we need today. We face our shallow,
secular era, and people who have a mind only for bread, money,
entertainment, and power. Somehow we need to encourage them
to think of God, soul, and eternity. How will we explain the Bible
to people today so that they will understand it? How will we
kindle the fire of the Lord in our churches? The answer to both
questions is: "Jesus only."

"No one knows the Father except the Son and those to whom
the Son chooses to reveal him" Mt 11:27. Let us not hate or
despise the "ungodly" of our day; let us not become bitter or
angry toward them; let us not despair over them. Remember our
battle cry: "Jesus only!" Only he can do it! And he will!

We do not need talented and trained, skilled and spiritually
powerful fathers and mothers, teachers and ministers, men and
women, old and young. We need weak, unskilled, and broken
sinners, who entertain no great hopes about themselves but
have concluded: "Jesus only!"

21 / The Healing Presence of Jesus

"For where two or three come together in my name, there am I with them" Mt 18:20.

IN MATTHEW Jesus promises: "For where two or three come together in my name, there am I with them." And Jesus has never defaulted on his promise.

But we must consider the context of this promise. At stake is the healing of a fractured relationship between believers through admonition and mutual forgiveness. The primary purpose of Christ's presence is not to provide us with blissful personal experiences, but to remove the evil from us that hampers and hinders mutual love.

Wherever people are concerned about reconciliation, wherever there is concern for the expression of the spirit of love in human relationships, there Jesus is present as Lord to implement God's will on earth as it is implemented in heaven. Matthew adds the wonderful promise that if two or three agree here on earth about any problem between them, and pray about it, the Father in heaven will hear them. This shows how strongly the first disciples struggled to live in mutual love.

All of us have reason to pay attention to these words, for nothing is more difficult to fulfill than the demands of love in interpersonal relationships. For corrupt human nature it is impossible. Perhaps we can generate a sense of good will, but we cannot truly love others. For true love covers the faults of others and helps them overcome their failures. None of us can do this by our own ability.

Jesus knows this, for he sees the human heart as it is. Yet, he is present as the Lord wherever people are struggling for love. If we agree to follow our Lord, then all the powers of redemption are at hand and available for our use.

Jesus is Lord! We must learn to be more obedient to the demands of love. We must not condone broken human relationships, but struggle to help and love one another. We must learn to pray in harmony with our brothers and sisters, and, above all, believe in the possibilities of Jesus and trust in him!

22 / God Creates New Hearts

"Create in me a pure heart, O God, and renew a steadfast spirit within me" Ps 51:10.

INWARDLY falling away from the Lord on David's part had resulted in a series of serious setbacks on the outside. The Lord caught up with him and ensnared him in a net of bitter remorse. "Have mercy on me, O God, according to your unfailing love; according to your great compassion blot out my transgressions. Wash away all my iniquity and cleanse me from my sin" Ps 51:1f.

The genuineness of David's repentance is revealed in his continuing to deal with the Lord even after the external problems had been solved. David understood that everything depended on the state of his heart. Concerned about similar setbacks in the future, he asked for a new heart, a pure heart. We also need a pure heart. But we receive it only through the forgiveness of sins.

Forgiveness is called absolution, which means loosening. Only forgiveness can loosen us from ourselves, from our own wishes and desires. Forgiveness alone loosens us from the desire for the approval of others, from bondage to and fear of other people. Forgiveness alone can cleanse our inner life and give us a new, steadfast spirit.

David prayed that the Lord would create in him a pure heart. When God creates, He creates out of nothing. There is nothing in us that God can use to give us a pure heart. He must, and can, create something completely new out of nothing. And that is the only way spiritual renewal is possible for us.

> Grant me, Jesus, that in you
> I may find a spirit new.

23 / Sin Is Selfishness

"Everyone looks out for his own interests" Phil 2:21.

ONE WAY sin shows its corrupting influence is in the weakening and distortion of our spiritual vision, our habit of judging things, of trying to distinguish between right and wrong.

The essence of sin is selfishness and self-centeredness. When we are selfish, we are unable to see things as they really are; we are not objective in our judgments. Everything is colored by our own feelings about how a thing or a person serves us. Our own interests determine our judgments and relationships.

Our lives are filled with self-centered judgments. We tear apart what we ought to put together. We combine what should be separated. We seek our own advantage, promote our own affairs, even if it means going contrary to the way things really are. Such lack of objectivity reflects a sinful attitude toward life. It is said of J. J. Nervander, a famous Finnish intellectual, that when he returned from a long trip abroad he was a strangely changed man. Earlier he had been an acknowledged leader of university students, but after his trip he continually found fault with people, until he finally withdrew from public life. A historian has suggested that Nervander had suffered an inner collapse on his trip abroad, with the result that he no longer saw anyone but himself. His view of life around him had changed. This is a significant statement. When the inner life collapses, one's vision becomes distorted and one's judgments skewed. Objectivity is replaced by subjectivity. Destructive repercussions are felt in all areas of one's life.

We desparately need people who are objective, factual and forthright in their thinking. In other words, we need people who have experienced redemption, and, therefore, can see straight and judge rightly. Each of us still has the spirit of self-centeredness. We need daily prayer, daily repentance and daily confession of sins. But we also need daily appropriation of our reconciliation through the blood of Jesus.

24 / Conditions of Peace

"If only you had paid attention to my commands, your peace would have been like a river" Is 48:18.

WE ARE NOT always conscious of how intimately inner peace is related to inner discipline. Yet the Lord says, "If only you had paid attention to my commands, your peace would have been like a river."

The matter becomes clear when we consider the words that flow from our mouths. How undisciplined we are in our speech!

We allow our tongues to engage in idle talk and, even worse, in evil and slanderous gossip. This talk creates all kinds of problems for us and often permanently damages our souls.

Thomas a'Kempis said we are seldom happy when we leave the company of others, meaning that, while with them, we slipped into idle talk that deprived us of inner peace. Wrong words hurt not only those to whom they are directed but also hurt the speaker. Whoever seeks inner peace must discipline his tongue.

The same is true with our thoughts. A person lacking inner discipline will easily entertain thoughts that go against God's will. These may be lewd fantasies, covetous thoughts about a neighbor's spouse or property, or fanciful images of self-importance and unrealistic daydreams. When we allow such images to occupy our inner world, we lose our inner peace. As we struggle to find inner peace, let us discipline our thoughts.

When God forgives us for Christ's sake, peace will fill our souls. But without struggle and discipline in our inner selves we can never maintain an inner balance and discover peace. Some personality types find it easier to gain and maintain this peace, but we all need discipline.

With good reason the psalmist points out that God chose Israel and gave her the land of the nations "that they might keep his precepts and observe his laws" Ps 105:45. When we obey God's laws we experience God's blessing in the form of a deeper peace of mind.

25 / Cornered for Cleansing

"Surely the arm of the Lord is not too short to save, nor his ear too dull to hear" Is 59:1f.

WHEN THE Israelites experienced divine punishment during their wilderness wanderings, "they remembered that God was their Rock, that God Most High was their Redeemer" Ps 78:35. They remembered God and turned to Him in their affliction. In our afflictions, no matter what they are, we must "remember" God and turn to Him in prayer and trust. But the psalmist also says of the Israelites that, in their prayers, "they would flatter him with their mouths, lying to him with their tongues; their hearts were not loyal to him, they were not faithful to his covenant" Ps 78:36f. They were unworthy supplicants.

What about your prayers? It is good that you pray, but what if your prayers are like the prayers of the Israelites, who in the very act of praying deceived the Lord with their lips and lied to Him with their tongues? When the Lord dealt harshly with you, you repented. When he enrolled you in the school of suffering, and brought you to a halt, perhaps by letting others see your corruption, you asked the Lord's forgiveness and promised to detest and reject sin in the future. With tears in your eyes you made a clean break with sin and the ways of the world. But, when the Lord removed His heavy hand, you began again, secretly at first, to pamper the same sin and to play with the world. Repentance was on your lips, but the Lord was not in your heart. You did not really want to break away from your sin, and you were an unworthy supplicant.

God cannot put up with the deceitful hearts of unworthy supplicants, and He must resort to renewed judgments. By punishing them He scrapes away their inner corruption, in order to save them, not to destroy them. Notice how often people who pray must suffer in many ways, while the indifferent and hypocritical get by.

Peter was honest, but he had often prayed unworthily. He suffered punishments at the hands of the Lord, as we see clearly in the letters he wrote. "Bear in mind that our Lord's patience means salvation" 2 P 3:15. Peter had learned from his experiences that if the Lord had not been patient with him, that he, an unworthy supplicant, would have been lost. The Lord's punishments are signs of His patience; He uses them again and again to corner unworthy supplicants for cleansing in Christ's blood.

26 / Do We Bring Praise to God?

"Your attitude should be the same as that of Christ Jesus" Phil 2:5.

JESUS did not withdraw from the uneducated, the ungifted or the unskilled, nor from the poor or unfortunate, nor even from the wicked. He did not live to please himself, says Paul (Ro 15:3) "Your attitude should be the same as that of Christ Jesus, who did not consider equality with God something to be grasped" Phil 2:6. "Accept one another, then, just as Christ accepted you, in order to bring praise to God" Ro 15:7.

These words state a noteworthy truth. We will bring praise to God when we set about to protect and defend the weak. That doesn't mean that we must put up with human weaknesses, much less wickedness. But, defending the weak and tending to the wicked brings praise to God.

Consider our attitude toward inexperienced and ignorant people, who bring trouble or cause suffering to their neighbors with their curiosity, idle talk, and short-sightedness. If we had the attitude of Christ, we would not condemn them, cut them down with our judgments, or belittle them behind their backs. "We who are strong ought to bear with the failings of the weak and not to please ourselves. Each of us should please his neighbor for his good, to build him up," says Paul (Ro 15:1f.)

How different the interpersonal relationships of Christians would be if this admonition were followed. How much more pleasant our common life would be. And how much more would God be praised.

"Learn of me," says Jesus, "for I am gentle and humble in heart" (not just in outward appearance or in pious words, but through and through) "and you will find rest for your souls" Mt 11:29. We find so little rest for our souls because we are neither gentle nor humble in our dealings with the needy and the weak.

27 / Strength in Our Weakness

"For in him we live and move and have our being" Ac 17:28.

AN ELDERLY Karelian refugee, on her difficult journey during the summer of 1944, remarked to one of her hosts, "In him we live and move and have our being." A remarkable statment of her faith. Surely this homeless pilgrim was happy and blessed. Surely her steps were lighter than those of many of her fellow evacuees, for she had a lively faith.

We need this kind of faith. We all have our burdens. How happy we would be if, with living faith, we could say, "In him we live and move and have our being." We would no longer have to depend on our own strength, our own spiritual endurance, or our material and physical resources. We would know, like the apostle, that "I can do everything through him who gives me strength" Phil 4:13.

This frame of mind comes when the Lord Jesus himself takes residence in our hearts through faith. The den of lusts, fears, and doubts becomes a temple of the Holy Spirit. Day dawns in the heart when Jesus enters. His strength is experienced in weakness. No longer need we stare hopelessly at the stormy sea; with eyes fixed on Jesus we can endure all kinds of afflictions.

Many religious people have a gnawing feeling of uncertainty that the affairs of their soul are not in order. Take your inner feeling of uncertainty, whenever you experience it, as a sign from God Himself to awaken you out of your indifference and laxity.

Ask yourself, "Why am I inwardly estranged from my Lord?" Let this fact terrify you. Weep over it at the feet of Jesus. And when the Holy Spirit reveals your sin to you, put it away in sincere repentance, trusting in the blood of Christ that was shed also for your sins. You will then inwardly partake of Christ, who through faith makes his abode in your heart. In this way we get to live and move and have our being in God.

28 / Life Has Its Dangers

"Neither death nor life...will be able to separate us from the love of God that is in Christ Jesus our Lord" Ro 8:38f.

IT IS NOT too difficult to understand that "trouble or hardship," as Paul says, cannot separate us from the love of Christ. Every day we see examples of how trouble and hardship drive many into God's hands.

The idea that "life" cannot separate us from God's love is something altogether different. There are times when life, with all its tasks, responsibilities, and problems, luxuries and comforts, threatens to lead us astray. How many, who at one time lived close to God, trusting in His love, have been drawn by the turmoil of life into the torrent that ultimately carries its victims into hell!

Most people are pious in some way or other. When they hear the summons to faith, they respond by beginning to believe on their own, as it were. But, true Christian faith is conceived in the womb of a frightened conscience. Constant tension is characteristic of living faith, which believes that God justifies the ungodly. We are in a state of being ungodly and righteous simultaneously, cursed and blessed, condemned and saved at the same time.

In His boundless mercy, God deprives a person of his fabricated faith, brings him to the brink of hell, and makes him call out and beg. We see this true faith in the Canaanite woman, who was willing to eat the crumbs of grace, under the table with the dogs. God destroys our natural piety, in order to save us, not simply from troubles and hardships, but also from the danger that life itself poses.

29 / Living Faith and Clean Conscience

"They must keep hold of the deep truths of the faith with a clear conscience" 1 Ti 3:9.

GOD REVEALS His truth to those who are ready to obey Him, but not to those who are merely curious. Ancient and familiar truths take on new meaning when the Holy Spirit gives them life. They acquire a sharp point that pierces the conscience. God talks to us.

Perhaps you know this from experience. There have been times when the word became alive and relevant for you. You felt that God had business with you, saying something that had to do with you and nobody else. God was interviewing you, appearing to you in His word.

In this way the hidden world of God is opened a little at a time. But we must remember, as Paul said to young Timothy, that one must "keep hold of the deep truths of the faith with a clear conscience." Words are meant to sustain and renew us. They contain the creative power of God. But, they remain without effect, unless we obey them. We must consent to the cleansing of conscience implied in God's word; namely, contrition, repentance, and rejection of sin. The mystery of faith can be preserved only in a clear conscience.

In the course of your life God may have revealed to you something about His hidden world. Do not try to preserve His revelations in an unclean conscience. You may suffer a shipwreck of faith and lose everything.

30 / Dying to Be Renewed

"Be transformed by the renewing of your mind" Ro 12:2.

CAN A PERSON improve himself? The Bible intensifies this question for the Christian by emphasizing that we have no choice. "Be transformed by the renewing of your mind. Then you will be able to test and approve what God's will is--his good, pleasing and perfect will" Ro 12:2.

On the other hand, the Bible clearly states that the human heart is wicked from birth and that we are justified by grace alone for Christ's sake. Christian experience agrees with the truth of Paul's statement in Ro 7:21, "Evil is right there with me."

We begin to understand the problem when we recall what the Bible teaches about the old nature and the new nature. The old nature is our natural self, corrupted by sin and the home of all kinds of lusts. The core of corruption is our estrangement from God, our enmity toward God, our failure to love and trust God. This old self "is being corrupted by its deceitful desires" Eph 4:22, and it is futile to try to change it.

The Bible does not teach that Christ will refine the old self, even though that is what many of us might think. The old self must die and be replaced by the new self, "created to be like God in true righteousness and holiness" Eph 4:24.

The new self is Christ, who through faith dwells in us. When Christ, through faith, lives in me, he begins to see with my eyes, to work with my hands, to walk with my feet, and to think my thoughts. "I no longer live, but Christ lives in me." Ga 2:20. This is what renewal of life is all about.

31 / Remain in What God Has Done

"Remain in me, and I will remain in you" Jn 15:4.

THE EXHORTATION in John 15 to remain in Jesus is repeated several times. "Remain in me, and I will remain in you." A branch will not bear fruit unless it "remains" in the vine. "If you remain in me and my words remain in you, ask whatever you wish, and it will be given you" Jn 15:7. Again it is said, "If you obey my commands, you will remain in my love" Jn 15:10.

Remain in Jesus! This exhortation can only be directed to people who have been united with Him.

Perhaps there was a moment in your life when you knew you were dealing with the Lord. The Lord spoke to you, you could not escape Him. You knelt down and said with trembling voice, "Lord, have mercy on me!" The Lord laid His hand on you and forgave you; you were His!

Years, perhaps many, have elapsed since that day. The Lord is no longer close to you. "Remain in Jesus!" This does not mean to remain in the lukewarm state in which you now find yourself. To remain in Jesus you must return to him. That is the point of our struggle. We must continually return to Jesus in order to remain in him.

But am I entitled to return to Christ simply because once upon a time I was consciously close to him? What if I was not completely honest when I surrendered to him?

Remember that you have been baptized into Jesus. The starting point of our faith is not our personal decision, but our having been united with the Lord through baptism. "You did not choose me, but I chose you" Jn 15:16. In baptism the Lord became your very own. Luther writes in his *Small Catechism* that baptism "effects forgiveness of sins, delivers from death and the devil, and grants eternal salvation to all who believe, as the Word and promise of God declare."

Remain in Jesus! Remain in that which you have received in baptism! You cannot base your hope of salvation on any spiritual experiences; rely on the fact that you have been baptized. You are chosen of God. You, too, have the right to remain in Jesus.

August

1 / The Futility of Opposing God

"He is the Lord; let him do what is good in his eyes" 1 S
3:18.

YOUNG SAMUEL told Eli what the Lord had said against Eli
and his sons. Eli replied by saying: "He is the Lord; let him do
what is good in his eyes." We will never know whether Eli
uttered these words in humility before the Lord, or whether he
spoke them because of his priestly habit of using religious
language. The advice he gave young Samuel suggests that he
knew how God works. We know that Eli had been lax in
cooperating with God in raising his sons and perhaps in other
ways. One would like to think that Eli's words had depth.

But, regardless of Eli's motive, these words express a deep
Christian truth. Anyone who can say these words from his heart
is living in faith, having seen the futility of opposing God. He
has learned that God is a God who implements His will without
fail and without mistakes. Faith means trusting that the best
thing that can happen to anyone is for God's will to be done.

If we keep in mind that God is God, and that we are simply
servants, our relationships with others will be different. In
family life, for example, we often insist on our own desires. This
instinct for power is deeply imbedded in all of us. We make
demands on others and attempt to determine the course of their
lives and their actions. But, we cannot even bring up our
children by our commandments. We must learn to leave others,
as well as ourselves, in God's care.

A person who believes in God must assume responsibility for teaching others. But, we must take our place before God and humbly submit to God's good and gracious will in all our affairs.

2 / Losing to Gain

"Don't try to act big" Ro 12:16 (LB).

THIS ADVICE sounds strange? It seems to reflect a negative attitude toward life. Shouldn't we set high goals for ourselves? What would happen if we followed it?

Just remember that this biblical advice is dictated by love. If bigness is your goal, you will recognize only the people who are "somebodies." Their goals will be your goals. You will adopt their way of thinking and you will compete with them. You will have no time for people who are "nobodies": the poor, sick, suffering, and afflicted. Striving for greatness goes against love, which compels us to keep in touch with the poor rather than try to become rich and famous.

Jesus states the Christian ideal this way: "Whoever wants to save his life will lose it, but whoever loses his life for me will find it" Mt 16:25. This was his personal goal. He did not distance himself from the poor for the sake of his own ambitious goals. He lost his life for their sake. In doing so he became our model. His ideal is radically different from common sense. Is this why so few really follow him?

Jesus said that we will save our lives only as we walk in the way he walked. This does not mean that we are obligated to develop the talents God has given us in every way possible. Rather, the emphasis is on serving and not on being served, regardless of any benefits.

Losing oneself in service rather than in the pursuit of greatness may appear as weakness. But, the divine order of life is contrary to natural, human ways of thinking. In God's economy, we gain only by losing.

3 / Your Prayers Are Heard

"I call on the Lord in my distress, and he answers me" Ps
120:1.

IN TIMES of distress the channel of prayer is often blocked.
Why should I pray when everything is going against me? Who
will listen to me? Things are at their worst when external
troubles are complicated by internal guilt and condemnation. If I
am a fallen creature, what right do I have to expect the Lord to
hear me?

The psalmist says that he called on the Lord in his distress.
He had no idea what would happen, but he knew no alternative.
And he experienced that the Lord really does hear the calls of
the distressed. He learned that the Lord answers His children,
and his motto became: "I call on the Lord in my distress, and he
answers me."

It is good to remember these words of Holy Scripture. Times
of distress come when we least expect. The distress itself is not
so bad, for we can expect distress sometime in life. The real
problem comes when distress blocks the way to the Father.

Is your soul distressed now? Are you tired of calling on the
Lord? Even if your accusing conscience tells you not to, leave
your troubles with the Lord. Do not counsel Him or tell Him
what to do. Only trust that He hears you. He will answer you,
perhaps in an unexpected way, and in His own time.

4 / God's Children Hear God's Word

*"He who belongs to God hears what God says. The reason
you do not hear is that you do not belong to God"* Jn 8:47.

THE JEWS WERE offended by Jesus; their hearts were not in
tune with his. They could not hear or accept what Jesus was
saying, because they did not belong to God. When they accused
him of having a demon, they were not angry at what he was
doing at the moment. They were really saying that there was no
room for Jesus in their lives. Jesus was blunt to point out that
they were the children of the devil, not of God.

Whose children are we? It is important that we be born
again. It is possible to be religious without new birth, and we

may give Jesus some kind of place in our lives. But unless we are born again, of God, we will be unable to hear and obey God's word. If we live without Christ, one day we will die without Christ.

Today many are searching for wholeness. Many people are on inward journeys toward the living God. This is good; the Lord Himself is behind this movement. But if spiritual searching does not lead to new birth, God's purpose is not achieved. We may look religous but we will not be awakened; we will not have Christ.

God's word is the irreplaceable source of life. We will not hear God's word, except for portions that appeal to us, if we do not belong to God and have not experienced new birth. We need to be born again to hear God's word and to live from it.

5 / The Art of Joyful Service

"Worship [serve] the Lord with gladness; come before him with joyful songs.... Enter his gates with thanksgiving" Ps 100:2, 4.

LUTHER SAYS the Christian is one who does God's will spontaneously and joyfully. When the gospel comes alive, what was once a chore becomes a joyful duty. "In my inner being I delight in God's law," says Paul (Ro 7:22).

We are to serve the Lord with joy. Experience shows that joyful servants are rare. We think we are doing the best thing when we do what we want, but the best thing is to do what God wants. How often do we become dissatisfied with God's purposes? Because of our running argument with God, a heavy curse hangs over our lives. We exhaust our physical and spiritual energies and pollute our lives and the lives of others. "For the wages of sin is death" Ro 6:23; meaning, sin is a kill-joy.

We rebel when God closes doors in our face. The door may have been to a particular job, to someone's heart, to promotion, well-being, or improved health. We stand behind these closed doors and argue with God, failing to see that God has always opened His own door, which is the best possible one for us. We do not care that He wants us to go through this door and follow the road of joyful service.

The good news is that God has reserved a personal door and a personal road for each of us. But the best news for disgruntled souls is that God in Christ has forgiven our sins, and is waiting for us to accept His gift. But, remember that you cannot accept God's forgiveness without also accepting His will for us. Faith without obedience, belief without surrender to God and submission to His will, does not save.

Entrust your life to the Lord and throw yourself and your failures into His hands every day, and you will learn the art of joyful service.

6 / Ripe Fruit Takes Time

"Do not conform any longer to the pattern of this world"
Ro 12:2.

IN WARNING Christians against conforming to the pattern of this world, Paul urges them to think soberly about who they are and what they can do. The spirit of the world is proud and haughty, given to exaggeration. A person who lives by the world's rules wants to be number one in everything. He also wants to feel universally necessary and useful. He thinks he knows everything, or can at least criticize anything. This kind of person stays on the surface of things, is noticed by the world, and becomes successful.

This shallow and worldly attitude militates against things like silence and solitude. It is impossible to become deeply involved in anything. There is no time to delve into anything. Our attention is splintered, our patience strained. We never set our roots deeply, so we never bear ripe fruit.

To resist the temptation of worldliness we must remember our personal limitations. We can't do it all. "By the grace given me," says Paul, "I say to every one of you: Do not think of yourself more highly than you ought, but rather think of yourself with sober judgment, in accordance with the measure of faith God has given you" Ro 12:3. Let each one be faithful in his own calling. Think soberly! God's Spirit makes us humble, quiet and compassionate. This is the best protection against the temptation of worldliness.

It is said that "an expert is known by his limitations." That is how a Christian, too, is known.

7 / Prayer Changes People

"As he was praying the appearance of his face changed"
Lk 9:29.

IN MANY WAYS modern life has become dreary. At times we feel like somebody has us by the throat. Reasons to rejoice have virtually disappeared. The search for substitute joys has intensified. The Bible offers Christians a program for life, exhorting them to shine like stars in the firmament in the midst of a crooked and depraved generation (Phil 2:15). Starlight is cold light. It is the light of Christians when they think they are special and try to help the unfortunate ones in their midst. This is cold light, for it leaves poor souls in the cold.

The apostle had another kind of light in mind when he wrote to the Philippians. In the course of the letter he says, "Let your gentleness be evident to all" Phil 4:5. In his letter to the Colossians he writes about the same matter: "As God's chosen people, holy and dearly loved, clothe yourselves with compassion, kindness, humility, gentleness and patience" Col 3:12. Apparently such exhortations were needed already in the early church. Only cold, hard-hearted, unfriendly and judgmental Christians need to be exhorted to be compassionate, kind and gentle.

There was no room in the heart of Jesus for harshness and cruelty. The words of our text suggest how we too might become compassionate, kind, and gentle, able to be a blessing to others. "As he was praying, the appearance of his face changed." What if someday our faces also became gentle and our demeanor friendly? Unless we persevere in prayer it will never happen.

8 / We Cannot Command the Spirit

"We are witnesses of these things, and so is the Holy Spirit, whom God has given to those who obey him" Ac 5:32.

THE GREAT need of all Christians today is a clear vision of the reality of the Holy Spirit. We all need the Holy Spirit actively to guide our lives. Both church and society need men and women, young and old, who are filled with the Holy Spirit. There may be an abundance of activity, but only work done in the Holy Spirit will show lasting results. The kingdom of God is a matter of "righteousness, peace and joy in the Holy Spirit" Ro 14:17. Without the Holy Spirit we merely talk about these things. By living in the Holy Spirit they become real.

The anemic character of our faith must be exposed; we must know what it is we lack. But, by itself, this will not correct the problem. We also need to ask, "How can we experience the power of the Holy Spirit?" And remember that we cannot command the Holy Spirit; we must obey.

We cannot expect the Holy Spirit to respond to our every wish. The Holy Spirit is more than frosting on the cake. We cannot discover spiritual power and joy, which the Holy Spirit alone can provide, if we insist on being in charge of our lives. Again, we cannot command the Holy Spirit; we must obey! Our faith will not be revitalized if we simply look for ways to satisfy our own needs.

The absolute prerequisite of spiritual blessing is the willingness to surrender our will and to listen to the voice of the Spirit.

The Bible warns us against grieving the Holy Spirit of God (Eph 4:30). We do this through our disobedience and, as a result, lose the gifts of the Spirit.

As we wait and yearn for a new blessing, we must be ready to obey the Holy Spirit.

9 / God Receives Praise Through People

"...to the praise of his glory" Eph 1:14.

IN HEAVEN God's glory will be everywhere. God will be all in all. God's plan of salvation will be fully realized. The tensions of sin will have been eliminated, and all things will declare the glory of God. Heaven will be beautiful because we shall see God as He is.

But already in this life we have been called "to the praise of his glory," as Paul says. What a marvelous goal for life!

You, too, can live your life in such a way that God receives praise. This will not make you special; people will not point to you and praise you. When others can clearly see what God is doing through you, even though you remain what you are, then God will be praised. God reveals the greatness and sufficiency of His grace in your life.

Take a good look at the reality of God's grace as you experience it in your life. Note how He receives sinners, how He forgives blood-red sins, and how He renews the unwilling so that they may serve Him in new obedience. It is not a question of us and what we can do, but of the Lord and what He can and will do. In this way God is praised through His people.

10 / God's School of Higher Education

"My ears had heard of you but now my eyes have seen you" Job 42:5.

WE TEND to ignore experience, from which we could learn much. Especially in the life of faith, experience gained in the school of the Lord, is invaluable. If we are to recognize the work of God, trust the Lord and have the sensitive conscience needed to avoid sin, we need experienced Christians. Knowledge is no substitute for experience.

God prepares experienced Christians in His own school. Job attended such a school. He lost everything, in the end even his confidence in God. But then came the day when he put his hand over his mouth and stood quiet, giving the glory to God (Job 40:4). In his great distress he had learned something: "My ears had heard of you but now my eyes have seen you" Job 42:5. Experienced people do not speak according to what they have learned from others, they have personally learned about things after paying a high tuition.

It often seems that we are wasting our time in God's school, regressing rather than progressing from grade to grade. We students often feel that the Lord has left us. Like Job, if we learn to be still before the Lord and quietly wait for our Redeemer's marvelous deeds, we will experience that the good will of God was hidden behind the seemingly incomprehensible trials we faced.

In its New Testament, the Bible states that "in all things God works for the good of those who love him" Ro 8:28; those who cling to Him no matter what "things" happen.

"Blessed is the man who perseveres under trial, because when he has stood the test, he will receive the crown of life that God has promised to those who love him" Jas 1:12.

11 / Receive the Word in Silence

"...humbly accept the word planted in you, which can save you" Jas 1:21.

A PERSON concerned about the salvation of his soul needs to hear this verse of Scripture. The word alone can save; not something originating in me, not something I do, not my prayers, my positive thinking, or my confession. Only the word; nothing else.

This word has the power to save me. But, the word does not save me because I learn to understand it. The word is not something I can recall in times of need to show that I belong to those who honor God. The word must do its work in me. "Therefore, get rid of all moral filth and the evil that is so prevalent and humbly accept the word planted in you, which can save you" Jas 1:21.

The goal of the word is to remove from our lives everything that is contrary to God's will. The word leads to us to confess and put away our sin. The word leads to repentance. This means that the word must be received in silence, so that we can hear what the Lord has to say. In silence we must submit to the word, to be evaluated and educated by it.

This word is the good news, "the power of God for the salvation of everyone who believes" Ro 1:16. The word of the cross is the power of salvation.

Do you want to be saved? Then silently receive the word God wants to give you. Study the word! Make reading of the Bible a priority in your life!

12 / The Power of Christ's Hand

*"Who has believed our message and to whom has the arm
of the Lord been revealed?"* Is 53:1.

THE BIBLE often speaks about the hands of Jesus. We are told,
for example, how Jesus healed the sick by laying his hands upon
them.

We know something about the wonderful power of hands. At
the funeral of an old pastor, parishioners remembered how on
various occasions he had laid his hand upon their shoulders or
knees. At times the hand had spoken words of admonition, at
other times words of comfort and encouragement, always saying
more than the mouth could have uttered.

How much more important are the hands of Jesus. They are
extended to us in the gospel and the sacraments. Perhaps you
have been blessed at worship services or devotional meetings by
the hand of Jesus touching you. You forgot all about the people
around you, feeling that you were alone with Jesus. When we
have been touched by his hands we rise blessed.

But they are also pierced hands, for they are the hands of
our Redeemer. A fallen sinner, confronted by God, is surprised
by the marks of the nails in Jesus' hands. The sinner then
realizes that he also has been redeemed; he knows that Christ
hung on the cross also for him and now acknowledges him as his
own.

God gives us His Holy Spirit and we, lost and condemend
sinners, realize that Christ's hands have reached out to save us.
We can say with Paul, "God has rescued us from the dominion of
darkness and brought us into the kingdom of the Son he loves"
Col 1:13. A change of rulers takes place within us, and the hands
of Jesus produce results. Someone is physically healed; another
is given a new, responsible attitude toward work; service
becomes the life's work of the saved.

Forgiveness always means that Christ receives us into his
kingdom under his personal rule. Christ exercises his lordship in
the world by working not only in our inner life, but also in our
outer life. Christ not only restores what we have broken but
remakes it. These wonderful hands possess the only power that
can change our personal lives, our family life, and the life of our
society and nation.

13 / Christ Gives Us His Joy

"Those who look to him are radiant" Ps 34:5.

Frost took the herbs of joy,
Life is very stingy.

THE ENEMY sneaks into the farmer's field, but also into the human heart, to carry away the best gifts of life. We need joy; without it life is barren and unsatisfying.

It is no coincidence that on Paul's list of the gifts of the Spirit joy is second. When we think of joy, we need not think of special joyful occasions, although they are certainly God's gift to His children. We can simply think of the free, joyous frame of mind which rises spontaneously from within a person. This joy shows in the corners of his eyes, his words and all his activities. It is a quiet, natural and unpretentious joy that expresses itself in the small details of everyday life.

Surely the Lord does not intend for us to go around with a depressing and sour look on our face, much to our own and others' sorrow. Life can be very stingy with joy. The Lord's people, however, have been called to live in ways that bring joy to their neighbors.

Where can we find the fountains of joy? It would be great to find joy in one's work, but the results of our work often provide little reason for rejoicing. Joy over children and loved ones is precious and enriching, but such joy can evaporate in the cares of life.

God's word invites us to rejoice over God's works. In them we have a solid source of joy. Nature is overflowing with divine works which, if we have eyes to see, greatly enrich our lives. Our main reason for joy, however, is God's grace in Jesus Christ. Belonging to God is the real reason for joy. Christianity gives life its new goal. Faith and hope are like a spring bubbling with joy in the drabness of everyday life. "Those who look upon Him radiate joy."

14 / Remember Your First Love

"Remember the height from which you have fallen!
Repent and do the things you did at first" Rev 2:5.

SPIRITUALLY lukewarm Christians are told to return to their first love. They are to do the things they did when their faith was new. From this familiar verse we learn that each person is to be faithful in that which the Lord gave him at the time of his initial awakening.

In the course of years the Lord surely gives additional gifts. All life is for learning and receiving new things; we never graduate from the Lord's school. But, each person is unique, and each must continue to be faithful to his or her initial awakening and blessing.

There are people who are adrift because they go with every new gust of spiritual wind. They have no time or opportunity to grow roots, so they never bear fruit for God's kingdom. We must remain faithful to our first love and do what we did at first. Our first love represents wholeness and spontaneity, qualities which the years tend to erode.

Purity and sincerity of heart sharpen our vision better than wisdom and experience. The "first works" often appear foolish, but the world needs God's fools who have the courage to risk offending others and to bear the shame of Christ.

15 / Jesus Is Our Life

"Because I live, you also will live" Jn 14:19.

BECAUSE of the resurrection of Jesus, those who believe in Him will live. Paul says in Galatians 2:20 that the life he lives in faith is no longer his own life but Christ's life in him: "I no longer live, but Christ lives in me." Accordingly, his thoughts and speech, his decisions and efforts, his goals and his whole lifestyle were no longer Paul's own, for Christ dominated everything.

This did not mean that Paul was without sin. "For we know that our old self was crucified with him so that the body of sin might be done away with, that we should no longer be slaves to sin" Ro 6:6. Rather, Christ was the new living center of his life.

It is terrible to die spiritually! A Christian is sorrowful over the loss of illusions of self-sufficiency and grandeur, for it colors who he is and everything he does. We must keep this in mind and not demand from the dead the works of the living. We cannot produce good out of ourselves; we are unable to love; we cannot fulfill God's will. But Christ can and does. If he lives in us, our lives will show evidence of faith that is alive.

"Jesus lives" is a message of joy to every Christian. We can rejoice in him who lives and loves--Jesus Christ. We cannot find life in self-improvement. But, if we accept the death of our old self, like Paul did, then life will be revived in us, too. Because Jesus lives, we also live.

16 / The Best Is Yet to Come

"What good will it be for a man if he gains the whole world, yet forfeits his soul?" Mt 16:26.

THE GOSPELS tell about a woman who, seeing the mighty works of Christ, became so excited she began to praise his mother. But Christ poured cold water on her efforts. He said to her, "Blessed rather are those who hear the word of God and obey it" Lk 11:28. The time for celebrating had not yet arrived, for the battle was still raging. Hearing and obeying God's word were the tasks at hand.

Today also we can become so delighted with Christ that we forget we are still in the midst of a war. Our attention is so easily diverted to nonessentials. We imagine that we have already arrived, and everyone is a true Christian and child of God. We forget that the world is still sinful and that the devil has the terrible power to seduce souls. The Lord must awaken us to a deeper realization of the fearful reality we live in. He must arouse us to be alert and to fight, so that our dearly purchased souls will not be lost.

We become satisfied with a Christianity filled with much activity but missing the essential item, namely, the eternal salvation of our souls. We do not struggle to take God's word seriously, considering only our own interpretation. Like the woman in the Gospel story, we become excited over temporal things but miss the eternal.

17 / God Justifies Sinners

"I tell you that this man, rather than the other, went home justified before God" Lk 18:14.

THE TAX COLLECTOR in the temple stood in the back, near the door, but the other one, the Pharisee, walked all the way to the front. But it was the tax collector who stood closer to the gracious God and went home justified.

The Pharisee had raised his eyes to heaven, but the tax collector had beaten his breast, afraid to raise his head. God is seen best with head bowed down, for He is near those whose hearts are broken and who fear His name.

Such is the gaze of faith; it is the sinner gazing at his helper. Sometimes he cannot even see the helper--as happened to the tax collector in the temple. No one passed judgment on this man. Secular authorities had not charged him with crimes. Perhaps he had cheated people, but they were not there to accuse him. He was his own accuser; he condemned himself as a sinner before God. But he went home justified.

This is how we too are justified. There is no other way. "If we judged ourselves, we would not come under judgment" 1 Co 11:31. The Pharisee did not accuse himself; he remained condemned before God. He went home with God's judgment hanging over him. The tax collector, however, began by accusing himself and went home justified.

Many suffer in their married life because a self-righteous, pharisaical spirit controls one or both of the spouses. Joy, contentment, and comfort flee the self-satisfied. But if a member of the family humbles himself as a sinner before God and gets help from the Savior, the whole atmosphere of the home is transformed.

18 / Where Can We Go From Christ?

"'You do not want to leave too, do you?' Jesus asked the Twelve. Simon Peter answered him, 'Lord, to whom shall we go? You have the words of eternal life. We believe and know that you are the Holy One of God'" Jn 6:67-69.

NO ONE can remain neutral in the Christian life. We must decide for or against Christ. But before a person reaches the point of decision, something decisive has already happened to him. God has decided for him; God has chosen him.

Just as Jesus called his disciples into his fellowship, but one of them, Judas, enrolled in the service of Satan, so even now Christ chooses his own, but one or another leaves him. First an inner estrangement takes place, then an external one, and the Lord's people are left behind.

Christ's followers must decide to receive God's grace or reject it. They must agree to stay in Christ's company, following him wherever he leads, or else choose the course of their own life. But, Christ's decision for us, Christ's election of us, came first. "You did not choose me, but I chose you," says Jesus (Jn 15:16).

Now and then Christ leads his own into a valley of decision, where he says to them, "You do not want to leave too, do you?" Who are the ones who leave? Very likely those who have joined his company by their own choosing.

Those remain who must say with Peter, "Lord, to whom shall we go? You have the words of eternal life!" In other words, those remain who have no other place to go, for Christ has become absolutely necessary for their lives. They are unable to get along without him. If they no longer sense his presence, they become frightened and cry out, "Where are you, my Jesus?" They call on the Lord Christ in all their daily activities. Even in the moment of death, Christ is still absolutely necessary, for we have no other refuge.

19 / The Spirit Makes the Christian

"No one can say, 'Jesus is Lord,' except by the Holy Spirit" 1 Co 12:3.

WHEN WE ADDRESS a person as "Mr.", which in Finnish means also "lord," no particular significance is given to the title. But in the New Testament the use of this title "lord" meant an acknowledgement of a dependence upon the person addressed. The speaker acknowledged the person's authority over him and ownership of him.

With this in mind, Paul says that no one can call Jesus Lord, be subject to him, and belong to him, except by the influence of the Holy Spirit. Luther says the same thing in his explanation to the third article of the creed: "By my own reason or strength I cannot believe in Jesus Christ, my Lord, or come to him" (Small Catechism). The Holy Spirit alone can do it.

Faith is often only self-initiated activity, where Jesus is not really the Lord of the individual. His life belongs to himself; he is selfish, self-seeking, and unable to sacrifice for God or neighbor.

How can we be freed from ourselves to do God's will as His servants? Only by receiving the Holy Spirit. No one can call Jesus as Lord, except by the Holy Spirit, not you, not I. It is essential that we receive the Holy Spirit, or as the Bible says, be baptized with the Holy Spirit. That must be our prayer!

20 / Christ Seeks and Saves the Lost

"I will search for the lost and bring back the strays. I will bind up the injured and strengthen the weak" Ez 34:16.

SHEEP GET LOST when they become too tired to keep up with the flock. Weariness also weighs heavily upon the Lord's sheep. The harsh reality of life dictates that we eat by the sweat of our brow (Gn 3:19). There are no exceptions.

There is another reason for our weariness, however. An unbelieving heart does not allow us to leave the cares of tomorrow to our heavenly Father. Were God to deal with us according to His law, He would leave us under the condemnation of our sins and in the bog of unbelief. But the Lord has the heart of a good shepherd, who seeks the lost, even the tired who were left behind.

But sheep can also get lost if they no longer listen to the voice of the shepherd. Disobedient to the Lord, we stray from his people, often so gradually that we are unaware of it. We begin to compromise in small matters, leaving the narrow way to follow the way of the world. The Lord's voice is muffled by other voices. But, the Lord seeks also these lost sheep and coaxes them back into his flock. Where would we be, if the Lord did not seek those who became lost as a result of their disobedience?

Finally, sheep can also become lost because rustlers or wild beasts invade the flock and carry them away. We have cruel enemies, enemies of God, who will not leave weak Christians in peace. Sin, death, and the devil are constantly on our heels. But, God has shown His pastoral love by sending His Son to make us His friends and to overpower our enemies.

21 / Happiness Is Thanking the Lord

"A man of perverse heart does not prosper" Pr 17:18.

EXPLAINING the fourth petition of the Lord's Prayer, Luther notes that God provides daily bread together with all other life provisions to all people, whether or not they believe in Him or pray to Him. Then he adds, "But we pray in this petition that God may make us aware of His gifts and enable us to receive our daily bread with thanksgiving" (*Small Catechism*).

The essential thing is awareness of God's goodness and a grateful heart. Many people forget God in their hurry to earn their daily bread. God's word and prayer are neglected. Why bother with them when days are filled from morning to night.

But not only is God forgotten, His commandments are ignored in the desperate effort to live in as much luxury as possible. Fraud and cheating, overpricing and underpaying, ignoring and trampling underfoot the needs and interests of others seem to bring the results we desire, provided we are sufficiently clever. Slander, gossip, and similar forms of evil-mindedness are used to one's own advantage, even if they hurt others. Furthermore, we think all of this is in sweet harmony with the occasional hymn we sing, the tear or two we shed now and then, and the dollar we drop in the offering plate. Strange as it may seem, piety and greed have often been bedfellows.

All of this is self-deception at which Satan smiles sweetly. A person's prosperity does not depend on money and property, much less on deceitfully acquired wealth. But, knowledge of God, awareness of His goodness, and childlike confidence in a merciful Father are something else. In our gratitude toward God we have true riches, more precious than anything else. Happiness is being able to say thanks to the Lord.

22 / It Is Christ or Nothing

"For sin shall not be your master, because you are not under law, but under grace" Ro 6:14.

THE SECRET of new life is Christ within, overcoming sin. We need not concentrate on fighting against particular sins, for sin will always be stronger than we are. Let us cling to Christ, who alone has power over sin.

How do we do this? The Bible says, "He who conceals his sins does not prosper, but whoever confesses and renounces them finds mercy" Pr 28:13. If you excuse or defend your sins, you cannot cling to Christ nor experience his power against sin. But if you humble yourself and acknowledge your sin, you will find mercy. God will empower you.

At this point we must look at the practice of confession and absolution. The Bible never says that confession of sins to God in the presence of another human being is a prerequisite of salvation. You may confess your sins directly to Jesus. But experience shows that confession in the presence of another person is necessary for many of us, if we are to know Christ's power.

The Bible also talks about rejection of sin. This means I must humble myself before God and others when the Holy Spirit rebukes me for my sin. I must be prepared to put away all excuses, drop my defenses and acknowledge before God and others that I am a poor miserable creature. When this happens, mercy is experienced, and Christ's power against sin is realized.

Why do we not experience this power of Christ more often? Because we are still too powerful! We struggle with our own strength. Christ refuses to enter into a cooperative arrangement with us. To enable us to experience Christ's power, the Holy Spirit shows us the impotence of our strength and piety. This takes place in the school of the cross with its courses in trials, afflictions, and sufferings.

23 / Everyone Is Religious

"All things were created by him and for him" Col 1:16.

THERE ARE two kinds of people: religious and irreligious. The latter often talk about this division. They claim that the diverse forms of religious life do not appeal to them and that they have no interest in the various demands of religious people. Still, as enlightened people, they relate respectfully to the religious convictions of others. Sometimes they will admit that religion has its benefits, provided it is practiced with moderation.

This division into religious and irreligious is based on an error. Every person has a religion. Everyone has something to which he attributes ultimate value, in which he puts his trust, from which he gains his happiness. Everyone has something which supports him, and which is the object of his worship. Luther once remarked: "Everyone has a god: either God or an idol."

Religious convictions take on many forms, and it is sometimes difficult to identify a person's god. The world is full of religions, because human beings have been created for union with God. We are creatures who cannot get along without some form of religion. The question is simply who or what serves as our god.

We must know this in order to have the proper outlook for Christian ministry and mission. Conversions, even among people who appear to be spiritually unreceptive, are not unknown in our day and age. It is still possible to move from unbelief to faith.

24 / Christist for Us in Us

"It is because of him that you are in Christ Jesus, who has become for us wisdom from God--that is, our righteousness, holiness and redemption" 1 Co 1:30.

TODAY WE have every reason to speak on behalf of the inner life. The lifestyle of most people does violence to the inner world, which contains powerful forces, not all positive and pure. Long before our time, before scientists uncovered the role played by the unconscious in all human actions and behavior, Jesus said, "Out of the heart come evil thoughts, murder, adultery, sexual immorality, theft, false testimony, slander" Mt 15:19. That is what the inner world is like. Whoever surrenders to it will become a victim of one or another of these evil powers.

Modern literature is filled with portrayals of human corruption, drawn from the inner life of people. Many have made the mistake of assuming that this inner life must be given free expression, thinking that in this way people will be healthy and happy.

The road to health and happiness is quite different. Simply delving into the depths will not save anyone. Salvation is found only in Christ. Only Christ can control and correct the corruption of our hearts. Christ must enter our hearts to live and rule in us. We must become rooted in him, grow in him and live in him.

Struggling Christians need to remember that our help is in the Lord. No matter how successful or unsuccessful we have been in the struggle with the wickedness of hearts, Christ is still the only Master and Lord. His power never fails. Do not struggle by yourself; leave your affairs again and again in Christ's hands. "Believe in the Lord Jesus and you will be saved" Ac 16:31.

25 / With Empty Pails to the Well

"For with you is the fountain of life" Ps 36:9.

GOD'S WORD directs us to the true oasis. "With you is the fountain of life; in your light we see light." All other rest stops leave our souls empty and weary. Like drugs, they may provide momentary relief, but not healing. Only with the Lord is there a fountain of life.

Christ offers life to you; he is the Savior of your body and soul. He does not expect you to give him anything, neither devotional exercises nor religious activity. He only wants you to receive from him. All we need to bring to the fountain is an empty pail and thirsty lips. Let us retreat from the troubles and cares of life, no matter what they may be and go to Christ. Let us go to him with our emptiness and weariness. Our lives, with all their problems, both external and internal, are his field of interest and expertise. Confident of this, the psalmist says, "All my fountains are in you" Ps 87:7.

Our imperfect faith includes legalism that robs us of joy and gives outsiders a false image of Christians. "With joy you will draw water from the wells of salvation" Is 12:3. Christians must claim this promise. Let us hasten with empty pails and unclean lips to the place where we are only and always receivers. Let us draw life and joy from the fountain that never runs dry. "The cross stands, the word endures, grace suffices."

26 / The Cross Is More than History

"Father, forgive them, for they do not know what they are doing" Lk 23:34.

ON THE WALL of a parish summer home in Finland there is a cross; below it is this prayer which Jesus uttered from the cross. How often is Jesus prompted to pray to the Father for us in similar words because of our treatment of the cross. We do not know what we are doing.

This doesn't mean just those who "live as enemies of the cross of Christ" Phil 3:18. Nor is it limited to those "who have tasted the goodness of the word of God and the powers of the coming age" but have fallen away and now "are crucifying the Son of God all over again and subjecting him to public disgrace" He 6:5f. There are such people, and their lives move us to tears.

We especially need to think about those of us who consider ourselves friends of the cross. We must hope that our attitude toward the cross does not give the Lord reason to pray for his Father to forgive us. God made the crucified Lord "a sacrifice of atonement, through faith in his blood...to demonstrate his justice at the present time" Ro 3:25f. But, talk about the cross is often merely doctrinal. Our faith in the cross must be more than historical knowledge; God has set up the cross as a present and continuing reality in our lives. God wants to demonstrate his justice and grace today.

The cross beckons you and me to seek refuge and cleansing in the blood of Jesus every day. It is God's will that your sins rest, not upon you where they will condemn, but upon the Son of God. God wants to save you from the misery into which sin has plunged you. The only question that remains is how you will treat the cross. Is it merely an object of knowledge, or do you visit it again and again with your sins?

27 / Through Death to Life

"For you died, and your life is now hidden with Christ in God" Col 3:3.

THE WORST thing for some Christians to deal with would be their death. Yet, death will always be part of their lives. They are aware of certain signs of death already in their lives. They realize how they are unable to be friendly and kind to everyone. That's understandable, they say, for people have all kinds of faults that are impossible to put up with. They can see signs of selfishness and hypocrisy in themselves, but they find comfort in recalling, often tearfully, the times they have been unselfish and honest.

As judged by their inner life, they are rather indifferent toward God and His word. But, against this indifference they set their church attendance and occasional Bible reading. In other words, these people see signs of spiritual death in themselves, but they will not admit that they have died. They continue to seek something to which they can appeal in the presence of God.

Paul said that he did not boast about himself, but proclaimed Jesus Christ. Certainly Paul had not really died, otherwise he could not have proclaimed Christ. In what sense are Christians really dead? Being dead and yet having life in Christ can be dangerous, for it might encourage a carefree lifestyle.

But, the life of those who have died is "hidden with Christ in God." Their life is in the Lord, but it is hidden life; in themselves they have no life. They are not aware of this new life, much less are they able to show it off to others. They stand before Christ, wanting to leave themselves in his hands, no matter how they feel. They dare not rejoice about themselves; their joy is in the Lord.

28 / It's What's Inside That Counts

"Remember, therefore, what you have received and heard; obey it, and repent" Rev 3:3.

CHRISTIANS experience times when they fall away. They still associate with fellow Christians, observe Christian customs, and participate in Christian activities, but inwardly they have fallen away from God.

In such times, Christians become impotent. Opposition to evil has ceased; matters are misjudged. Others get a false picture of Christian discipleship. The great tragedy is that bitter disappointments await them. They will experience what the foolish virgins did when they were left outside the banquet hall when the bridegroom arrived because of the lack of oil in their lamps.

We fall away from God in two ways. First, we befriend a sin, perhaps a particular fault which we once rejected with tears. We easily entertain forbidden thoughts. We do not resist temptations; we even seek them out. We accept in ourselves things which we know in our conscience are sins. We muffle the voice of our heart. These sins were washed away in the blood of Jesus, but we have welcomed them back.

We also fall away from God when we get caught in the snare of self-complacency and self-righteousness. We become enthusiastic in our piety, but think of it as an advantage over other people. We pray, read the Bible and attend church, but these represent only our personal activity and we know of no need to deal with the Savior of sinners. We do not have true self-knowledge or a broken heart.

Falling into self-satisfied piety is much more dangerous that falling into overt sins, for it is more difficult to see the former. The biographer of a well-known church leader states that during a certain period of his life the man had apparently fallen away from God and for that reason made some bad decisions. If a biographer can note such things, how much more accurately are times of falling away from God noted in heaven.

What do the records in heaven show about you? "Wake up, O sleeper, rise from the dead, and Christ will shine on you" Eph 5:14. Every Christian who lives inwardly in sin is lacking the light of Christ.

29 / Dynamics of Spiritual Renewal

"Therefore, if anyone is in Christ, he is a new creation" 2 Co 5:17.

UNDER WHAT conditions might something new be born in us? Both new converts and old Christians want to know. For the latter the question is painful, for they think the gracious work of God should already have produced new life in them. But, in so many instances the old continues to have the upper hand. Surely this cannot be God's will for any of His children.

Paul observes, "If anyone is in Christ, he is a new creation; the old has gone, the new has come!" The prerequisite for renewal is stated in the words, "If anyone is in Christ." There is no other way. Apart from Christ, left to ourselves, we are under God's wrath. In Romans 1:18 we have a frightful picture of life under God's wrath, life without Christ. And Paul helps us to realize that God's wrath has rested not only upon the people of ancient Rome or the ungodly world of our own time, but upon many who are called Christian but who are so entangled in sin that no renewal seems possible.

Christ's atonement is the prerequisite of all renewal; it is necessary for transfer from God's wrath to God's grace. "You see, at just the right time, when we were still powerless, Christ died for the ungodly" Ro 5:6. Christ's death has to do with the ungodly, the children of wrath and hell. "God made him who had no sin to be sin for us, so that in him we might become the righteousness of God" 2 Co 5:21. We are lost and condemned sinners, but if we flee from God's wrath and seek Christ's blood daily, we will find freedom from the guilt and condemnation of sin. We will find ourselves at home as children of God. The powers of Christ's love will take over in us and compel us to live a renewed life (2 Co 5:14).

30 / Fruit Trees Are Meant to Bear Fruit

"He is like a tree planted by streams of water, which yields its fruit in season" Ps 1:3.

THE BIBLE compares the ungodly to chaff that the wind blows away (Ps 1:4). Without contact with the true reality of life, out of touch with God, the wicked person fits very well into a variety of surroundings. At times he even drops in on the people of God. A strange ability to be at home in all kinds of places and to adjust to all kinds of circumstances is characteristic of the ungodly. Being light as chaff he moves easily from place to place.

It all happens painlessly. His piety too is painless, since he knows nothing about the travail of new birth. He does not understand the tears of an awakened conscience, or the bitter shame and self-accusation of a wayward child of God. The life of the ungodly bears the stamp of ease, which on the surface seems a distinct advantage.

On the other hand, the Bible compares the person living in the Lord to "a tree planted by streams of water, which yields its fruit in season." He has a permanent point of contact with life. He does not fit everywhere. There is an edginess about him, which in the world's view is incomprehensible, unwise, and old-fashioned. But, he is bound by God's word. "His delight is in the law of the Lord, and on his law he meditates day and night" Ps 1:2.

God's word draws boundaries; there are limits to self-determination. The godly person is bound in all things to the Lord and His word. He is not always ready for just anything, he does not always have the right words, he cannot always give the right advice. There are times when he must remain silent and be satisfied to pray for the Lord to open the way. But, he bears fruit "in season." When the season comes, when advice and help are truly needed, God will use his weak friends to exhibit his power and to bear fruit for the achievement of his gracious goals.

31 / Reasons for Praise

"Praise the Lord, O my soul, and forget not all his benefits" Ps 103:2.

EVERYONE understands that joy and praise to the Lord arise from the heart of a person whose sins have been forgiven.

My soul does not cease
To sing and rejoice,
That a poor creature
Has lost his burden.

The soul has times of feasting. The Christian's joy and praise, however, are not limited to special sacred moments. God's good works surround every human being all the time, but only a believer recognizes them. Therefore, only a believer knows whom to thank.

What's more, everything is a gift. Every piece of bread that nourishes his body comes from the Lord. All the necessities of life are from the hand of the Lord. Even his health is a gift. We do not always remember this and we often fail to praise the Lord. Only after God has taken His gifts from us do we begin to learn.

How often have you remembered to praise the Lord that you have entered a new day with your health intact? When we arise in the morning, do the tasks of the day weigh upon us so that we approach them fearfully? Or do we enter the routine of the day without much thought. Do we realize that, in either case, it is the Lord's grace that enables us to start the day in good health and to complete our work?

God is constantly at work in our world. His hand sustains all things. Were He to withdraw it even for a moment, everything would collapse. Because of the Lord's grace we have all that we really need. "Praise the Lord, O my soul."

September

1 / The Time of Miracles Is Not Over

"So there was great joy in that city" Ac 8:8.

CITIES LURE people who are in pursuit of pleasure, but the pleasure they find is not the great joy spoken of in this verse from Acts. The frantic pursuit for entertainment exploits the human desire for happiness, victimizing people instead of helping them. Gaudy advertisements that promise thrills cloud the mind and confuse the conscience. People are driven to live beyond their means in a futile and sometimes fatal pursuit of pleasure.

This mad pursuit of pleasure has spread from urban centers to rural areas and drawn youth in droves into cities in search of joy. But it is precisely in the cities, where unbelief is at its greatest, that God wants to reveal His power. Let us not lose hope. From cities, true happiness can spread into the countryside.

What happened in the city of Samaria can still happen today. Wonderful things had taken place there when Christ was preached. The Bible says, "With shrieks, evil spirits came out of many, and many paralytics and cripples were healed" Ac 8:7. "So there was great joy in that city." The word of Christ drives out evil spirits, so that the creative power of God can begin to renew people's lives. Healing of the sick results when this creative power of God is at work in our world. Have we preached Christ in our cities as we should? If so, then the power of God will work miracles even today.

Where the will of God is obeyed, people will always have reason to rejoice. Think of the many homes in the city of Samaria where people burst into joy upon seeing the miracles of God in the lives of the unfortunate. Our cities have become nests of secularism, but spiritual renewal can take place in them, as happened in the time of the apostles. Let us expect God's miracles! Let it be said: "So there was great joy in that city."

2 / Matter of the Heart

"Create in me a pure heart, O God" Ps 51:10.

THE LIFE of a human being is full of danger. Our sins have polluted our interpersonal climate, just as toxic wastes have polluted the air. Without realizing the consequences, we have polluted the inner world our children must live in. We usually avoid dirty language in the presence of our children, but in our hearts we harbor unclean spirits, along with their lies, deceits, and other evils. Our children will catch these spirits like the common cold.

We are surrounded by corruption in the world, but we must fear even more the corruption of our hearts. Jesus says, "For out of the heart come evil thoughts" Mt 15:19. We have reason, therefore, to humbly pray, "Create in me a pure heart, O God!"

We are apt to think that God will answer our prayer by using some kind of magic to work a miracle. But God does not work that way. Of course, when we experience God's amazing grace it seems like a miracle. For we know that we are sinners who, again and again, must ask God for a new, clean heart. We do not merit God's favor. Yet God performs a great miracle in us, cleansing us from our sins, our inner pollution.

The cleansing of the heart, however, also has a significant effect on our conscious life. We must go through the death of the old self and the birth of the new self. When God works in us it hurts; but it also heals and energizes. We know of external, physical dangers; we may be aware of the very real danger of an unclean heart; but if we do not know the struggle and pain which accompany God's work of renewal, we have not really experienced God's grace. Without a desire to repent, understood as cleaning up the pollution of our wicked heart, our faith is merely intellectual assent.

3 / Growing Spiritual Roots

"...take root below and bear fruit above" Is 37:31.

THIS IS the order in the kingdom of God: if you wish to bear fruit, you must be ready to grow roots. Jesus teaches this law in his comments about the kernel of wheat which must be sown in the ground and die in order to produce more seeds. John the Baptist puts it this way, "He must become greater; I must become less" Jn 3:30.

Growing downward, being humbled, can be described as the "low road." We may talk piously about such spiritual poverty and enjoy the appearance of being humble, but no one enjoys the low road. We feel pain and humiliation if, in our own eyes and the eyes of others, we become lesser instead of greater. Our whole nature rebels when we are put down and our will is thwarted.

But, we can easily list reasons why God must humble us. The psalmist points to one of the more important ones: "Before I was afflicted I went astray, but now I obey your word" Ps 119:67. Again, "It was good for me to be afflicted so that I might learn your decrees" Ps 119:71. To bear fruit for the kingdom of God we must live by the word of God, draw on its power and follow its instructions. We must become rooted in the word. The word must have the last say.

Only as we travel on the low road in life do we learn to rely on God's word. God's word becomes precious to us only when we are deprived of our grand illusions about ourselves. Perhaps we read the Bible before, but only in an attempt to master it. Now, having been humbled by God, we seek to submit to it's teaching with a sensitive conscience.

The Book of Psalms opens with a description of the person who meditates on God's word. He is "like a tree planted by streams of water, which yields its fruit in season" Ps 1:2f. "In season" means when harvest time has arrived, not just any old time. Fruit must have time to grow! As we wait for the fruit to ripen, we must take root and delve deeply into the Word.

4 / Community and Unity in Christ

*"May the God who gives endurance and encouragement
give you a spirit of unity among yourselves as you follow
Christ Jesus"* Ro 15:5.

JESUS PRAYS that his own may be one. The numerous
exhortations to unity in the Bible indicate that it is not easy for
those who belong to Jesus to achieve unity. There are special
temptations in this regard that need to be overcome.

In part this is due to the limitations of human
understanding. "Now we see but a poor reflection as in a mirror"
1 Co 13:12. Problems and conflicts, however, are usually caused
by the corruption of our hearts. We admire and exalt ourselves,
and try to get by on our own. We think we know better than
anyone else and act accordingly. We are suspicious and,
therefore, unwilling to listen to what others have to say. Corrupt
people find it hard to achieve unity with others.

The Bible adds the words, "as you follow Christ Jesus," to
the exhortation to unity. Whoever seeks to follow Christ Jesus
will struggle to be agreeable and to live in harmony with others.
"Your attitude should be the same as that of Christ Jesus" Phil
2:5. This is the norm that must be honored. But, we do not
always achieve unity by following Christ Jesus; he himself did
not agree with everyone. When Paul wrote of unity, he assumed
that everyone would not think alike. But, he left the matter in
God's hands and believed that God would make it clear (Phil
3:15).

The main thing is that we "go forward according to the same
rules we have followed until now" Phil 3:16 (TEV). To achieve
unity it is essential that we all follow the same rules as we
"press on toward the goal to win the prize for which God has
called me heavenward in Christ Jesus" Phil 3:14. We will then
live according to the attitude of Christ Jesus. The unity achieved
will not be a matter of the individual surrendering to the group
spirit, nor of compromise, but unity created by Christ.

5 / We Are Unique, Not Special

"In your light we see light" Ps 36:9.

EACH OF US has his own fate and the problems that accompany it. Each of us has stumbles and sins along life's path. "Each of us has turned to his own way" Is 53:6. No wonder that, as we learn more about ourselves, we tend to conclude that our position is so unique we need special help with our problems.

If we listen to God's word, and ponder it, in this frame of mind, we can easily conclude with sadness that, because of our unique situation, the word does not apply to us. And we continue to wait when we ought to obey.

The word of God has been given to us not to ponder but to obey. As we ponder, we can quickly feel that the word is not for us and set it aside. In doing so we will also set aside God's saving grace. We ought not let Satan interpret the Bible, as he once did in the Garden: "Did God really say that?" Gn 3:1.

It is not hard to understand the Bible, but it is hard to obey. Yet only as we obey it will we understand it. The problem is the one Paul Nicolay pointed out: "It is not hard for us to receive the Holy Spirit; it is hard for the Holy Spirit to receive us." Matters become clear only on the road of obedience. "In your light we see light."

6 / Heart Knowledge and Prayer

"You are always on their lips but far from their hearts" Jr 12:2.

CHRISTIANITY is a matter of the heart. It is our hearts for which God asks. We are in constant danger of falling into the kind of piety described by Jeremiah: "You are always on their lips but far from their hearts."

Such an attitude toward life results, first of all, in a hardening of the heart. We have no doubts about ourselves or our wishes and desires. We pursue our own will, not asking about God's will. Perhaps we pray to God but all we ask is that our plans prosper. We want God to implement our desires, rather than asking about His will and the strength to do it. We become angry or depressed when we do not get our way.

We should be suspicious of ourselves and our agenda. It is dangerous to travel with our own map. We end up going backward rather than forward (Jr 7:24). With this kind of self-guided piety "no one repents of his wickedness, saying, 'What have I done?'" Jr 8:6. There is no knowledge of sin.

Christians have all kinds of problems; we are anxious and sad. But do we really consider what we have done and repent of our sins? If not, we have no need of forgiveness from God or anyone else. Prayer is conversation of the heart with God. If we merely mumble with our lips we are not praying and the Lord will not listen.

Jeremiah is a strong proponent of religion of the heart. He says that if religion is only concerned with ritual, the Lord will no longer be listening to His people (Jr 11:11). As a man who suffered intensely, he had gained depth to his perception of life. He looked to the Lord for "singleness of the heart and action" Jr 32:39. The relationship of our heart to God is of utmost importance. We need to have God close to our hearts.

7 / The Blessing of Insomnia

"You kept my eyes from closing" Ps 77:4.

TIMES OF insomnia, when sleep escapes us for some reason or other, can be frustrating and tiring. The psalmist, who had spent many sleepless nights, understood that it was the Lord who kept him awake. So he does not become impatient but accepts insomnia as God's gift, using these moments to pour out his heart to the Lord in prayer and to hear what the Lord has to say. Unable to sleep, he talked to the Lord who never sleeps.

In the midst of life's endless turmoils we need sleepless nights to listen to the Lord's voice speaking as our conscience. During the day we are too busy; our inner life is too chaotic, and our environment too unsettled for us to listen. But, the Lord comes to our rescue by keeping our eyes open as we lie in bed, so that we might hear what He wants to say to us. Let us not complain when sleep escapes us, but let us make good use of these precious moments.

"Man does not live on bread alone, but on every word that comes from the mouth of God" Mt 4:4. To live as we should with our neighbors, we need to hear what God has to say. Time spent to that end is time well spent, even if it is valuable time robbed from sleep.

8 / Prayer in Spirit and Truth

"Yet a time is coming and has now come when the true worshippers will worship the Father in spirit and truth, for they are the kind of worshippers the Father seeks" Jn 4:23.

WHAT IS worship in spirit and truth, as Jesus talked about with the Samaritan woman? The English translation suggests an answer by using a small "s" in spirit rather than a capital "S." When we read "Spirit," we know that the reference is to God's Spirit. Therefore, to pray in spirit and truth is to pray in such a way that the human spirit, the inner core of the person who prays, is active and involved. Then the prayer is genuine.

This interpretation, however, is not the only possible one, nor perhaps the most convincing. Everyone who practices religion prays, whether they are Jews or Gentiles. Christians are by no means the only ones who pray in a serious manner with their inner beings. Jesus further enlightens us by saying to the woman of Samaria, "Yet a time is coming and has now come when the true worshippers will worship the Father in spirit and truth." He is saying that the time for a new kind of prayer has arrived. Where he is present people pray new prayers. Christ makes us into people who utter prayers of truth. He does this by working in us through his Spirit.

If your prayer life needs renewal in order for you to be able to pray in spirit and truth, keep in mind that it will not happen through your own striving to get your inner spirit involved. Turn yourself and your poor prayers over to Christ and ask him to give you the grace of the Holy Spirit to see your faults and sins, to repent, and to believe in forgiveness for Christ's sake. Without an inner experience of faith and an awareness of God's mercy, you will be in no position to use the precious privilege of prayer given to all who pray in spirit and in truth.

9 / Do We Talk Too Much?

"It is good to wait quietly for the salvation of the Lord"
Lm 3:26.

SOMEONE has said, "When a person talks, God is silent; when a person is silent, God talks." Of course, silence by itself does not prompt God to talk. There is a differece between merely not talking and keeping silent. Whoever is silent before the Lord and perseveres, even when nothing happens, is on the right track and will not be disappointed.

God silences a person in many ways. The case of Job shows one way. In the midst of suffering Job had many things to say, including things that were improper. But he finally ran out of words: "I put my hand over my mouth. I spoke once, but I have no answer--twice, but I will say no more" Job 40:4f. When we find ourselves in situations where we have no explanations or excuses, where even God's word sheds no light on our problems, where we become dumb before God and others, even Christians may consider our case as hopeless. But Job's example teaches that such enforced silence may contain a blessing. When Job finally shut up, God was able to teach him. Having found his tongue again, Job was able to say, "My ears had heard of you but now my eyes have seen you" Job 42:5. In the school of silence Job had learned to know the Lord in a new way. The time of enforced silence was not wasted time.

God silences a person also by awakening in him true knowledge of sin. A person who is troubled with the state of his own life has neither reason nor time for idle gossip. He is unable to judge others, for he must judge himself. He is silenced. This is not a pleasant experience, but it helps us to take our proper place before the Lord, and that is always good.

Being silent before the Lord means that we leave our affairs in His hands and wait for Him to act. Those who do so are never disappointed. Be still before the Lord, O my soul! His will be done!

10 / Judges Too Will Be Judged

"Do not judge, or you will be judged" Mt 7:1.

A PERSON who judges and finds fault with others creates an uncomfortable and gloomy atmosphere. He is like an icy glacier that leaves death in its wake. With this negative attitude toward life, however, he becomes his own greatest victim. Refrain from judging others and you will escape many problems and unpleasant situations.

There is no room for joy in the critical heart, and critical people will lose spontaneity and freedom in their lives. There is a root of bitterness in one's heart, which bears fruit in various forms of critical fault-finding. The person who judges also suffers, because he will lose his friends, who are precious gifts of God.

Friendships are not genuine until they have been tested, and this testing begins when we see our friend's faults. It is not difficult to see faults in others, but if we allow full freedom to the spirit of judgment, friendly relationships will begin to break, we will lose our friends and we will find ourselves alone.

A critical person suffers in yet another way. If our critical attitude is expressed in words of condemnation we will fall victim to sins of the tongue. Once again, we hurt ourselves the most, as the evil tongue activates the very powers of hell. We suffer greatly because of our undisciplined tongues. One lie leads to another and we are finally caught in the web of deceit.

When Jesus says, "Do not judge," he is speaking as our Savior and has our salvation in mind.

11 / Warn But Don't Judge

"There is only one Lawgiver and Judge, the one who is able to save and destroy. But you--who are you to judge your neighbor?" Jas 4:12.

DO NOT JUDGE, for no one has appointed you to be judge! The Lord does not intend that we close our eyes to the evil rampant in the world. On the contrary, He wants us to be shocked and horrified by the wickedness we see. The Spirit of God will draw the boundary between God and the world. "He will convict the world of guilt in regard to sin and righteousness and judgment" Jn 16:8.

Only those who have the Holy Spirit will respond seriously to their conviction of guilt. The Holy Spirit, for example, will open the eyes of fathers and mothers to see the evil sprouting in the lives of their children. Augustine said that no one pulled the weeds of youthful sinful desires in him, and that they suffocated the work of God's grace in his life. Must our children some day make the same complaint? God's Spirit will also prompt friends to warn each other of their character weaknesses.

The Spirit of the Lord is neither neglectful nor compromising, but holy and intolerant of evil. Therefore, the Holy Spirit reprimands like salt. The deep wounds of sin will sting, but a person controlled by the Holy Spirit will have the salt of truth in him. This does not mean, however, that a person filled with the Holy Spirit has been appointed judge over others. There is but one who judges, and He does not judge according to what He sees and hears but according to what He finds in the heart.

We are not qualified to judge others. Even as our fault-finding attitude is condemned, it is liberating to know that we have not been appointed to judge!

12 / Grace Makes Us Gracious

"For God did not send his Son into the world to condemn the world, but to save the world through him" Jn 3:17.

DO NOT condemn your neighbor; help him! It is easy to condemn; but we must have the mind of Christ to help those whom we find to be at fault. His keen eyes saw the evil in people, but he never gave up on them. On the contrary, we are told that when he saw the crowds "he had compassion on them, because they were harassed and helpless, like sheep without a shepherd" Mt 9:36. Jesus' own disciples, in spite of the miracles they had witnessed, became hard-hearted, but he did not forsake them. He joined them on the dangerous trip across the lake (Mk 6:52f.)

Jesus did not come into the world to condemn but to save. He had the attitude of a shepherd. Don't give up on your

220 THE STRUGGLE FOR WHOLENESS

neighbor and become angry at his faults. That attitude will help
no one. You need the attitude of a shepherd. In a hymn we sing,

> In everyone let me see
> A picture, Lord, of thee.

If we could only see in each other, beneath our faults and
weaknesses, the work of God! Then it would not be hard to help
one another.

God's grace envelops also the person whose faults infuriate
us. He is also a victim of sin! You will only add to his burden
with your judgments. He needs you to encourage him and lead
him into the care of Jesus. In order to do this, you need special
grace to see in other the work of God and share in that work.

Many people cannot hide their sins, and are desparate for
people to help them. Those who have learned under Jesus'
tender tutelage to be like shepherds will be able to help. He who
has needed and received much grace is gracious toward others.

13 / Our Sins Are On Christ

*"Christ was sacrificed once to take away the sins of many
people"* He 9:28.

CHRIST'S DEATH is unique. "He entered the Most Holy Place
once for all by his own blood, having obtained eternal
redemption" He 9:12. This is the theme of the Letter to the
Hebrews. "But now he has appeared once for all at the end of the
ages to do away with sin by the sacrifice of himself" He 9:26. The
final decision in the matter of humanity's salvation has been
made.

What does this mean for us? It means above all that in the
matter of our ultimate concern something final and fully
satisfactory has happened. "It is finished!" In our minds, the
matter is still up for grabs; again and again we start from
scratch. But we need not tire or despair, for in Christ the matter
is clear and his work is finished. "Christ was sacrificed once to
take away the sins of many people." Do you think some sins
were left behind when Christ took away sins? "The blood of
Jesus, his Son, purifies us from all sin" 1 Jn 1:7. "You will hurl
all our iniquities into the depths of the sea" Mic 7:19.

Sin can be lodged in one of two places, Luther said. Either sin is on you or on the Lamb of God. There are no other places. Look at the Savior dying on the cross. Do you see how your sins, ugly and still very much alive, push him into death? He does not avoid them, he bears God's wrath and punishment in your place. He suffers your condemnation so that you will be free! "The punishment that brought us peace was upon him" Is 53:5.

But, you still commit sin in full awareness of the suffering Christ. How could he have taken your sins away? He removed your sins in the sense that they are no longer between God and you. You are free from the condemnation of sin. "He came and preached peace to you who were far away and peace to those who were near" Eph 2:17. Since Christ has removed God's wrath, you have the right to approach the Father without fear. You have peace with God through the death of Jesus. Before others you are, and will be to the end, a sinner. Your self-examination will reveal sinful desires and stirrings within you until death. But before God you are without sin, for all your sins were on the Christ of Calvary. He died once to take away the sins of many.

Open wide, O narrow heart,
Receive the priceless treasure!

14 / God Is Our Comforter

"Be joyful in hope, patient in affliction, faithful in prayer" Ro 12:12.

GOD DOES NOT want us to be depressed. A depressed person is useless; his grasp on life is weak. He pollutes the environment with his depression. The Lord, however, does not reprove the depressed person but comes to his rescue. He is a God who "comforts the downcast" 2 Co 7:6.

There are three ways in which God comforts us. First, through His own word. "Your word is a lamp to my feet and a light for my path" Ps 119:105. Study the Bible! If you ignore God's word, you have no reason to complain about darkness. God has given you a light for your path. How marvelous is God's word which encourages the wanderer caught in darkness!

The second form of comfort is hidden in the affliction itself: "Your rod and your staff, they comfort me" Ps 23:4. When the Lord uses His rod it means that He cares about us. A father disciplines only his own child. "Endure hardship as discipline; God is treating you as sons. For what son is not disciplined by his father?" He 12:7. If only we were able to accept our afflictions from God's hand!

Lastly, our troubles are light and momentary (2 Co 4:17). Even though the remaining years of our life were pain, affliction, and tears, they would still be light and momentary. "For his anger lasts only a moment, but his favor lasts a lifetime; weeping may remain for a night, but rejoicing comes in the morning" Ps 30:5. Therefore, "Be joyful in hope, patient in affliction, faithful in prayer."

15 / Free and Full Forgiveness

"...if you hold anything against anyone, forgive him" Mk 11:25.

FORGIVENESS is difficult. We stubbornly cling to our rights which we feel have been violated. The loftier our opinion about ourselves, the more difficult to forgive one another from our hearts. But if God has been able to humble us, so that we know we need to be forgiven, it is easier to forgive others. If I am aware of my own faults, I cannot judge others. To be able to forgive we need to trust that God is ready to forgive the one who has sinned against us. How can we entertain harsh thoughts about a person whom God is ready to forgive?

God forgives for the sake of His great love, and He does it freely and without cost. God's love is neither calculating nor miserly. He does not even consider the possibility that the person whom He forgives will soon squander the grace he has received.

God is love, infinite and extravagant love! The very essence of true love is to give itself freely, without expecting anything in return. God is like that when He forgives. We also need confidence that God is able to change and correct the natural weaknesses of our neighbor and to keep him from future lapses. The psalmist knew this confidence: "The Lord upholds all those who fall" Ps 145:14.

The Lord performs His miracles with those who are most helpless. If we focus only on the inability of the other person to change his ways, we will not find it in our hearts to forgive him. We fear that, given the opportunity, he will wrong us again. But if we consider God's possibilities, we are encouraged and freed to believe in divine miracles in the most hopeless cases.

In summary, to be able to forgive we must have God in our line of vision; we need living Christian faith.

16 / Meeting Expectations

"May those who hope in you not be disgraced because of me" Ps 69:6.

IN MANY WAYS we disappoint one another. We prove to be unworthy of trust; we fail to meet expectations. This can cause deep sorrow for parents who have high hopes for their children, but it can be tragic when the people involved have been entrusted with a special task. For example, the leader of a battalion assigned to hold a section of the front line may fail to meet the expectations of his commander and jeopardize the outcome of the battle.

Every Christian has an assignment as a soldier of Christ. He has been given an important task; his section of the front must not collapse. Christian warfare never makes newspaper headlines; it is a silent struggle in humility, self-denial, truth, love and service. But, how easy it is to fail in our mission. Every proud thought we harbor is desertion. All self-aggrandizement, all living for self, resulting in impatience in difficulties, is betrayal of the Lord's cause. All falsehood, whether in words, overbearing manners, or hypocritical behavior is also desertion. And, finally, the lack of love and failure to serve are high treason! How often the enemy infiltrates on this front. We have every reason to keep on praying in the words of the psalmist, "May those who hope in you not be disgraced because of me."

17 / Love Needs to Be Learned

"Be patient, bearing with one another in love" Eph 4:2.

THE CURSE of sin weighs heavily upon us and our life together is difficult. People's nerves are worn to a frazzle, not only by sinful living, but also by the struggle for a livelihood and the problems of life in general. Their struggle has reached the breaking point.

The first thing we notice is each other's faults, which begin to drive wedges into our friendships. In the course of time, however, a sincere person begins to see also his own faults and how they create problems for others. Taking this into account, the Bible urges us to bear with one another, to be patient and not grow weary. Because life is difficult, we simply cannot make it unless we are long-suffering toward one another. It is futile to hope for a life of ease.

If at present you are struggling with family problems or vexing personal relationships, be patient! We are more likely to succeed in our daily relationships if we accept the inevitability of life's difficulties. We are called to bear with each other in love, not unwillingly and reluctantly. We should stop complaining about the wickedness of others and avoiding unpleasant people. We should be patient with one another in love, empathizing with others, forgetting the hurts inflicted on us, and forgiving the faults and failures which we all have.

But where can we get such love? "Accept one another, then, just as Christ accepted you" Ro 15:7. That is the secret! If we are forced to go to Christ daily with our faults in order to be loved, we will learn to be long-suffering toward others. And, in the midst of life's difficulties and fragile human relationships, we will even learn to love.

18 / When the Stream Runs Dry

"He is like a tree planted by streams of water" Ps 1:3.

ACCORDING to the Bible, Christians are not meant to live in a dry river bed. Jesus says, "I have come that they may have life, and have it in the full" Jn 10:10. He also says, "Whoever drinks the water I give him will never thirst. Indeed, the water I give him will become in him a spring of water welling up to eternal life" Jn 4:14.

There is no drought when Jesus is present. The Old Testament uses rich figures of speech to describe people who trust God: "They will be like a well-watered garden" Jr 31:12. "He is like a tree planted by streams of water, which yields its fruit in season" Ps 1:3.

If our inner life is like a dry desert, we need to examine ourselves, for there is some reason why the Holy Spirit has left us. To find out we must ask God to examine us and to reveal to us the truth about ourselves. We cannot afford to be negligent in such an important matter. The freshness and vitality of our spiritual life depends on our relationship to God's word. Surely the Lord, who wants to bless His own with all spiritual blessings, will show us the reason for the drought in our inner life, if we honestly ask Him.

19 / Grace Is New Each Morning

"Satisfy us in the morning with your unfailing love, that we may sing for joy and be glad all our days" Ps 90:14.

DURING THESE beautiful autumn days we have awakened morning after morning to delight in God's marvelous works in nature. "What a rich harvest your goodness provides! Wherever you go there is plenty" Ps 65:11 (TEV) Do we know how to be grateful for the rich bounty of God's mercy? Do we who believe acknowledge the wonderful works of God and sing His praises for all to hear? Where would we be, if God had not prospered our land and blessed our efforts?

In his morning hymn J. L. Runeberg, the Finnish poet, sings the praise of the Lord for the bright new day, but concludes:

As dawns the day without,
Dispel the night within!

That's why we fail to praise God for His good creation. Within our hearts it is night. There is a darkness that the sun in the sky cannot dispel. It is good to relax with early morning walks during these fall days, but that cannot help our inner life.

God must shine the light of His grace for our souls to be refreshed and renewed.

The fog of sin obscures our inner vision. Idle, loveless, deceitful talk pollutes the human environment, but even more so it corrupts our souls. Duplicity weaves a web that entangles us in our relationships with one another. Impure, sinful desires, which we nurture, seem to provide momentary pleasure, but eventually deprive us of true joy. Unbelief--the mother of all sins--taxes and depresses us more than anything else, robbing us of grace and the joy of life. We have reason to ask God to blow the fog out of our souls every day. Unless God lets His light shine from the face of Jesus Christ, we will never be able to see and rejoice over the works of His creation. "Where there is forgiveness of sins, there are also life and salvation" (Luther, Small Catechism).

20 / Christ Heals, Not Prayer

"Simon's mother-in-law was in bed with a fever, and they told Jesus about her" Mk 1:30.

IT IS MISLEADING to talk about healing by prayer. Prayer heals no one! The power is not in our prayers; Jesus is the Great Healer. Our task is to tell Jesus about the unfortunate who need his healing, as he was told about Simon's mother-in-law.

Yet we often imagine that in order to accomplish something our prayers must be special. I have witnessed attempts at healing the sick by prayer that have been pure sham. The leader waved his arms back and forth over the patient, with the voices of those who prayed undulating in strange patterns. The room was filled with the air of magical rites. Such performances can have some meaning, and the sick are sometimes healed by purely psychological techniques. However, what Mark relates is something altogether different: "They told Jesus about her."

We may not have tried strange and magical prayer techniques, but we must humbly acknowledge that there have been times when we have tried to make our prayers as pleasant and moving as possible, thinking they would have special power. We try, so to speak, to inflate our prayers.

Do we believe in our prayers? Or do we believe in Christ, who hears our prayers and makes the impossible possible? He has power to heal the sick, if he sees fit.

Forget about impressive and artificial prayer techniques! Tell Jesus about our problems, simply, naturally, and in humble faith. If some person or problem is on your heart, trust in his power and tell Jesus about it.

Also note that the disciples joined together to tell Jesus about Simon's sick mother-in-law. Let us also pray together more often. Jesus has said that such prayers do carry special weight.

21 / The Place of Suffering and Healing

"Come, let us return to the Lord. He has torn us to pieces but he will heal us; he has injured us but he will bind up our wounds" Ho 6:1.

GOLGATHA is the place where God suffers for us. He suffers because He is love. To comprehend this we must distinguish between God's alien work and his proper work.

Do you remember how you had to take bitter medicine when you were seriously ill? From the weight of God's blows we know the seriousness of our situation. God does not wound and tear for nothing. This is His alien work. He is forced to do it, but it does not yet reveal His true nature. But when He heals and binds up our wounds, then He is about His proper work. The Lord is merciful and gracious, long-suffering and altogether good.

We are invited to Golgatha, but who wants to accept this invitation? To make our way to the Cross, we must realize that we are returning to the place from which we have strayed. We who have been torn and injured return to Golgotha to be healed and to have our wounds bound up by Christ.

We go to Golgatha so that God might perform His proper work also in us. If we are to be helped, the Lord must do His work. Human efforts will not do, neither our own nor our friends. Lest we remain lost, the Lord must break the wickedness of our hearts. The Lord must heal and bind the results of our sins; no one else can do it. "Come, let us return to the Lord." Back to Golgatha!

22 / Repentance of the Unrepentant

"No one sews a patch of unshrunk cloth on an old garment. If he does, the new piece will pull away from the old, making the tear worse" Mk 2:21.

THROUGHOUT the Bible we hear the call to repentance. It is a task from which we must not shirk. But, what is repentance? Some say it means giving up bad habits and improving one's life. People who believe this will try their utmost, struggling to the point of shedding blood, to overcome their sins. In some respects they seem to succeed, some sins are actually overcome.

But if they are conscientious they quickly realize their task of repentance is far from finished. New sins appear and even the old ones, once put away, rear their ugly heads again. It becomes clear that, although certain external vices have been overcome, the heart has remained unchanged. And that is where the same old wicked, loathsome, and filthy lusts have their nesting place. The scrupulous person picks up the task once more and proceeds to prune the bad branches of his tree. Such repentance is wearisome, and eventually hopeless.

Jesus describes such a person when he talks about patching an old garment with a new piece of cloth. It will not work. The old cloth will tear; the cure will be worse than the illness. Who knows how many Christians today are wearing themselves out with such repentance. They are engaging in a futile repentance, which inevitably leads to self-righteousness. The true and righteous God cannot accept such repentance. He is being merciful to people who engage in such futile repentence when He allows them to fail so that others will see the futility of their efforts. When God's word exhorts us to repent and return it means something radically different from such self-healing activity.

23 / What Is True Repentance?

"He who conceals his sins does not prosper, but whoever confesses and renounces them finds mercy" Pr 28:13.

REPENTANCE takes place when a person honestly sees who he is and acknowledges that God is right to condemn him. As one sick unto death, he turns to this same God for mercy.

God's Spirit seeks to lead a person to know his sins, revealing not only certain individual sinful acts as sinful, but our entire lives. Our whole being appears sinful in the light of the Holy Spirit. Even our piety, our half-hearted attempts to please God, are polluted by sin. We try to escape from the admonitions of the Holy Spirit. But, God wants us to come to ourselves like the prodigal son in the distant country. We must bow to God's judgment, acknowledge it as true, and submit ourselves into His hands.

Confession of sins is part of true repentance. First, it is essential that we confess our sins to God. The Bible states that whoever confesses his sins and renounces them will experience mercy. Then, there are things we need to confess to those we have hurt. Finally, God's Spirit directs us to make confession to God in the presence of another person. Nowhere does the Bible insist upon this latter form of confession as a condition of salvation, but it has often proven to be helpful.

Renouncing sins does not mean just giving up sinful practices but submitting to God's judgment over my sins and acknowledge myself as a sinner before God.

24 / Cosmic Reconciliation and Individual Repentance

"Repent, then, and turn to God, so that your sins may be wiped out" Ac 3:19.

EVEN THOUGH the prodigal son came to himself in the distant country, was sorry for his sins, and renounced them in response to the summons of his conscience, he still needed to return home in order to become his father's child again. Repentance involves returning.

Returning for a sinner means that, under condemnation for his sins, he turns to the merciful God and asks for help. We cannot expect to approach God with the virtues that belong to true Christians, such as prayer, contrition, and repentance. In utter helplessness we turn again and again to the Lord, to ask him to give us true repentance. We must not listen to our minds which insist that we must somehow heal ourselves, or do this or that. We must keep turning to the Lord with the mess of our lives. Repentance has to do with being in the hands of the healer.

Three things are clear concerning repentance. First, it is not for just anyone. An indifferent person cannot repent. The awakening of the conscience is a prerequisite of repentance. Second, repentance is essential. The cosmic reconciliation and cleansing from sin accomplished by God in Christ will not achieve its purpose if we do not submit to God's judgment over sin, confess our sins, and turn to our helper. Third, repentance is not an isolated event, for the entire life of a Christian is an unending process of repentance. Repent and return to God.

25 / Donated Righteousness

"All have sinned and fall short of the glory of God, and are justified freely by his grace through the redemption that came by Christ Jesus" Ro 3:23f.

BELIEVERS AND UNBELIEVERS alike find it difficult to acknowledge the truth of this Scripture: "All have sinned and fall short of the glory of God." By nature we all want to be someone important. Each of us imagines that we have some kind of halo. We compete with one another; we admire ourselves. Secret self-admiration is a common human characteristic.

The Bible is blunt but realistic in its diagnosis of the human situation. All of us, without exception, have sinned and fall short of the glory of God. All of us are without true glory and true worth. Our piety is but a poor cover for the shame of our nakedness. "There is no one who understands, no one who seeks God" Ro 3:11.

Perhaps you think that you seek God. All Christians say this. The fact remains, however, that we really seek ourselves, not God. If this is true, where can we find salvation? Paul says that we "are justified freely by his grace through the redemption that came by Christ Jesus." It is free; it is a gift. Righteousness comes to the selfish enemies of God as a gift, for the sake of Christ. It is a gift, not only when we first believe, but continues to be donated righteousness to the very end.

Grace means that a sinful and condemned creature is also, at the same time, a saved saint for Christ's sake. The deeper the consciousness of condemnation produced by the Holy Spirit, the more real the experience of the saving power of God. The atonement by Christ has indeed overpowered sin. On the cross God has manifested as much of His glory as we are able to behold in this sinful world. From the cross, divine glory radiates into human life.

26 / God Is My Analyst

"Search me, O God, and know my heart; test me and know my anxious thoughts. See if there is any offensive way in me, and lead me in the way everlasting" Ps 139:23f.

WHEN YOU feel well you do not think of going to a doctor. As soon as you begin to feel sick the thought of going to the doctor enters your mind. That is how it is also in regard to our inner, or spiritual, life. We give no thought to what inner peace, or peace with God, is all about until we run into trouble. We may be involved in spiritual activities, but we are not interested in examining ourselves or being examined, until something happens to destroy our peace.

The psalmist concluded that he was not qualified to examine himself. He knew that what he could find out about himself could never put him on the right track. He decided to get into analysis with the Lord. So, he prayed: "Search me, O God, and know my heart; test me and know my anxious thoughts." He took his problems to the Lord: "If my way is one that leads to destruction, lead me to the way everlasting."

This person is in God's hands. The Lord has allowed the sickness of sin to weigh on him, and he has been forced to see the doctor. Now, he finds himself under the Lord's care. He does not fully understand his situation, but he trusts that the Lord understands and wants to help. He has chosen to leave his precious soul in the hands of the Lord, and is willing to let the Lord do what needs to be done for his salvation. This person is a true struggler who refuses to offer his struggling or even his faith in exchange for salvation, but leaves everything to God.

27 / Face to Face With God

"Taking the five loaves and the two fish and looking up to heaven, he gave thanks and broke the loaves. Then he gave them to the disciples, and the disciples gave them to the people" Mt 14:19.

IN TELLING about the miracle of the feeding of the multitude, the gospel writers mention that while giving thanks Jesus looked up to heaven. These words have a special message, preserved for us in the first three gospels.

Perhaps they simply portray the way in which people of that day prayed. In any case, they suggest that the person who prayed stood eye to eye with the heavenly Father as he presented his case. He expected help only from God. He knew that he was always in God's presence, so he placed himself in that position as he prayed.

We who pray want to be united with God and submit to His will. Jesus is the only person who submitted completely to God's will in his prayers. He is the only one who has been able to stand face to face with God, allowing nothing to come between them. This explains his bitter anguish on Golgatha, when, under the load of God's wrath for our sake, he felt he had been forsaken by God. "My God, my God, why have you forsaken me?" Mt 27:46.

What about our prayers? Do we look up to heaven? Do our prayers leave us with God, or do we leave our prayers with Him? Are we willing to face Him? Unless we are, we will never see His face full of grace nor receive His peace. Is it possible that the ineffectiveness of our prayers stems largely from our not looking up to our Father when we pray? Jesus says that when we pray we must believe we have received what we ask and it will be ours (Mk 11:24). Such prayer is impossible, unless those who pray entrust themselves to God, so that His face can shine upon them.

28 / Saved to Serve

"The Lord redeems his servants" Ps 34:22.

CHRIST'S REDEMPTION includes the whole world, but the psalmist says only the Lord's servants benefit from it. This does not mean that we earn a share in redemption by our service. Salvation is by faith alone, by grace alone. "To the man who does not work but trusts God who justifies the wicked, his faith is credited as righteousness" Ro 4:5.

But there are two kinds of faith: mere knowledge of, and assent to, certain doctrines; and living Christian faith. Luther states in his Preface to Romans: "Faith, however, is a divine work in us which changes us and makes us to be born anew of God. It kills the old Adam and makes us altogether different men, in heart and spirit and mind and powers; and it brings with it the Holy Spirit." It is impossible for true faith not to engage in service to the Lord and the neighbor.

In the light of the New Testament, this is how we are to understand the words of the psalmist: "The Lord redeems his servants." It is amazing that insignificant creatures like you and I can be servants of the Lord. But true faith assures us that, in spite of all sense of unworthiness, we have been redeemed by Christ. We are so precious to God that He did not spare His dear Son to make us His own. When this unmerited grace of God is experienced by a sinner, he is freed from inner bondage and filled with the desire to serve his Lord wholeheartedly.

29 / Suffering As an Assignment

"So then, those who suffer according to God's will should commit themselves to their faithful Creator and continue to do good" 1 P 4:19.

WE TRY TO AVOID suffering, for we assume that suffering is useless and worthless. And yet, experience shows that those who have suffered are of great benefit of others. The Lord Christ himself is our best example.

Who has experienced his kind of suffering? Christ suffered so that Scripture might be fulfilled, and redemption finished. In suffering and being obedient to death, he fulfilled God's will.

There was no other way for him to accomplish the task he had received from the Father, except by suffering.

We should think of this more often, when suffering in any form, large or small, overtakes us. Suffering is God's redemptive task for us. He has reserved the heaviest burdens for His own. In the course of doing the Lord's will we often have to walk through suffering, sorrow, and affliction. Let us not insist on knowing to what purpose God wants to use the suffering He has assigned to us. Let us ask only for humility to do our part in the midst of suffering. The Lord will answer for the rest. He knows to what purpose He is using our pain.

I would rather serve the Lord in some other way. It would be far more pleasant to do something that promises success, something that would test my talents and show what I can accomplish. But perhaps the Lord has reserved for me another kind of task, that of a sufferer. If you suffer in silence, trust that you are about the Lord's business! Your life is not wasted; in your suffering you are doing the Lord's will.

30 / Our Public and Private Selves

"Your life is now hidden with Christ in God" Col 3:3.

THE LIFE of a Christian is hidden with Christ in God. It begins with the exhortation to pray to God in the secrecy of one's room. "Your Father, who sees what is done in secret, will reward you" Mt 6:6. Life has two sides, the public side, which is in full view of others, and the private side, which others see only fleetingly.

Jesus has no intention of eliminating these two sides of our life. He deepens our whole life by urging us to spend more time in prayer in the privacy of our room. It so happens that this private side of our life is the more crucial side. Its defeats and victories are of greatest significance. The spirit of our times does not encourage such privacy, but God does. If He doesn't succeed in any other way, He will try sickness or other difficulties to draw us away from the public eye into private consultation with Him.

Our Christian faith is hidden, suggesting at times that it has slipped through our fingers. We no longer talk about it with others. Perhaps you had in mind things you wanted to talk about with a more experienced Christian. You wanted to ask for advice in your struggle for wholeness. But when the opportunity arose you discovered you had nothing to share. Everything had vanished into thin air. You felt it would be hypocritical to start talking. Do not be surprised when this happens, for your life is hidden in the Lord. It is not in our power to discuss our struggle for wholeness whenever we please.

But this much you can do: you can join with your friend in prayer to the Lord. He knows all your needs and reads even the secret thoughts you are unable to put into words. Simply meeting a friend often lessens our burden.

The hidden nature of Christianity as a whole stems from the hiddenness of God. Luther puts it this way: God is closest to us when He seems to be the farthest, and farthest when he seems to be the closest.

October

1 / Gone With the Wind

"We all shrivel up like a leaf and like the wind our sins sweep us away" Is 64:6.

WATCHING THE WIND toss dry leaves around the yard may remind you of the prophet's words: "We all shrivel up like a leaf and like the wind our sins sweep us away." The image is powerful. Sin separates us from God and His holiness. Without such reference points and a sense of eternity, our lives become unstable, blown whichever way the wind dictates.

The essence of sin is selfishness. Wrapped around ourselves, we shrivel like a dry leaf with no choice but to go with the wind. As the prophet declares: "Our sins sweep us away." The ungodly person knows no peace. His lifestyle sweeps him away like a strong wind, without mercy. With his inner life so badly out of balance, nothing truly satisfies him.

This prophetic picture casts new light on the true cause of our own lack of stability and peace. Only the peace of God can guard our hearts and our thoughts.

2 / Prayer and Problems of Power

"In the same way, the Spirit helps us in our weakness. We do not know what we ought to pray for" Ro 8:26.

WE ASSUME that a lack of power creates our anemic spirituality. We would like to pray but lack the strength. Our remedy is to exert greater effort to produce better prayers.

The Bible proclaims a remarkably different perspective: "The Spirit helps us in our weakness. We do not know what we ought to pray for, but the Spirit himself intercedes for us with groans that words cannot express" Ro 8:26. The persons Paul has in mind are simply ignorant about what those things for which they should pray. They don't lack power for they have the Spirit's power. The Spirit will help them in their weakness.

What do we make of this? God's thoughts are not our thoughts, God's ways are not ours. We do not counsel Him or tell Him how He is to help us in each circumstance of life. Understanding that we are slaves of sin, we admit we have no way to tell how God will help us. All we know is God's desire to do so.

When we pray as sinners, our only choice is to leave everything in the Lord's hands. We must depend on the Lord and wait for Him to act. At this point the Holy Spirit comes to our aid, encouraging us to stay with the Lord, no matter what. All may appear hopeless to us, but the Spirit speaks differently. Though the poorest of creatures, we experience the Spirit's help in our weakness. Without knowing why, we cling to the Lord. We trust he knows how to help.

Let us leave the care of our souls entirely to the Lord and trust Him no matter what happens.

3 / Anticipating the Lord's Arrival

"He who testifies to these things says, 'Yes, I am coming soon.' Amen. Come, Lord Jesus" Rev 22:20.

THE LORD'S COMING was a lively issue for the early Christians. Of utmost significance for them was waiting eagerly for "our Lord Jesus Christ to be revealed" 1 Co 1:7. In Greek, "eagerly waiting" conveys a sense of nervous tension. Early

Christians were people waiting fervently and anxiously for their Lord.

If we believe in the living Lord, we wait for him. Dead faith is exposed by the fact that it gives no thought to Christ's return. If Christ is only a teacher or model, why should we wait for him? But he is our living Lord, calling us to live with him. Available, he speaks and listens, raises and carries, bruises and heals. Christ does his work in order to reveal his great power and glory. He cannot remain hidden forever; he will show himself. We move toward that day at an accelerated speed. The heavenly horizon is in view!

The radical power of our Christian faith stems from the thought of Christ's return. The light of the Lord's imminent return changes forever our view of the world and all its values. Christ's return remains the most powerful motive for mission work. It is preparation for the day of Christ's arrival.

What if He returned today? Are you prepared? Is your house in order? Would you be ready to welcome him today?

4 / Conversion for Change

"Turn to me and be saved, all you ends of the earth" Is 45:22.

WE DO NOT have two Gods, one who requires conversion and another who does not. To be saved, everyone must be converted. We often deceive ourselves, living as if traveling through the narrow gate of conversion were not necessary for entrance into God's kingdom. But unless we turn around, we are not saved.

Conversion does not earn credit with God or make us worthy of Him. Conversion does not mean adopting certain Christian customs to be different. This is not what conversion is all about. Nor do we attempt on our part to become better people, all of a sudden honest, humble, pure, and unselfish. God does not expect us to change ourselves. God knows we cannot.

Conversion is just what the word suggests. It is turning to the Lord just as we are. We give the Lord an honest report about ourselves, without embellishment or excuse. Unable to change ourselves, we turn to the Lord as He draws us with His grace. Then the Lord Himself begins the work of changing us. Without conversion, the Lord's work cannot begin in us.

5 / Darkness Is for Listening

"What I tell you in the dark, speak in the daylight" Mt
10:27.

THE LORD leads His disciples into darkness so that He might
speak to them. Separating them from others, thrusting them
into suffering, He allows them to experience the horrors of the
night. The waters deepen with no help in sight.

By nature we dread these afflictions, preferring to travel in
the security of daylight. We try our best to evade difficulties,
labeling it a great tragedy when things do not go our way. But
God knows we need these misfortunes. Christ enters our
darkness and speaks to us.

The Bible declares we must be still before the Lord,
submitting to Him, quietly hoping in Him. Well-intentioned
people may try to help us in such tribulation. We must guard
against that and against lending ear to voices of self-pity within
us. If we begin to think of ourselves as martyrs or surrender to
self-pity, we become useless to the kingdom of God and a burden
to others.

As the Lord speaks in the quietness, he teaches us what we
can learn no other way. For that reason God must deal with His
own through suffering; for that reason the messengers of Good
News whom God sends to save others must themselves
experience difficult times of affliction.

6 / Evil Is in the Eye of the Beholder

*"We are confident of better things in your case--things
that accompany salvation"* He 6:9.

ORDINARILY a person imagines others to be like him. He who
is evil sees others as evil. A schemer thinks everyone is a
schemer. The one who is insincere attributes insincere motives
to others. Wicked hearts sow distrust, bitterness, and
corruption!

The disciple of Jesus acts differently. He prepares to believe
good things about others. Outward appearances present an
incomplete and deceptive picture. The disciple seeks the good in

people whose lives and actions are bad. Fault-finding and criticism of others is replaced by empathy with them.

Our natural response is to shy away from and condemn those in whom we witness faults. In this way we push them deeper into their misfortune. As Christians we seek the good even in the worst of persons. We do so believing in God's seeking love, which responds most tenderly to the most unfortunate. Believing that the Lord works in people, the Christian seeks to lift up the good and the best in them. For this reason, as Luther says, he "apologizes for him, speaks well of him, and interprets charitably all that he does" Small Catechism. What a triumph it would be, if each person would focus on the best in others. We would then be less apt to take offense. Good will would reign in us.

7 / Jesus Knows What to Do

"He said this only to test him, for he already had in mind what he was going to do" Jn 6:6.

JESUS ASKED his disciple Philip about feeding the multitude that had followed him into the desert. To this question John adds a brief parenthetical comment: "He said this only to test him, for he already had in mind what he was going to do."

How often disciples of Jesus have run into similar situations! There seems to be no way out. The road ahead is completely blocked. The fund of ideas is exhausted. But Jesus knows what he is going to do, even though the disciples have no way of anticipating his next move.

We assume that we must understand what needs to be done. We become frantic as we ask repeatedly, not realizing that it is not important for us to understand fully. The crucial thing is believing that Jesus knows what he is doing. An old hymn stated it this way: "Jesus has a way out always."

Submission of this kind requires us to let go of our own well-laid plans and to depend solely on the wisdom and power of the Lord Jesus. But this implies that we let him do all the deciding. We let him do what he sees best. He is the Lord; he can handle our affairs, too!

8 / Awakened to Alertness

"Wake up! Strengthen what remains and is about to die, for I have not found your deeds complete in the sight of my God" Rev 3:2.

ANANIAS and Sapphira of Acts 5 are familiar characters. They represent individuals who join enthusiastically in Christian fellowship and participate in Christian activities, but for selfish reasons. Hiding their deceitful hearts under cloaks of piety, their Christianity lacks inward alertness. Their hearts are not right before the Lord.

We know what happened to Ananias and Sapphira. Peter said to Sapphira, "The feet of the men who buried your husband are at the door and they will carry you out also" Ac 5:9. Any person whose heart is not right before the Lord, who is a Christian through deceit, will find others eager to carry his spiritual corpse into the bosom of the world. That world of the dead rejoices over every former Christian added to its midst.

This is how the falling happens. First, we fail to be on the alert; second, we adorn our failure with piety. The falling away happens in the presence of God's word and the company of believers. Worldliness, so prevalent today, is a natural result. The dead find their place among the dead!

Would that God gave all Christians His grace, so that souls that are asleep might be awakened into a state of alertness. Our failure to be inwardly alert not only destroys us spiritually but also leads others, by bad example, to join us in the same destruction. Experience teaches us that Christians who are not inwardly alert, who minimize and defend their sins, are the most dangerous saboteurs in the Lord's church.

9 / The Son Brings the New Day

"The Lord's compassions are new every morning; great is your faithfulness" Lm 3:23.

"EACH DAY has enough trouble of its own" Mt 6:34. No day passes without contributing its own troubles. We are unrealistic if we do not take this into account. But each day also offers new strength. Our compassionate Lord's grace is "new each morning."

We tend to label our outward afflictions as the most troublesome. Poor health, lack of money, difficult living conditions and similar problems weigh heavily on many of us. Our greatest problem, however, is separation from God. Our greatest misfortune is a failure to trust God.

Each morning God seeks us, even though we do not know how to seek Him, offering us new grace to overcome our unbelief. God draws us to His Son Jesus Christ so that we might be free.

How can I know the incredible truth that God renews His grace toward me every morning? Life appears unchanged; old questions remain. While others gladly welcome the light of a new day, we feel the sorrow and depression of the continuing darkness.

Is grace new each morning for you? Our only hope is the Lord Jesus Christ and his holy cross. Each new morning Christ sits on the mercy seat receiving sinners. Each new day his blood purifies from sin. It is because of Christ's sacrificial love that God has mercy on us.

10 / The Pause that Empowers

"Stay in the city until you have been clothed with power from on high" Lk 24:49.

FROM OUR point of view Jesus should have reprimanded the disciples who were hiding behind locked doors. "What are you doing here, as though I were still in the grave? Go out to the people and tell them I have risen from the dead!" Instead, Jesus tells his disciples to stay behind locked doors. "Stay in the city until you have been clothed with power from on high."

The Savior's teaching method says something important to us. At times, his disciples can only wait in silence. Witnessing to the Lord does no good without the prerequisite "power from on high," the Spirit of the Lord. Our own power is useless in a business requiring divine power. Our own power cannot advance the Lord's cause, not in our homes nor among our friends nor in our congregation, much less in the rest of the world. Only the Spirit can do it. So the Lord says, in effect, "Go into your prayer chamber! Pray and fast!"

Someone observed that when the Lord's cause is losing, Christians are like mushrooms hidden out of sight, gathering strength to burst forth with the coming rain. Behind locked doors is the place to gather strength from God's word, the sacraments, and mutual conversation and consolation. The risen Lord moves among his friends behind the locked doors. Do we use this time properly? Do we hear the Lord saying to us, "Peace be with you?" The wounds Jesus cleanses can then be healed.

Waiting behind locked doors, the disciples do not lose hope in the final victory. No matter how thick the gloom outside, the disciples wait for power from on high, for the risen Lord opens their minds to know the promises of the Bible will be fulfilled. Therefore, they gather strength for the day when the Lord will again "pour out his Spirit on all people" Acts 2:17.

11 / Divine Free Delivery

"Deliver us from the evil one" Mt 6:13.

JESUS HAS TAUGHT us to pray, "Deliver us from the evil one." Luther writes: "Thus you see how God wants us to pray to him for everything that affects our bodily welfare and directs us to seek and expect help from no one but him." Large Catechism. Luther explains that as Christians we do not glory in sufferings and evil, nor wish them upon ourselves or others, even though we know that God uses them to train us. Behind evil the Christian sees the Evil One against whom he must fight in faith and prayer.

"Since the devil is not only a liar but also a murderer, he incessantly seeks our life and vents his anger by causing accidents and injury to our bodies. He breaks many a man's neck and drives others to insanity; some he drowns, and many he hounds to suicide or other dreadful catastrophes. Therefore there is nothing for us to do on earth but to pray constantly against this arch-enemy. For if God did not support us, we would not be safe from him for a single hour" Luther, *Large Catechism*.

By pointing to our need to combat these evils, Jesus implies that our situation is dangerous. Behind evil is the Evil One, the Devil. The danger is not to be minimized. Against us is a powerful enemy, whose purpose is to destroy us. Human resources are not enough to deliver from the Evil One. We need God. God wants to be our refuge and strength. Trusting God is not in vain. Seeking His kingdom through unconditional surrender, we trust God to deliver us from evil.

The Lord's Prayer ends with "Deliver us from evil" for good reason. It can be properly prayed only after the preceding petitions. Luther says, "This petition he has put last, for if we are to be protected and delivered from all evil, his name must first be hallowed in us, his kingdom come among us, and his will be done." Large Catechism.

12 / Believing in the Holy Spirit

"If anyone does not have the Spirit of Christ, he does not belong to Christ" Ro 8:9.

DO YOU REALLY believe in the Holy Spirit? Do you believe, for example, that only the Holy Spirit reveals Christ? If you did, then you would be constantly praying that the Spirit would reveal Christ to you. You would not be satisfied with your present state, knowing your Savior only vaguely from a distance. You could not say that Christ does not belong to a poor sinner like you.

If the Holy Spirit reveals Christ, you would pray constantly for God's Spirit to help you. You would constantly ask the Lord's Spirit to do what you cannot, to reveal Christ to your family and congregation. Our Lord promises that no one asks for the Spirit in vain.

If you believe in the Holy Spirit, you believe with Paul that he who walks in the Spirit overcomes the flesh, all the evil that dwells in him. Do you believe this? Do you admit you are totally dependent on the Lord for victory over sin? Then you will not bother with good resolutions. Instead you will daily call for the help of the Spirit, who alone can cleanse your heart.

Finally, if you believe in the Holy Spirit, the Lord's church is dear to you. The Holy Spirit is always the Spirit of the church; He calls and gathers the Lord's people. The sectarian spirit, born of the flesh, and not the Holy Spirit, causes us to elevate our own group as the only true church. The Holy Spirit endears us to Christian friends and draws us to corporate worship in the church.

13 / The Master's Voice

"But they will never follow a stranger; in fact, they will run away from him because they do not recognize a stranger's voice" Jn 10:5.

THE EAR of the disciple accustomed to the Savior's voice distinguishes it from other voices. The true disciple of Jesus is sensitive; hearing strange voices, he runs away fearing they will lead him to destruction.

We have much to learn in this regard. Have our ears learned to distinguish the voice of Jesus from other voices? Do we have the gift of discerning the spirits? On the contrary, don't we often look upon those people who know everything, appeal to everyone, and are drawn to everything, as ideal? According to Jesus, that is not what his disciples are like. They choose between voices, seeking to hear the voice of Jesus and fleeing from strange voices. This is what it means to struggle on the narrow road. Even Christian friends do not always understand such lonely strugglers. But that is not important. The important thing is that Jesus recognizes his own, even the most lonely among them.

How does the disciple learn to recognize and distinguish the voice of his Lord from other voices? He spends a lot of time alone with his Lord. Ordinarily this happens during times of suffering. Alone, enveloped in silence, he hears his Master's voice. He learns to love that voice. He finds direction for his life.

We all yearn to be people who recognize the voice of Jesus, ready to run away from those who would have us turn away from his way.

14 / Outer Success, Inner Bankruptcy

"What good is it for a man to gain the whole world, yet forfeit his soul?" Mk 8:36.

MOST PEOPLE strive to gain the whole world in some form. All their efforts, financial struggles, vocational goals, and choice of friends focus on this goal of life. The results can be remarkable: important positions, power, money, reputation and other similar benefits. But Jesus says that such gains are illusory, that in reality these gains are a terrible loss to the soul.

Ambition and lust for power and money motivate people powerfully. But lust and greed enslave a person and, though they seem to lead to outward success, work inner devastation. In our society, from the lowest to the highest levels of life and position, we find people who have succeeded, but only at the cost of their souls. This applies also to the church. The church loses its soul and becomes spiritually powerless when its leaders, great and small, are driven by their lusts.

The opposite way of life is surrender to God and contentment with what He gives. "God opposes the proud but gives grace to the humble" Jas 4:6. God indeed gives to the humble: tasks, the necessities of life, friends, a future, life, everything.

Is it your lusts that drive you? Are they the real motives behind your plans and projects? Or does God lead you and give you what you need? What a pity if, in the course of this life, we gain vast amounts of human praise, while all the time the Lord is against us. In the final accounting we discover that we are bankrupt, with nothing to show for all our efforts as slaves to our greed.

15 / Jesus Blesses Children and Parents

"And he took the children in his arms, put his hands on them and blessed them" Mk 10:16.

WHAT A NEAT PICTURE! Jesus blesses children. These children were fortunate. But they were just ordinary children, cranky, contradictory, forgetful, disobedient, just like our own. We would not be wrong in assuming that the mothers had a good reason for bringing their children to Jesus. Perhaps they were concerned about them. Perhaps they were aware that their children had inherited their weaknesses and faults. Perhaps they were worried about how environmental factors, peer pressure, and other things impacted the children they loved. Perhaps they were conscious of their own inadequacy as teachers of their children.

What could they do with their children when they themselves were inconsistent, argumentative, irritable,

rebellious toward God and His ways with them! For this reason
they brought their children to Jesus. They wanted the best
possible future for the children they loved. Out of their own
inadequacies, they brought their children to Jesus.

This "children's gospel" opens up its richness for us. It
becomes also "mother's and father's" gospel. When Jesus "took
the children in his arms, put his hands on them and blessed
them," we are promised that Jesus is still prepared to receive
children, to bless them and, in the process, to solve the most
critical problems of child-rearing.

But the Lord will not solve these problems without us; his
hands, laid in blessing upon children, are a sign to show how we,
risking failure, are to train our children. Shouldn't we take the
naughty child in our arms, put our hands on him, and bless him?
Love is more powerful than sternness. God's love, neither soft
nor lacking in firmness, is not only for children, it is for unloving
parents, too.

16 / Christ Heals the Whole Person

"Do not be anxious about anything" Phil 4:6.

IS THERE another word in the Bible that we need more than
this invitation to holy unconcern? Is there another word that
sounds more unrealistic than "Do not be anxious about
anything?"

This encouragement is deeply rooted in the reality of Paul's
life. He was free from all temporal goals and ambitions. Our
worries are largely worldly concerns. If free from property,
money, dreams of glory, and private plans for the future, we
would certainly not fuss as we do now. As our hearts turn from
worldly to heavenly treasures, we are freed from false anxiety.

A second reason for Paul's holy unconcern was his faith in
the risen, living Lord. "The Lord is near" Phil 4:5. No matter
what happened, the apostle was assured that the Lord was near.

When a modern doctor examines a patient, he is not
satisfied to know about a particular organ. The doctor studies
the whole person, his habits, his past, anything that helps him
understand the cause of the illness. The illness itself is merely a
symptom. The hidden causes of illness are the inner drama of
the patient, factors which shake the foundation of his life.

Anxiety and nervousness indicate something is wrong with our life. Important in their own right, medication, fresh air, or sound sleep will not improve our condition. We cannot overcome anxiety by being told not to worry. Our wrong kind of worry indicates a wrong relationship to God. The Great Physician must examine and care for the whole person. The Physician may use a sharp scalpel as he works on us, but we have no choice, if we want to be healed and gain peace for our souls.

17 / Mercy for the Repentant

"How priceless is your unfailing love! Both high and low among men find refuge in the shadow of your wings" Ps 36:7.

JESUS HAS priceless grace in mind when he tells about the men who sold everything they had in order to buy the treasure hidden in the field and the pearl of great price (Mt 13:44f.) Today we seldom think of these parables of Jesus. We talk a lot about our own ideas of grace. But we will never experience grace, unless we are willing to give up something for it. And not only something, but everything! Christianity without self-denial and world-denial knows nothing of God's priceless grace.

The Lord points to priceless grace when He invites us to ask, to seek and to knock. We want quick results and find it unpleasant to stand, perhaps a long time, knocking and waiting behind a locked door. Impatient with God's plan for justifying the ungodly, we remain spectators without grace.

The most shattering words about priceless grace are those that present the Savior with bleeding wounds, and describe his road of travail from Gethsemane to Golgatha. As God's grace comforts us in our trials, let us not fail to pause before the suffering Savior on the cross. There the proud heart is broken, and God's mercy begins.

We often talk about grace as though the God of all grace simply accepts our misery and sins. In truth, the righteous God approves of no sin, even though He accepts the repentant sinner. We cannot forget that God's grace is priceless, and that we must make peace with our sins.

Ignorant of the true nature of God's grace, we fail to find solutions to problems, release from afflictions, and joy in the security a sinner finds under His wings. Only those who truly struggle can take refuge in God's grace wholeheartedly and find joy. Struggle and joy belong together.

18 / Blessed to Be a Blessing

"Praise be to the God and Father of our Lord Jesus Christ, the Father of compassion and the God of all comfort" 2 Co 1:3.

SOMETIMES we assume that people who need to be comforted belong to a weaker race. Must we not harden ourselves and endure without whimpering whatever comes our way?

The Bible tells us otherwise when it calls God the God of all comfort. True comfort comes from God; His role is that of a comforter. Let no one say that comfort is of little or no significance, for His gracious purpose in the world is realized when the sorrowful and afflicted are comforted.

If you have seriously tried to comfort a person in grief, you have undoubtedly experienced how difficult, if not impossible, it is. Our words have little weight and our empathy is weak. Then it is good to remember that God is both able and willing to comfort. Entrust your friend to God. You may not know how to comfort, but God does. Remember this and you will be freed from trying to squeeze out of yourself what will seem artificial and irritating to your friend. Depend instead on God as the only Comforter.

The Bible calls this world a "valley of tears," and God uses people as His agents to comfort this world. Paul praises God, "who comforts us in all our troubles, so that we can comfort those in any trouble with the comfort we ourselves have received from God" 2 Co 1:4. Only those who have needed much comfort know the art of comfort. So God takes the people He prepares as comforters through deep waters. It is they who are of greatest blessing to others, and many call them blessed.

19 / Taken By the Lord

"Your hearts must be fully committed to the Lord our God" 1 K 8:61.

WHEN THE LORD asks us for our hearts, we may take Him seriously. We may respond positively, desiring sincerely to surrender to Him in our inner life. Have you made this decision and remained faithful?

But many have promised their hearts to the Lord more than once, learning to their shame that good resolutions are often broken. In our hypocrisy we try to reassure ourselves, appealing to human weakness and to the fact that other Christians are no different. We stop our spiritual struggle, and follow the road to spiritual apathy. But if God's gracious work does not allow us to become satisfied with the half-way measures of a divided heart, it dawns on us that we are incapable of giving our hearts to the Lord. The Lord Himself must take our hearts; we do not give it to Him.

This happens in the school of the cross. The Lord teaches us what our heart is really like. Through the internal and external circumstances of life, the Lord shows us that because of our fallen state all we can do is oppose him. We become acquainted with a heart cold toward the Lord and dissatisfied with His ways. We learn the depth of our corruption and sinfulness. We learn with Paul that nothing good lives in us (Ro 7:18) until God reveals to us our corrupt hearts through the cross, adversity, suffering and distress. This is precisely the way the Lord claims our poor hearts. He breaks in by gradually crushing our selfish and proud egos. It hurts our old nature, but it is good for us, for if the Lord does not take our hearts we will remain without the life Christ alone can give.

20 / Pleasing People or Obeying Christ

"If I were still trying to please men, I would not be a servant of Christ" Ga 1:10.

WHY DO WE try to please people? Do we try to be good because we think well of each other? That would be genuinely Christian and right. But, this desire to please people really stems from our lust for power, our pride and our ambition. Personal advantage takes priority over faithfulness to truth and prompts us to do what we think will please others.

At other times, out of laziness, we shy away from anything that makes us uncomfortable, taking the path of least resistance. It is often a struggle for us with our friends, for we depend on them and do not like to cross them. We may find it easier to resist strangers.

The difficulties in trying to please people are obvious. The worst thing is that by seeking to please people we cannot be servants of Christ. The Bible is quite clear about seeking the praise that comes from people: "How can you believe if you accept praise from one another?" Jn 5:44. The two do not mix.

Flattery is the fog of sin that obscures our inner life. Living in a fog, we do not see things as they are. We go astray and become lost. The Bible says that sins can be swept away like the morning mist (Is 44:22). Only forgiveness can bring us back into the sphere of truth and purity, where life is lived realistically in obedience to God. True and noble thoughts arise out of pure hearts. Obedience to God is always more important than pleasing people.

21 / Be Aware of Your Enemy

"For we are not unaware of his schemes" 2 Co 2:11.

ACCORDING TO Jesus, Satan is "a liar and the father of lies" Jn 8:44. That is why he prefers to hide. If nobody believes he exists, Satan accomplishes more.

Satan works in secrecy to seduce and destroy souls that once were awakened. Everything happens quietly, easily, and gradually. The slow road is the sure road to hell. Satan has nothing against your continuing to attend church and even the Lord's Table, as long as he keeps you from noticing changes that occur in your relationship to your Lord. He knows how to arrange things so that there are no signs along your road that point to hell. In this way he cunningly adds to his list of victims.

How necessary then that we uncover Satan's schemes. Paul was familiar with them. Time and again he had encountered the old schemer. In his body he bore the marks of the tormenting power of Satan's messenger (2 Co 12:7). God's Spirit had opened his eyes to see how the schemer worked. Awareness of his schemes is the first condition of victory over Satan. Let us study the Bible, talk to experienced Christians, and examine our own lives, lest Satan's schemes remain hidden from us.

But above all: "Put on the full armor of God so that you can take your stand against the devil's schemes" Eph 6:11. Treacherous schemes, no matter how devilish, can be thwarted, of that we are certain.

> When the forces of Satan
> Do battle against me,
> They cannot hurt me,
> In You I overcome.
> When Your blood they see,
> They shake in their boots.

22 / God Is Faithful

"Have faith in God" Mk 11:22.

IT IS NOT EASY to believe in God with minimal faith. Jesus says the faith of the disciples was the size of a grain of mustard seed (Lk 17:6), so small that it was not worth mentioning. Elsewhere it is said that the Lord will not snuff out a smoldering wick (Mt 12:20). Such is the faith of the disciple. Because faith is so weak, the Lord encourages us to hang on, even though our faith may seem futile and weak.

The mystery of faith is stored in a pure conscience. Whoever tries to be a Christian without obeying his conscience will undermine his faith, as the Bible puts it in 1 Timothy 1:19. Whoever seeks faith must learn to obey.

"In addition to all this, take up the shield of faith, with which you can extinguish all the flaming arrows of the evil one" Eph 6:16. Until the end of life the "flaming arrows of the evil one" fly around us. The Lord says, "Have faith in God." Only the shield of faith can extinguish these flaming arrows.

But how can I have faith in God? Can a person even do anything, for isn't faith totally the work of God? Our question is answered when we note that "Have faith in God" can also be translated, "Look upon God as faithful." Think of God as faithful and you will find evidence of God's faithfulness in your own life and experience. Pay attention to the Bible's declarations about God's faithfulness and you will dare to entrust your entire life in the hands of this faithful God.

23 / Prayer in the Name of Jesus

"You may ask me for anything in my name, and I will do it" Jn 14:14.

IN READING the Bible we often comes across words of Jesus such as these: "I will do whatever you ask in my name" Jn 14:13. "My Father will give you whatever you ask in my name" Jn 16:23. "Until now you have not asked for anything in my name. Ask and you will receive, and your joy will be complete" Jn 16:24.

Obviously a prayer is not acceptable simply because it concludes by mentioning Jesus' name. He did not intend his name to be some magic formula. Rather, Jesus invites us to pray in his name with confidence, so that we ask God to hear us for Christ's sake. Whenever we plead our case before God, unless He is merciful to us for Christ's sake, we have no assurance our prayers will be heard. For that reason we must pray, trusting in Jesus, standing behind him in the safety of his grace.

But clearly these words, "in the name of Jesus," mean far more. Someone who permits us to act in his name shows great trust in us. We can get money from a bank in someone else's name, if that person trusts us. Jesus trusts his disciples when he invites them to pray in his name. He assumes that the disciples ask for things in harmony with his will. Using someone's name means we are prepared to submit to his will and promote his cause. That is what Jesus expects of us. If we are prepared to do his will, no matter how vaguely we understand it, he gives us the right to use his name when we pray.

In the explanation to the *Small Catechism* published by the Church of Finland we are told: "When in our prayers we place our confidence in what Jesus Christ has done in our behalf and at the same time submit to God's will, we pray in the name of Jesus."

24 / Have You Declared Bankruptcy?

"Jesus looked at him and loved him. 'One thing you lack,'
he said. 'Go, sell everything you have and give to the
poor" Mk 10:21.

ONLY ONE thing more! Is this also true of you? Hasn't your
conscience demanded that you let go of many things you did not
think you could relinquish? God's word illuminated the dark
places in your conscience and you discovered new sins in
yourself. God's word has been opened up to you in a new way,
and you are being drawn into the presence of the holy God.

Jesus loved the young man who struggled honestly. Jesus
loves those who want to keep his commandments, rejecting all
sin, deceit, and compromise. This means that a Christian must
take God's law seriously. It must be obeyed unconditionally.
How fortunate we would be to reach the place of the rich young
man with only one more sin remaining!

We notice, however, that this one sin was so dear to the
young man that he could not deal with it. Jesus says, "With men
this is impossible, but not with God" Mk 10:27. A divine miracle
is needed. Struggling against our sins, we reach the point where
we give up. We become bankrupt in regard to our own resources,
including all spiritual striving and even repentance. If we refuse
to admit our bankruptcy, we will walk away sadly from Jesus.
Like the rich young man we will be left outside the kingdom of
God.

25 / Empathy or Sympathy?

"Accept one another, then, just as Christ accepted you, in
order to bring praise to God" Ro 15:7.

WE NEED to willingly and patiently care for one another in the
spirit of Christ. "Accept [take care of] one another, then, just as
Christ accepted [has taken care of] you."

But we must guard against allowing mere human good will
or pity to determine and direct our actions. We often try to help
someone, but not in the spirit of Christ. We are strict where
Christ is gentle, or gentle where Christ is strict. Lacking the
divine spirit of holiness and love, we allow our limited human

emotions to guide our efforts at counseling. We harm rather than help our neighbor.

A person may ask others for advice, even though he knows in his conscience what God wants of him. He asks in the hope that his counselors, feeling sorry for him, will give him permission to do what the Lord has clearly labeled as sin. We need the gift of spiritual discernment, lest we direct people further away from the Lord.

What are we to tell a person who asks for help? He must be directed to inquire from the Lord Himself, to struggle with the Lord until the Lord gets the upper hand, and to surrender to the Lord's will. Directed in his wrestling with God, the person must say to the Lord as Jacob did: "I will not let you go unless you bless me" Gn 32:26. The road to God's blessing includes both struggle and surrender.

26 / There Is Love That Never Fails

"Love never fails" 1 Co 13:8.

WE ARE OFTEN misunderstood or even attacked by people we try to help. We become easily discouraged, and even bitter about our attempts to do good. This should not happen. "Love never fails." Although we feel failure in our attempt to help and understand others, our efforts are not in vain. Even when the forces of hatred and evil in this wicked world appear to be in control, the power of love is stronger.

Christians must not lose confidence in the power of love. If our love is misunderstood or misused, let us remember him whom love led to the cross. The crucified one is our Savior and fountain of blessing. Let us not be afraid if, even in a small way, we are given the privilege of carrying a cross in his company. No matter how it looks, love never fails. Every loving deed, every loving thought will have a positive influence in this world.

As we move through life, we are apt to become stingy with love. We fear impoverishment if we sow love and it produces no harvest. But, love never fails. True Christian love is not diminished or squandered, for its source is not in us. "God is love" 1 Jn 4:16. God is the true fountain of love, a fountain that lasts forever. The hardness of our hearts, our lack of love and our wickedness, have failed to extinguish His love, radiating from the cross of Golgatha in the dark night of humanity.

Sensing that our hearts are empty of true love, our efforts to love will produce purely human and short-lived results. Let us take our place at the foot of the cross, acknowledging our poverty and unworthiness, repenting of our lack of love, and casting ourselves upon God's inexhaustible love.

27 / Power to Endure

"This calls for patient endurance and faithfulness on the part of the saints" Rev 13:10.

GOD'S WORD does not promise easy times and sunny days. "There will be terrible times in the last days" 1 Ti 3:1. But "we have the word of the prophets made more certain, and you will do well to pay attention to it, as to a light shining in a dark place until the day dawns and the morning star rises in your hearts" 2 P 1:19. Today we have reason to give special attention to the prophetic word.

According to the Book of Revelation, "the beast was given a mouth to utter proud words and blasphemies" but only for a limited time (Rev 13:5). "He was given power to make war against the saints and to conquer them. And he was given authority over every tribe, people, language and nation" Rev 13:7. Tribulations overtake the nations. But affliction is not the greatest danger. The worst thing is for people to forsake God inwardly and, in some form or other, to worship the beast. These are the ones "whose names have not been written in the book of life belonging to the Lamb" Rev 13:8.

"This calls for patient endurance and faithfulness on the part of the saints." Only the powerful weapons of endurance and faithfulness will ultimately open the way through the darkness. "The Lord may try us but never forsake us."

Jesus is the Lord. Either he has all power or no power. Since he is the Lord, outside him there is nothing. But such living faith is possessed only by the saints, those set apart for God, cleansed by the blood of Christ, so that they are "blameless" Rev 14:5. When our faith wavers, all we can do is seek the company of God's saints on the narrow way for renewed cleansing in the blood of Jesus. Only these saints have what we all need, patient endurance and faithfulness.

28 / As Within, So Without

"But seek first his kingdom and his righteousness" Mt 6:33

ORDER IS important on all levels of life. From the outward appearance of a person we can judge whether his inner life is in order. If the inner life is in disorder, the person appears restless and all his activities are marked by chaos and weariness. External training must go hand in hand with the training of the inner person.

Disorder is most destructive when it involves the very center of life. Luther explained that the core of humanity is exposed in the presence of death. Death reveals the realilty of at least two things: 1) We can neither control our death nor master our life. No one can "add a single hour to his life" Lk 12:25. Being human means being absolutely dependent upon God in life and in death; 2) Everyone must die his own death; similarly everyone must live his own life. Everyone is responsible for his own life.

These two things, dependence upon God and responsibility before God, constitute the inner core of human personhood. But if this inner core is in disorder, if the person denies his dependence and responsibility, his entire life is off course and in chaos.

Jesus says, "Seek first his kingdom and his righteousness." That is the proper order for life. God must have top priority. Only when this is the case does proper order prevail; only when a person keeps constantly in mind his dependence on God and his responsibility before God does he live his life as a human being. God first!

We must talk about this with those who are spiritually indifferent, so that they might be awakened to seek God in everything. But we must also discuss it with Christians, for even believers are tempted to let other things take the place of their relationship to God.

29 / Conflict Management in the Church

"Make my joy complete by being like-minded, having the same love, being one in spirit and purpose" Phil 2:2.

WE STRUGGLE to express the varying points of view in what we experience in this imperfect world. We differ in levels of development and spiritual endowment. Personal factors, which point to our natural depravity, selfishness, and lack of love, also come into play. With all of these limitations it is no wonder that we cannot avoid differences of opinion among Christians.

But differences of opinion also result in conflict. Throughout history Christians have fought bitter wars over matters of faith. As a result, the Lord's cause has been severely damaged. In the church in Corinth, religious parties were in conflict with each other. Paul had to write to them, "I appeal to you, brothers, in the name of our Lord Jesus Christ, that all of you agree with one another so that there may be no divisions among you and that you may be perfectly united in mind and thought" 1 Co 1:10.

Some people did not take these conflicts seriously, but Paul could not tolerate them. Paul and Apollos got along very well, even though their viewpoints were not alike. Both lived close to the Lord; they had one faith and one baptism. But their disciples and followers no longer understood each other. They clung to certain forms of expression, failing to delve into the meaning of their experiences. These friends of the apostles argued with each other and formed parties. This, says Paul, must not be tolerated. By discussing matters they must learn to understand each other's thoughts. Drawn closer to the Lord, although they do not think alike, they will understand and love one another.

We have reason to follow Paul's advice. We must move beyond doctrinal language which separates us, to the unifying life of faith which that language seeks to express. The closer to the Lord we are, the better we can avoid conflict among believers and love one another despite our differences.

30 / Do Not Go By Your Feelings

"Train yourself to be godly" 1 Ti 4:7.

CHRISTIANS used to talk about "dry repentance." This phrase seems to suggest that one must continue to read the word and pray regardless of how one feels. This is sound psychological advice.

It is well known that every experience leaves its mark on the soul, affecting our whole inner life. We may not have been aware of what was happening but the impressions stayed with us. Our inner life is like a thick pad of extremely thin sheets on which are printed all that we have experienced. When the opportunities arise, even things from the distant past are brought to mind without invitation,hsometimes against our will. Then it becomes clear what we have unknowingly carried within us all along.

If faithful cultivation of the word and prayer has filled the secret containers within us with impressions from God's world, we carry them with us, even though unconsciously. God, whose grace has made it possible, can in His good time bring this wealth into our consciousness. When that happens we will harvest what we have sown in the Spirit.

It is not a waste of time, therefore--even from a psychological point of view--to engage in "dry repentance." God rewards faithfulness in little things. The importance of Christian customs to our spiritual life is greater than we think.

31 / We Are Not Alone in Death

"Do not let your hearts be troubled. Trust in God; trust also in me" Jn 14:1.

WHAT IS the most horrible thing about death? The pain and anguish which open death's door? Or that death puts an end to life and cuts off our plans? The love of life, after all, is characteristic of human nature.

The deepest reason for the horror of death is the conscious and unconscious realization that death ushers us into the presence of the almighty and righteous God. We are taken into

God's judgment hall. Here we experience "victory of death" with its sharp and painful "sting" 1 Co 15:55.

But Jesus has broken off the "sting of death." Death still threatens and pressures us with it, but Jesus has made it ineffective as far as his believers are concerned. Through his blood and death Christ has become our righteousness and has prepared peace with God for us. When death approaches the believer, Jesus Christ approaches God as the sinner's righteousness. Our own righteousness will fail us, but if we believe in Christ, we will be clothed with Christ's righteousness just as we were clothed with Christ in baptism (Ga 3:27). We will be safe, for "there is no condemnation for those who are in Christ Jesus" Ro 8:1.

Jesus guards and protects us in death. Because of his merit we are safe in the presence of God. "He himself is our peace" Eph 2:14.

November

1 / Everlasting Rest Starts on Earth

"These are they who have come out of the great tribulation; they have washed their robes and made them white in the blood of the Lamb" Rev 7:14.

SINCE ANCIENT times Christians have used the first week of November to remember the departed saints. We need the encouragement which comes from remembering the saints. The memory of the blessed deceased gives confidence to those whose warfare is not yet ended. "So do not throw away your confidence; it will be richly rewarded" He 10:35.

Past generations of Christians used Richard Baxter's devotional book The Saints' Everlasting Rest. This everlasting rest is not something that awaits us on the other side of death. Everlasting life begins on earth where God already offers rest for our souls. The dead whom we remember enjoyed this rest already in the midst of their struggles on the earthly journey.

In the life of our Savior we can see what a soul at rest is like. At times Jesus' struggles were bitter. His Father's face was hidden from him on Golgatha, but even then he committed his spirit into the Father's hands. The panic-stricken disciples struggled to save their storm-tossed boat, but Jesus calmly slept. When he was maliciously attacked and reviled, he remained calm. Everlasting rest has to do with finding peace with God by living in union with Him.

When people live by the grace of Christ's atoning blood, their souls find a haven of rest in the midst of storms. "Therefore,

since we have been justified through faith, we have peace with
God through our Lord Jesus Christ" Ro 5:1. This peace is not
based on special feelings and experiences, but on the sure
promises of Holy Scripture. If you desire rest for your soul, open
your heart to these promises and cling to them. Do not neglect
the moments of quiet for prayer and meditation you have every
day, or you will lose inner peace and rest.

2 / Practical Results of Prayer

*"We have not stopped praying for you and asking God to
fill you with the knowledge of his will"* Col 1:9.

EVERYONE who reads the Bible will note how often it
underscores the importance of prayer. Think of Paul, whose days
were filled with activity. Constantly surrounded by people, he
experienced difficulties that taxed his energies. One would think
he had neither time nor energy for intercession. Humanly
speaking, the whole future of the church had been placed on his
shoulders. Yet his letters show clearly that he had time for, and
interest in, individual friends. He prayed for them on a daily
basis.

This emphasis on prayer says that, above all, Paul believed
in a God who listens to prayers. He believed more in God than in
what his own words could do. Unless God maintained the faith
of his friends, nothing could keep them in Christ. Therefore,
Paul remembered his friends when he prayed, trusting that the
Lord would complete His work in them.

Prayer is our most important task. Nothing can replace it.
The place which prayer has in our struggle for wholeness shows
what value we place on our faith as a whole.

What practical results would there be in your life, if you
really believed that prayer is your most important task? Among
other things, frustration with people would change into
conversation with the Lord. Accusations and complaints about
others would change into self-accusations and self-complaints.
You would recognize that your own unbelief was the main
reason things are the way they are.

3 / Measuring the Worth of People

"So this weak brother, for whom Christ died, is destroyed by your knowledge" 1 Co 8:11.

IT IS DIFFICULT to know how to relate to people with whom we are in daily contact. Because of our inner corruption, we tend to elevate ourselves above others, look for faults in them, belittle their good qualities, offend them, and misinterpret even their best intentions. If someone is, in some sense, weak, poorly endowed, and struggling to make it, we feel justified in looking down on him. We pay no attention to his way of thinking and doing things. We relate to others according to the value we put on them. We may not show this outwardly, but the look on our face and the tone of our voice tell what we think about them.

The Christian attitude toward others is based on the value we see in people. But the measure Christians use to establish human worth is different from the natural one. Paul has this measure in mind when he warns the Corinthians about their haughty attitude toward people less enlightened in matters of Christian faith. It is important, he says, not to offend the weak brother, for whom Christ also died. The worth of an individual cannot be measured by his spiritual, moral, or other qualities. His worth is established by Christ's death. Through the blood of God's Son he, too, is God's child.

How different our fellowship and common life would be if we always kept this in mind! We would neither despise nor look with contempt on anyone who lacked knowledge or training or who, in other ways, we considered to be below par. Even though I do not like another, since Christ died for him I must relate to him with all possible respect, patience, and tact. Christ has loved him with the same love he has given me. I must love him as myself. As a certain hymn puts it:

The ship must always lie
In anchor near the cross.

We need to spend more time near the cross, if we are to learn to relate to one another in the right spirit.

4 / Sincerity and Spontaneity

"The Lord protects the simplehearted" Ps 116:6.

BEING SIMPLEHEARTED does not mean being ignorant or stupid; it means being sincere and straightforward. The New Testament sees simpleheartedness as an important Christian virtue. Wherever there is sincerity of heart, we can experience joy even though life's provisions may be meager. The early Christians "ate together with glad and sincere hearts" Ac 2:46. In fact, true and spontaneous joy comes only when our hearts are sincere.

Christian simpleheartedness is, first of all, sincerity in relationship to Christ. Paul was afraid that his friends' minds might "somehow be led astray from...sincere and pure devotion to Christ" 2 Co 11:3. For, only in Christ's care can the heart become and remain sincere.

The ways of the world are devious, but "the Lord protects the simplehearted." Even on his best behavior a Christian finds it difficult to maintain the sincerity of his heart. True sincerity gave Paul Nicolay the motto for his life: "Never do anything that feels doubtful."

Many gifted people make serious mistakes and become corrupt because they do not strive to do what is right, but do what seems advantageous instead. A sincere heart that does not try to calculate one's own profit will keep a person on the right road, for "the Lord protects the simplehearted."

5 / God Forgives--and Forgets

"If you, O Lord, kept a record of sins, O Lord, who could stand?" Ps 130:3.

SOMETIMES it happens that things on our mind prevent us from conversing freely and spontaneously. We know something about an individual that disturbs us. Others may think he is important and honorable, but we know that is not the whole truth. Perhaps by accident we witnessed something about which others know nothing. No matter how we try to forget it, we cannot erase it from our minds, and it disturbs our conversation.

"If you, O Lord, kept a record of sins, O Lord, who could stand?" The Lord has witnessed everything about us, even the things no one else has seen. He knows our secret thoughts and desires; He sees our inner life, so badly bruised by sin, which we are ashamed to reveal to others. What would happen to us, if He kept it all in mind? We could not breathe easily for a moment; we could not approach Him in prayer; we could not put our trust in Him.

The remarkable thing is that God does not keep our sins in mind; rather, He forgives them. For Christ's sake we have forgiveness of all our sins. "In him we have redemption through his blood, the forgiveness of sins" Eph 1:7. God erases them from His records, so that they are no more! In spite of our sins, we can live with Him as children with a Father who does not remember the bad things His children have done. Christ came "to redeem those under law, that we might receive the full rights of sons" Ga 4:5. And now, God treats us as His "darlings", for the sake of Christ.

6 / A Small Word That Means Everything

"Go and sell all you have" Mk 10:21 (TEV).

"All things are ready" Mt 22:4 (KJ).

IT IS JUST a small word, but how rich in meaning: "all." "Go and sell all you have."

When the word of God touches our conscience we tend to begin haggling. We accept what suits us; refusing to submit unconditionally. Yet that is what the Lord expects. It's all or nothing.

True spiritual awakening means that a person is inwardly constrained to stand unconditionally before God. Such a person cannot even imitate a half-hearted, lukewarm Christian. Everything must be sold when the Lord commands. All sins must be put away; every temptation must be resisted.

In the course of years, especially if they have been spent in half-hearted struggle against sin, the conscience loses its edge and the person finds loopholes in what the Lord means by "all." Experience teaches us that the direction of life is set during the early years, making it especially important that young people are taught the absolute necessity of unconditional obedience. If we are not honest with the Lord in our early years, it will be virtually impossible to become true followers of the Lord in later years.

So, "throw off everything that hinders and the sin that so easily entangles" He 12:1. And that means every sin, with no exceptions.

In the demand of "all" we hear the harsh sound of the law. However, it really is a very liberating word. As long as we haggle, we are in inner bondage to both God and people. "The sorrowful soul simply cannot sing, as long as it's caught in the snare of sin." The person who haggles with the Lord has neither inner harmony nor joy.

But, let us take a closer look at the way the Bible uses the word "all." "All this is from God, who reconciled us to himself through Christ" 2 Co 5:18. God will hurl "all our iniquities into the depths of the sea" Mic 7:19. "You have put all my sins behind your back" Is 38:17. Just as we are asked to sell everything, unconditionally, we are told to leave our salvation in the hands of Christ, also unconditionally. The call goes forth, "Come to me, all you who are weary and burdened" Mt 11:28. All things are in God's care.

7 / Fruit Has Seeds of New Life

"If a man remains in me and I in him, he will bear much fruit" Jn 15:5.

WHAT KIND of fruit is Jesus talking about? Many misunderstand, assuming that Jesus means something that is very spiritual: inner piety and quietness, constant prayer, humble acceptance of God's ways, powerful spiritual experiences, and similar things. They are wrong.

Consider the fruit of a tree like the apple tree. What is its purpose? Is the purpose of the fruit found in itself or in its beauty? Hardly! When the fruit is ripe, the tree drops it, so that it might produce new life, a new apple tree. In this way the tree loses its fruit in order to propagate life in the form of an apple tree. This is what Christ expects of the fruit his disciples are to bear.

Christian fruit is a matter of service to others, of love and help. Remember what Jesus said about the final judgment? It will have nothing to do with our spirituality, but only our service. The people on the right side cannot even recall any good works; they had dropped their fruit and lost it.

A person who constantly observes his spirituality and strives for deep experiences is egocentric, incapable of living for others. Unaware of what he is doing, he seeks, in his spirituality, to collect stamps to trade with God. But one who is aware of his total corruption and state of condemnation is forced to live by grace for Christ's sake. He is changed into a quiet and humble person who begins to live for his neighbor. Such a person bears fruit for Christ.

8 / Grief Can Be Good for You

"It is better to go to a house of mourning than to go to a house of feasting" Ec 7:2.

PEOPLE nurture hopes that are in harmony with their desires. We hope for what we want. We are fortunate, however, that we do not always get what we hope for, because we are unable to see clearly when the time comes to choose. God must often lead us through the ruins of our hopes to teach us to put our trust in Him.

The Bible points this out when it says that "it is better to go to a house of mourning than to go to a house of feasting," and that "those who sow in tears will reap with songs of joy" Ps 126:5. God does not discipline just for the fun of it. He does not trouble a person just to tease him. He has no other way to stop us in our tracks when we are on the wrong road. He disrupts our plans and crushes our hopes only to help us understand that His road is the right one.

As we sit among the ruins of our hopes, we need to be encouraged to remain silent and reflect on what God wants to teach us. Silence must not be idle silence, spiritual inactivity, but inner reflection on God's word and the state of our heart. The goal of our inward look is that the evil of the heart might be revealed and the wrong road rejected. We need to be encouraged to remain silent so that the Lord might speak to us.

In the house of mourning we learn to cry to the Lord with our whole heart. We also learn to value God's word. "Trouble and distress have come upon me, but your commands are my delight," says the psalmist (Ps 119:143). Precisely in times of trouble and distress, God's word becomes more precious than one's own thoughts.

9 / Has the Holy Spirit Got You?

"So I say, live by the Spirit, and you will not gratify the desires of the sinful nature" Ga 5:16.

THE BIBLE teaches about the Spirit of God that works in our lives, guarding us at all times. It is a new and strong spirit that strengthens the mind, enabling us to withstand temptations. It is a willing spirit that disciplines the selfishness within us, creating a desire to serve others. It is a spirit of grace and prayer that revives dead faith, loosening the tongue of the child of God to speak His word. This spirit gathers dead bones and breathes life into them.

These are Old Testament testimonies about the spirit which God gives His people. We who live in the New Testament era know that God has given all this to us with the Holy Spirit. "Those who are led by the Spirit of God are sons of God" Ro 8:14.

Let us not make the mistake of thinking that we must grow inwardly to the point where we are able on our own, albeit it with God's help, to live as God's children. This will never happen. We will never have the kind of inner self that will discipline itself, protect us in temptations, make us willing to serve, prompt us to pray, or revive our dead faith. The Spirit we need is God's Spirit. Everything depends on God's Spirit, which still wants to do God's work in us.

We must guard our hearts, but we are to pray for and await the Spirit. If the Lord does not give His Spirit, all of our efforts are for nothing. If He withdraws His Spirit, everything collapses.

As someone wisely put it: "It is not hard for us to get the Spirit, but it is hard for the Spirit to get us."

10 / The Church Grows from Within

"Great fear seized the whole church and all who heard about these events.... Nevertheless, more and more men and women believed in the Lord and were added to their number" Ac 5:11, 14.

IN THE PRAYER of the church we pray: "Save and defend your whole Church..., and strengthen it through the Word and holy sacraments." These words say something fundamental about the life of the Church. The Word of God and the sacraments are the tools we use for the building of the Church, as well as for maintaining it.

Sometimes we do not think so. Instead of Word and sacraments, we keep an eye on the size of the membership of the congregation. We set up various activities to draw people into the life of the church. We rely on wisdom, learning, and talents. We ask, "What do the educated or the working people think about the church?" before we plan our programs. The fact of the matter, however, is that God Himself maintains His Church. And He does it with His Word and sacraments.

The church is threatened by enemies on the outside, but the greater danger is within. The story of Ananias and Sapphira in the Book of Acts illustrates this internal danger. The fault is in us, our insincerity and selfishness. We cannot blame outdated forms of organization or programs, lack of gifted ministers, or lack of funds. Our hearts are not right with the Lord, even if we are pious and blameless on the outside.

We can fight such internal enemies of God's church only by letting God's Word and sacraments do their work in us. The word must be allowed to expose the deceitfulness of our hearts, the filth and guile that parade in cloaks of piety. The word must crush our hardened hearts to the point of tears. The word needs to convey to us that in God's church the wounds of Christ still cleanse from all sin and corruption, and that in the sacraments Christ himself seeks us to unite us with himself.

We must open our hearts to God's Word and sacraments.

11 / Heart to Heart with God

"Pray continually" 1 Th 5:17.

PRAYER is heart to heart talk with God. Just as true prayer cannot be limited to particular places, it cannot be restricted to special occasions. Of course, regular times for prayer have their place. It is said of Daniel that "three times a day he got down on his knees and prayed, giving thanks to his God, just as he had done before" Dn 6:10. The early Christians observed the Jewish hours of prayer (Ac 3:1). Numerous Christians since then have disciplined themselves to observe regular times of prayer.

The importance of Christian custom in the matter of prayer must not be minimized. When we are told that Jesus went into the synagogue on the Sabbath day "as was his custom" Lk 4:16, we see him as the model of faithfulness for Christians of all times.

But true prayer cannot be limited to special occasions. Prayer is constant fellowship with the Lord. We yearn for the Lord day and night. Our sorrows and worries turn our faces toward God. As we take up our tasks we leave them in the Lord's hands. Our hopes for the future turn into prayers. When we approach another person, we pause before the Lord for the right words and the right loving attitude. No matter the problem, everything becomes an invitation to prayer. Perhaps this constant prayer is more than our talking to God. Our constant prayer is listening in silence as the Lord talks to us and gives us what we need at the moment.

12 / The Powerless Need Power

"Yet to all who received him, to those who believed in his name, he gave the right to become children of God" Jn 1:12.

THE GREEK word can mean both "right" and "power." But, power conveys the original meaning more accurately. Those who receive Jesus and believe in his name are given power to become children of God. If John had meant the right to become children of God, we might think that a person can become a child of God if he has the proper credentials.

The use of the word power indicates that to become children
of God we need to overcome powers that will not yield to our own
strength. Only those who believe in Jesus are put in contact
with a source of power greater than the powers of evil. Only
God's power can overcome sin, death, and the power of the devil,
which hold us captive.

You feel powerless; even your family and friends are aware
of it. You do not need a stronger ego, so that you might live a
more powerful Christian life. On the contrary, give up your
attempts at self-help and believe in the blessed name of the Lord
Jesus. His power will become evident only when your power
becomes non-existent. His power alone is able to free you from
Satan's bondage so that you can enter the kingdom of God. He
will give you his own power to enable you to live as a child of
God.

13 / Bearers of Peace

"When you enter a house, first say, 'Peace to this house'"
Lk 10:5.

"THE BISHOP arrived on Saturday, and we had a special
festival. We received much encouragement from him. It was as
though the peace of God had entered my room with him. How I
wish I could be with him more often." These words are from a
letter written by Wilhelm Malmivaara in 1888; the visitor was
Bishop Gustaf Johannson. On this pastoral visit, as on all his
visits, the Bishop was a bearer of peace to homes and hearts.
The Lord must have had something like this in mind when he
briefed his disciples: "When you enter a house, first say, 'Peace
to this house. If a man of peace is there, your peace will rest on
him.'"

Beautiful greetings of peace have no meaning, if the
messenger himself has no peace to share. The peace of the Lord
is not something we can share with just anybody. The oriental
shepherd understood peace as including two elements:
boundaries that were safe and neighbors that were near. The
shepherd feels insecure if he knows that things are not in order
along the border of the fields where his sheep are grazing. He
feels restless if he is not on friendly terms with fellow
shepherds, who in a moment of danger could come to his rescue.

This helps us understand the peace of the Lord. There must be no border problems, and we need to be on friendly terms with God. After all, our only true helper and friend is the living God.

Whoever tends to these two things in his own life becomes a child of peace and a bearer of the Lord's peace to restless souls.

14 / God Is Alive and Active

"Jesus said to them, 'My Father is always at his work to this very day, and I, too, am working" Jn 5:17.

IT OFTEN SEEMS that God is inactive. We see the works of people around us. We see our own works. But there seem to be no signs of the works of God. What a relief it would be to see God at work in our world in both important and unimportant matters. But we do not see Him.

In our struggle for wholeness, we become depressed when we see only our own works and how they turn out to be evil. It is hard to imagine that God is active in such a life. God remains hidden.

But, God is a living God, even though He is out of sight. Luther, from whom God often hid Himself and whose soul was often on the verge of despair because he could not see the works of God, learned a vital truth in these experiences. In a sermon he said, "God is closest when He is farthest, and farthest when He is closest." People will grow tired and weary, withdrawing into solitude because they need rest. But God "will not grow tired or weary, and his understanding no one can fathom" Is 40:28. When God conceals His works from us, it is part of His plan.

The Lord finds no pleasure in hiding from us. He does it with our welfare in mind; He wants to put our old nature to death. The times when the Lord allows us to languish in awareness of His absence are necessary and wholesome for us. When the Lord seems to be far away, He may actually be close at hand, very active in our behalf.

In the Book of Job this truth is stated in words that have given great comfort to those who are struggling: "For he wounds, but he also binds up; he injures, but his hands also heal" Job 5:18.

15 / The Divine Order of Salvation

*"Those who belong to Christ Jesus have crucified the
sinful nature with its passions and desires"* Ga 5:24.

PAUL DOES NOT SAY that we belong to Christ by crucifying
our sinful nature. That would be the way of the law. He says
that we first belong to Christ and then, as we live as his people,
we will crucify the sinful nature with its passions and desires.

The first step is to belong to Christ. "You are all sons of God
through faith in Christ Jesus" Ga 3:26. The same truth is
expressed in Eph 2:8: "For it is by grace you have been saved,
through faith --and this not of yourselves, it is the gift of God."
Note that it is not faith that saves us, Christ does. Through faith
we are God's children, united with Christ. This happens through
the Word and sacraments in which Christ lives and acts. Paul
adds: "...for all of you who were baptized into Christ have clothed
yourselves with Christ" Ga 3:26. We belong to Christ because of
our baptism.

This means that all who have been baptized have "crucified
the sinful nature with its passions and desires," if they are living
in the grace of baptism. Baptism means "not the removal of dirt
from the body but the pledge of a good conscience toward God."1
P 3:21.

Because Christ's blood will "cleanse our consciences from
acts that lead to death" He 9:14, we have hope. As the sinner
returns daily to the safety of Christ's blood, appealing to the
grace that is his through baptism, his conscience is cleansed. In
this way the sinful nature is crucified with its passions and
desires.

Our sinful nature does not die; until the very end it spews.
forth its filth. But if we live under the protection of Christ's
blood, daily asking for and receiving forgiveness, the flesh is
crucified. And then, when we die, we will get rid of it
permanently.

16 / The Creator Is Still Creating

"For us there is but one God, the Father, from whom all things came and for whom we live; and there is but one Lord, Jesus Christ, through whom all things came and through whom we live" 1 Co 8:6.

WHEN WE TALK about creation, we often think of the dawn of time when God created the heavens and the earth and everything in them. The Bible, however, teaches that God continues to create. Every flower of the field and bird of the air is in His hands. Were He to withdraw His hand everything would disappear. But, God continues His work of creation.

God's purpose is realized through the natural orders that express His will. He wills, for example, that people work. That is one of the fundamental laws of His world. Marriage is another natural order. God wills that a man and a woman be united for life. In marriage they fulfill God's purpose, especially through children for whom they provide a home. The state is another order of creation. It is God's will that order and justice prevail in society. God has entrusted the maintenance of a just order to the state. We must realize that God continues to achieve His purpose in this world through these orders.

God is always active in our lives. As the Bible says, "In him we live and move and have our being" Ac 17:28. But, we sin when we willfully break His divine laws. In a world created by God we rebel and turn from Him. The redemption which Christ accomplished is intended to save us from our disobedience, so that living in God we might observe His orders. We are meant to be co-workers with God, servants in His work of creation. When this truth dawns on us, we find a wonderful and thrilling goal for our lives.

Some day God will make everything new. Suffering and tears will be no more; afflictions will be a thing of the past. Eternal Sabbath rest is assured for the Lord's people. For now we have war, struggle, trouble and toil, not merely because of our sins, but also because we are in the midst of God's current activity, His continuing creation.

17 / What Are We Waiting For?

"What kind of people ought you to be? You ought to live holy and godly lives as you look forward to the day of God and speed its coming" 2 P 3:11f.

THE EXPECTATION of Christ's return pulsated among the early Christians. "Time is short!" They felt that the Lord's return was near!

Modern Christians do not seem to feel this way. No wonder our lives lack the richness and vitality of the New Testament writings. Christ's return is not an afterthought but an essential element of Christian faith. The church that is not waiting for its Lord is living far from him.

What does it mean in practice to wait for the Lord's return? It means that we must ask how all our affairs will look in the light of the day when Christ is Lord over the whole world. Consider today's tasks, joys and sorrows, defeats and victories. What significance will the things you do today have on that Great Day? Will they hold up under scrutiny? Were they worth the trouble? Will your defeats of today appear as defeats then? Will your victories remain victories?

Someone has suggested that biographies ought to start with a person's death, not birth. The end of life shows what has endured in the person's life. Similarly, the history of the world ought to be evaluated from the vantage point of the end, the day of the Lord's return. This is exactly what the Bible does. It does not give a detailed history of the world, but it teaches us to view life in the light of the Great Day, the day of the Lord's enthronement.

"That day is coming!" How fortunate it would be, if we who are so vain, who imagine ourselves to be so important, would wake up and await the coming of the Lord's day. A new season of spiritual blessings would be ours as a church and as a nation.

18 / The Lord Takes the Initiative

*"Jesus reached out his hand and touched the man. 'I am
willing,' he said. 'Be clean'"* Mt 8:3.

A POET DESCRIBES the hands that are needed to do the Lord's
work. My hands were filled with jewels, which sparkled like
diamonds in a golden ring, he says. But then the blood-red and
scarred hands of the Lord touched my hands. The jewels, which
were of this world, dropped to the ground. The Lord said to me,
"Empty are the hands of him who does my works."

My hands were dirty, the poet continues. They had become
dirty in the work I had been doing. Once more the blood-red
hands of the Lord touched my hands and they became clean. The
Lord said, "Clean must be the hands of him who does my works."

Then the poet tells about his restless hands. They had been
in a hurry; no time to fold in prayer. But the Lord touched them
with his peaceful hands and said, "Quiet the hands of him who
plans to walk my ways."

Finally, the poet tells about powerful hands needed for
heavy work. But when the Lord touched these hands with His,
the garlands of glory dropped to the ground. And the Lord said,
"Your hands must be in my hands, only then will my work be
done."

With these thoughts the poet has called attention to
something we easily overlook. With what kind of hands are you
working? God's work can be done only with empty hands, clean
hands, peaceful hands, and hands placed in the Lord's hands.
Furthermore, the poet has seen into the depths of the matter:
the Lord touches human hands and makes them empty, clean,
and peaceful and takes them into his own. Many try to empty
and cleanse and quiet their hands and place them in the Lord's
hands. It does not work. In this matter, the Lord must take the
initiative.

19 / The Cross Has a Purpose

*"If anyone would come after me, he must deny himself
and take up his cross and follow me"* Mk 8:34.

A CROSS belongs in the life of every Christian. The Lord
himself sees to it that each one has a cross.

The cross brings solitude by calling its bearer out of the
hustle and bustle of life. It brings humility by teaching us to
think soberly about ourselves. Normally, we entertain only
positive thoughts about ourselves. We assume we are wiser than
others, able to judge everything and everybody. Assuming we
know what needs to be done, we stick our nose into everybody's
business. Under a cross, a person learns to recognize his
limitations.

God crushes our pride by giving us a cross. Under the cross
we become aware of our impatience and our unwillingness to
submit to God's ways. We may hold a high opinion of ourselves
and our piety; under the cross we realize, to our sorrow, that our
heart seeks and loves only itself and rebels against God. Such
realization humbles our proud egos; we run out of words and we
stand defenseless before God and others.

These lessons are not easy. The cross bears the cross-bearer,
bringing quietness into our lives. "God loves the humble and the
quiet." And quietness conceals a great blessing.

20 / God's Rules Are to Be Followed

*"If anyone competes as an athlete, he does not receive the
victor's crown unless he competes according to the rules"*
2 Ti 2:5.

THE BIBLE has a lot to say about discipline. Instructions and
commandments must be learned and remembered. As Paul
wrote, "For you know what instructions we gave you by the
authority of the Lord Jesus" 1 Thess. 4:2.

Lutheran Christians like to talk about the total depravity of
human beings, which makes us incapable of good deeds. We can
be saved only by God's grace. That is correct, but grace does not
negate God's commandments! A child of God, living by grace,
needs to live under the discipline of God's law every day.

Paul "read the law" to the early Christians. "Do you not know that the wicked will not inherit the kingdom of God? Do not be deceived: neither the sexually immoral nor idolaters nor adulterers nor male prostitutes nor homosexual offenders nor thieves nor the greedy nor drunkards nor slanderers nor swindlers will inherit the kingdom of God" 1 Co 6:9f. Paul adds to this list of carnal sins, in Galatians 5, the sins of "hatred, discord, jealousy, fits of rage, and selfish ambition."

Throughout the New Testament letters we read: "Whoever does not love does not know God, because God is love" 1 Jn 4:8. For the Christian the new commandment of love is first and foremost.

Do not try to be a Christian without the commandments of God! Learn them, remember them, and follow them. And how do we learn them? The psalmist answers: "It was good for me to be afflicted so that I might learn your decrees" Ps 119:71.

A self-confident person cares little about God's will. But, when God humbles us, knocks us off our high horse, and disillusions us, then His commandments become sweet to us, no matter how sharply they pierce our self-love and pride.

The Bible describes the life of a watchful Christian as a disciplined life. We must follow God's discipline, which lays a heavy hand on the proud soul and binds him to His holy law.

21 / We Are Responsible

"Give an account of your management" Lk 16:2.

SOME CHRISTIAN groups classify certain of their members as committed. They are the ones who bear responsibility for the affairs of the group with prayers and offerings.

But responsibility does not belong only to a certain select group of individuals. God has given each of us responsibilities, creating us as responsible beings.

This becomes clearer when we consider family life. Spouses cannot be freed from their responsibility to each other. Parents cannot escape responsibility for their children. No decision of a court can nullify the fact that this man and this woman are the father and mother of this child. Together they constitute a threesome, even if divorce breaks up the family. From this perspective, divorce is seen as contrary to the order of life established by God.

Responsibility extends beyond mutual satisfaction of physical needs. It includes our spiritual need, too. Even if mother and father do not believe in God, they are responsible for the spiritual life of their child.

As the church year draws to a close, we are asked to reflect on the judgment that Christ will eventually carry out. Each person will then become fully aware of the responsibility he had during his lifetime. We will be asked to give an accounting of how we handled our responsibilities. It is God's intention that we will rise from our indifference and realize the immense responsibility placed on our shoulders.

> Sleep no more, O sinner,
> Be aroused in time.

22 / You Are Not Alone

"I will search for the lost and bring back the strays. I will bind up the injured and strengthen the weak" Ez 34:16.

THERE ARE TIMES when you feel that no one cares about your soul, that no one prays for you, that no one grieves over your defeats; in other words, no one cares about you or your life's journey. It makes no difference to anyone where and how you live, whether you are a victim of sin on the road to hell, or whether you are a straggler on the narrow road. Even among Christians, the mutual care of souls is badly neglected. As a result, many souls are withering in loneliness, falling ever deeper into the mire of sin. When people get together they talk about everything but the most important thing.

In the absence of mutual love and care, those who suffer can be comforted by the word of the Lord. They have no human friend to seek them out, bind their wounds, or strengthen them. Sometimes they are not even aware of their own predicament. But there is one who is concerned; the Lord, who does not want a single sinner to be lost. He says, "I will search for the lost." That's a promise!

If you are such a lonely soul, focus on the words, "I will." You have a Helper who can and wants to help you. It helps when we can bare our souls to a fellow human being and share our troubles. But that is not an absolute prerequisite of salvation. We have the right to open our hearts to the Lord himself. "For there is one God and one mediator between God and men, the man Christ Jesus, who gave himself a ransom for all men" I Ti 2:5f.

23 / Fear God and Hate Sin

"To fear the Lord is to hate evil" Pr 8:13.

"GIVE ME A HUNDRED MEN who fear only God and hate only sin, and I will perform miracles with them," said John Wesley. These words express God's plan for His own.

Fear only God. Our lives are filled with false fears. Fear of people is a common agent of destruction. It causes us to be silent when we ought to speak and to speak when we ought to remain silent. We are each others slaves.

He who follows the Lord must fear only God. But let him truly fear God. Let him honor the Lord's commandments. The great modern tragedy is not that the fear of God has generally disappeared but that those who acknowledge the Lord do not honor God's truth. Those in greatest danger are the Christians to whom eternity is not real and God's will not the highest priority.

But also hate nothing but sin. We know how to hate, but too often we direct our hatred at people who for some reason or other repel us. A child of God must hate only sin. He must really hate sin, especially the sin he carries within himself. Instead of defending our weaknesses and faults, we must learn to hate our sins. What a fantastic house-cleaning would take place among Christians, if they really hated nothing but sin.

Only those who fear God and hate sin are useful tools in the hands of the Lord. Their number may be small, but their accomplishments are great in spite of their weaknesses.

24 / When Feigned Faith Fails

*"Immediately Jesus reached out his hand and caught
him. 'You of little faith,' he said. 'Why did you doubt?'"*
Mt 14:31.

THERE WAS nothing strange about Peter's sinking into the
waves as he walked across the lake. Jesus had given him his
word, and if he had clung to it his wonderful walk would have
succeeded. But it was not strange that Peter failed to cling to the
word. After all, he was only a beginner in his faith. The wonder
of it is that, when Peter began to sink into the waves, Jesus
reached out his hand and caught him. He could have left Peter
to his own devices, but he didn't.

Jesus was ready to help his friend, whose faith had failed.
Peter himself was unable to reach out to Jesus, so Jesus reached
out to him and caught him. And the story says he did it
immediately.

That's the kind of Lord we have. With his word he has tried
to arouse faith in us. With the strength of our faith we could face
our difficulties. But he does not forsake us when we run out of
faith. He comes to our aid immediately, reaching out to catch us,
since we are unable to reach out and catch him. He saves us.

So let us not struggle to save ourselves. When other
techniques fail, we are tempted to help ourselves by inflating our
faith. We have done that many times, pretending to believe even
though our faith was gone. But, such feigned faith is of no value;
it will not carry us across the waters. Better that such faith fails
us and we feel ourselves drowning. For then Jesus will
immediately come to us, reach out his hand and save us.

Our problem is not that we have too little faith, but that we
have too much feigned faith. When faith runs out, Jesus will
appear and show his power.

> Jesus won't forsake,
> When troubles overtake.

25 / From Dead Works to Living Fruit

"How much more, then, will the blood of Christ... cleanse our consciences from acts that lead to death, so that we may serve the living God" He 9:14.

DEAD WORKS clutter the lives of many Christians. Their faith lacks the pulse, the power, and the joy of life. According to the Letter to the Hebrews, the reason is that their consciences have not been cleansed. The conscience is the core of human personality. If confusion reigns there, all of life is in chaos.

Satan controls a person by establishing himself in the conscience. He appears there as the accuser, robbing the person of inner peace, taking the conscience captive, and enslaving the whole person. It is pointless to try to help such a person by urging him to change his life. He cannot do it! Satan has charge of his inner life.

The renewal of our lives, becoming children of God and walking "in newness of life" Ro 6:4 (KJV), depends on the overthrow of Satan's power in the conscience. That can only occur when the conscience is cleansed. How does this happen? The blood of Christ cleanses our conscience when the Holy Spirit reveals that Christ has redeemed us. Our very real, ugly and unconquered sins have already been borne by the Lamb of God. "The punishment that brought us peace was upon him" Is 53:5. In ourselves we are unworthy, but Christ is worthy and his righteousness suffices to cover all our sins. Satan has lost his claim on us.

Whoever shares in the power of Christ's blood is free to serve the living God. Satan the accuser can no longer keep him from trusting in God. God has become a living reality, and our hearts rejoice in the Lord.

26 / Peace Beyond Understanding

"I myself will tend my sheep and have them lie down" Is 34:15.

WHY ARE OUR SOULS so restless, our hearts so turbulent, and our lives so out of balance? Because we set aside so little quiet time for ourselves, our lives are hectic, requiring more time than we have. But what is the point in running around in our tasks, if we are unable to do them properly because of our inner sickness? "Well prayed is half learned," said Luther. We might add, "Well prayed is half done." We must spend more time in quiet prayer in order to be healed within ourselves.

When the Savior needed quiet, he went up on the mountain to pray alone. We should follow his example and find a place for solitude in the beautiful outdoors, and go there on a regular basis to spend quiet time with God's word. "In quietness and trust is your strength" Is 30:15. Remember the exhortation of the psalmist: "Be still before the Lord and wait patiently for him" Ps 37:7.

The peace of our soul is also disturbed when we entertain the idea that we can do better when we are in charge. Our hectic pace is our own fault; we have not allowed God a part in planning our day. Certainly God does not intend for us to be in several places at the same time.

We stubbornly insist on our own will, thinking we must succeed in everything. But where is it written that we must succeed in everything we attempt? Leave success to God and concentrate on being faithful in the task at hand. He is better qualified to handle the results.

We are tempted to want to be independent and refuse God's help. But, as long as we try by ourselves to remove the ugly stains of sin from our lives, thoughts, language, and actions, we will lack inner peace. Paul says, "Therefore, since we have been justified through faith, we have peace with God through our Lord Jesus Christ" Ro 5:1. Inner peace is for those who believe in the God who justifies the ungodly.

27 / Spending God's Time

"What I mean, brothers, is that the time is short" 1 Co 7:29.

TIME FLIES! Fall is changing into winter. Don't forget that time is short!

The years and decades are from God, but so are the days and hours, even the minutes and seconds. We, on our part, are responsible for the way we spend time; responsible before God, who gives us time to spend according to His will.

Pay attention to how you spend your time. You may not spend your days and nights in sinful pleasure. But do you still waste your time? Of course, God has given you time for rest and leisure. The day of rest was His idea; He wants you to make use of your breaks and vacations. He is especially concerned about mothers, whose days are often much too crowded. But all of us must be concerned about how we use our time. We are to do it properly, that is, according to God's will.

It is not always easy to know what the proper use of time is. Our jobs and family chores often compete for our time with our devotional life and Christian activities. Which shall I do, stay home to do my chores or go to church? Shall I attend committee meetings or various Christian functions? These questions have to be answered, and it is not always clear what we should do.

Be still before God and ask Him to guide you also in the use of time. God has a plan for your life; do not take charge yourself. Let the Lord lead you. But never forget that the time is short!

28 / We Can Be Changed

"Live by the Spirit, and you will not gratify the desires of the sinful nature" Ga 5:16.

OUR LIFE will not improve by our trying to improve ourselves. Self-improvement never produces the desired results. We are to live by the Spirit. Only God's Spirit is able to take control of our sinful nature. Love, joy, peace, patience, kindness, goodness, faithfulness, gentleness, and self-control: these are the virtues we so desperately need in interpersonal relationships. These are "the fruit of the Spirit" Ga 5:22. We may have lost hope because we lack these virtues. From our point of view it is indeed hopeless. But for us Paul's words are true: "Live by the Spirit, and you will not gratify the desires of the sinful nature." Renewal can indeed take place, but only in the Holy Spirit.

Sometimes people get tense when they talk about the Holy Spirit. They have forgotten what Jesus said about the Spirit: "He will bring glory to me" Jn 16:14. To him who lives by the Spirit, Christ will be revealed. If you want to know what happens when Christ is revealed to a sinner, consider what occurs when we "turn our eyes upon Jesus and look full in His wonderful face."

Jesus is glorified when a sinner who has hurt and offended his neighbor looks into the face of Jesus and finds forgiveness and peace. This is what it means to live by the Spirit.

It is not we who are glorified; on the contrary, in our own eyes we become less worthy. But Jesus becomes more precious and more necessary. The ego is crucified; the sinful nature is mortified. But Christ begins to live in us. And our life is renewed through the Holy Spirit.

29 / Now and Not Yet

"Christ in you, the hope of glory" Col 1:27.

HAVING and hoping belong together in Christian faith. A Christian not only has what the Lord has given him, at the same time he longs to enter more fully into the experience of the reality of God. His longing stems from already having received grace.

Faith is constantly changing into hope; hope grows out of faith. The more room Christ finds in the human heart, the more fervent will be the hope of glory. "Christ in you, the hope of glory." The most devout Christians have always yearned most fervently in hope. If the hope of glory is diminished, it is a sign that our life in Christ is not right.

The same holds true of Christian congregations. When Paul wrote to the Colossians, he was thinking of Christ's Church among them. He was thinking about the gospel, which was circulating among the gentiles through the preached word. But Christ does not just circulate in the pagan world; he wants to settle down and take his place in his Church. That is where he wants to live. Churches are, so to speak, the bases for his military operations.

When Christ is allowed to live in his churches, the hope of glory enlivens them. Hope sustains the church in its spiritual warfare, as it tackles its appointed tasks. In hope new possibilities open up in the darkest moments. In hope the church also scans the horizon for signs of the Lord's coming.

30 / Churches Need Pious Awakenings

"Wake up, O sleeper, rise from the dead, and Christ will shine on you" Eph 5:14.

AWAKENING is God's work. The gracious work of God that seeks to awaken people out of the sleep of sin is what we know as God's call.

When God calls, He is not inviting us to embark on a journey toward some kind of Christian ideal. Natural, unregenerate man is in no position to heed such a call. When a person is pressured to make a decision for God and to surrender to Him, the idea seems to be that Christianity is a program that one must adopt. Such thinking does not take into account the sinful corruption of the human heart. Individual evil deeds are seen as sin, but the idea that human nature is sinful, opposed to God, and in love with sin is not recognized.

When God calls us, He confronts us; we see exactly what we are like. We have no place to hide from His holy presence. God sets His unconditional demands before us, and they drive the sinner to the verge of despair. It dawns on us that we love sin and hate God. Our very piety turns out to be sin.

This is what awakening is all about. The eyes of the blind are opened to reality. Beautiful illusions evaporate. But only then does Christ become necessary as a redeemer and reconciler.

There is spiritual movement among us; people talk about awakenings. But, what kind of awakening is occuring? Is God drawing us into His holy presence, where we experience bankruptcy? Or are we pulling away from Him, unaware of the depravity of our hearts and our need for the Redeemer?

December

1 / God's Emancipation Proclamation

"The Spirit of the Lord is on me, because he has anointed me to preach good news to the poor. He has sent me to proclaim freedom for the prisoners and recovery of sight for the blind, to release the oppressed, to proclaim the year of the Lord's favor" Lk 4:18f.

SIN IS a tyrant; it enslaves people. The corrupting influence of sin reaches into the very cells of our bodies. Think of the fear of being caught that haunts the criminal. However, it is not just individual sins that oppress a person; the very essence of sin, unbelief--the desire to be without God--is a millstone around his neck.

Christ came to free us from bondage. He is not interested in patching us up; he wants to turn us "from the power of Satan to God" Ac 26:18. He wants to take charge of our lives.

Luther said that whoever releases a person from a bad conscience performs a greater work than he who conquers an entire city. It is in the conscience that sin, with its accusations, maintains its throne. The gospel, as God's power, overthrows this tyrant. When the Bible says that "the blood of Jesus, his Son, purifies us from all sin" 1 Jn 1:7, it means that the gospel frees a person from his bad conscience. It proclaims that Christ died in our place. At the same time, the gospel brings Christ to dwell and work in our hearts.

Advent points to the Lord's coming. In the message of the gospel Christ comes to us "to release the oppressed."

2 / The Beautiful Christian

"Your beauty should be that of your inner self, the unfading beauty of a gentle and quiet spirit, which is of great worth in God's sight" 1 P 3:4.

PAUL'S ENEMIES in Corinth had explained that he could not be a true servant of God because he was so undemanding and unassuming. Certainly the representative of such a great cause should demand greater attention and respect for himself. He should not be earning a living as a manual laborer. If his was the right cause, he would take his place among the spiritual elite. That is how the agitators sized up the situation and the man. And there were those who listened to them. They knew that through the years people of influence have demanded respect and admiration.

Paul responded to his detractors with the observation that his behavior witnessed to his apostolic authority. "As servants of God we commend ourselves in every way: in great endurance; in troubles, hardships and distresses; in beatings, imprisonments and riots; in hard work, sleepless nights and hunger" 2 Co 6:4f. In another letter he spoke in the same vein: "The Lord's servant must not quarrel; instead he must be kind to everyone, able to teach, not resentful" 2 Ti 2:24.

Christian greatness consists of quietness and humility. He is first who is last and the servant of the rest. Jesus taught this, asking that we should "follow in his steps" 1 P 2:21.

The Advent season calls attention to the meaning of true Christian greatness. The world has its own ideas, and its spirit threatens to contaminate the few who want to watch in spirit and in truth. Much more important than any talk or testimony a Christian can give are patience and quiet, which God recognizes but few others value very highly. Christ comes to us "gentle and riding on a donkey" Mt 21:5. May his image become deeply impressed upon us as we once again sing:

Humility, quiet
God loves.

3 / Leave the Impossible to God

"With man this is impossible, but not with God; all things are possible with God" Mk 10:27.

PERIODICALLY each of us comes up against the impossible. We are given tasks that are beyond us. We run into situations in which we get stuck. These things may have to do with everyday needs and duties, but they may also involve our moral and spiritual life. In either case, they serve as dead end signs. They also give new meaning to the words of Jesus, "All things are possible with God."

We often comfort ourselves with these words, using them as an out in matters that appear impossible. But do we truly grasp the truth of these words? Jesus says that some things are impossible for humans. Despite our experience that this is the case, we do not really want to admit that some things are impossible for us.

Deep within us dwells a spirit of self-reliance. No matter how fenced in we may feel, we insist that we will manage without God's help. Before we can truly learn that all things are possible with God, before we can discover the unlimited possibilities of God, we must thoroughly learn and acknowledge our utter helplessness.

God will show us our capabilities. Whatever impossibility we face, God wants to extend His almighty and rescuing hand. But we will not accept His help until we have declared both moral and spiritual bankruptcy. Only as poor beggars will we be saved by Him. In the Lord's hands we are perfectly and eternally safe, no matter how high the waves and strong the wind.

4 / The Lord Sees Us

"Abraham called the name of that place 'Jehovah-jireh' [the Lord sees]" Gn 22:14.

THE WORDS "the Lord sees" encapsulate Abraham's spiritual experience as he was tested by God. Abraham faced many crises in his life, but, as it is said of him, he walked with the Lord. He was a great spiritual giant, who relied courageously and obediently on the Lord's word. But even he stumbled when he followed his own reason. His heathen neighbors noticed his failings, but what they did not see was how he had stumbled and fallen away from God inwardly. Not even his own family saw this.

The Bible does not give the details of this inward falling away from God which prompted God to test him by asking him to sacrifice his son Isaac; but something had happened. Obedient to God's command, Abraham made his way to Mt. Moriah as through a fire. By the time he returned he had met the living God in an entirely new way, for he called the place "The Lord Sees."

This is how God deals with His people. He does not leave them in their estrangement. "I am very jealous for Zion; I am burning with jealousy for her" Zec 8:2. He will not easily give up on the spirit He has put into His people. Do you find yourself going with heavy steps to your own Mt. Moriah to offer a costly sacrifice? Remember that the Lord is aware of what is happening. He has seen you stumble and fall, both inwardly and outwardly. He wants to put you on your feet again. He sees the heavy steps you are taking. But He also sees how things will come out and how you will rise again.

The Christian who is conscious of God's presence is blessed in his faith. Often we do not see evidence of the Lord and His guidance in our lives. But remember, it is more important that the Lord sees us than that we see Him.

5 / Witness Is Overflow

"For out of the overflow of his heart his mouth speaks" Lk 6:45.

WHATEVER is inside us comes to expression in what we say and do. Take a close look at your speech and your pursuits in the light of this truth stated by Jesus. What do you talk about when you meet people? What direction does your conversation naturally take? Is it not true that, more often than not, our own, dear ego occupies the center of our lives? We prefer to talk about ourselves. Even when we are not ready to reveal our inner secrets, our ego dominates the conversation. We want to suggest that we are special. Perhaps others have not yet noticed it; if they have, they are envious, or they ignore us. So we must display our merit and worthiness. Or maybe we pester people by talking about our illnesses, adversities, and problems. A person full of himself talks about himself.

Our topics of conversation may be harmless, everyday things, which are uppermost in our minds, or they may be obscene things that tag along with the frivolous and the trivial. Why do these topics flow so easily from our lips? Is there nothing better inside of us? Is there only emptiness, vanity, shallowness, and filth?

Christ says he came that we might have life, "and have it to the full" Jn 10:10. Christ's intention is to become our inner treasure. When he comes to live in us, our topics of conversation are radically changed.

6 / Human Weakness and Divine Power

"Once more the humble will rejoice in the Lord" Is 29:19.

HUMILITY brings joy; the proud are never satisfied. Pride is the kiss of death to joy. Proud people are easily provoked and irritated. They see clearly the speck in their brother's eye, but are not aware of the log in their own. Whatever they own and receive they feel they have deserved; they do not know the joy of receiving gifts. Humility teaches a person to be happy about little things. "Once more the humble will rejoice in the Lord."

Humility guards us against temptations. "Pride goes before destruction" Pr 16:18. The proud person is lulled into false security, trusting himself and his own qualifications. But in the decisive moment, when temptation must be resisted, his lack of power becomes evident. Only those who have been humbled will overcome temptation, for awareness of their weakness keeps them close to the Lord. His "power is made perfect in weakness" 2 Co 12:9.

Furthermore, "humility is the guardian of the gifts of grace" (Thomas a'Kempis). Spiritual life is, from beginning to end, the work of God. It is the gift of God's grace. Even the most insignificant signs of spiritual life in you point to God's work in your life. But even God's gifts are quickly lost if you begin to focus on the gift rather than the Giver.

"The precondition of spiritual life," says Thomas a'Kempis, "is not only in your experience of the grace of comfort, but also in your humble and patient endurance of its absence, provided you do not give up prayer or neglect your duties. Do not neglect yourself because of your coldness and paleness." Were we willing to walk the low road in life, on which a person is stripped of his own spiritual resources, we would be much richer. For "humility is the guardian of the gifts of grace."

7 / Spirituality Is Not Enough

"Hold on to what you have" Rev 3:11.

ABOVE THE violent conflicts of history the voice of Jesus is heard, "I am coming soon. Hold on to what you have, so that no one will take your crown." He would say to his own, "Do not focus on what you see around you. Do not let it fill your hearts. Do not find your joy in it; but neither let it frighten and depress you. I am coming. I am coming soon."

The Christian lifts his gaze above the violent storms, not to look upon ideologies and theologies but upon the living, glorified, and almighty Lord. Being a Christian is not a matter of certain thoughts and feelings, but a personal relationship and a struggle. This makes Christianity something both simple and serious at the same time. Above all, though, it is something very liberating. Christ comes and sets everything in place.

"God will put things in order," said Gustaf Johansson, former archbishop of Finland, in talking about God's universal rule. The Lord will do it, and the Christian's share in it is this: "Hold on to what you have, so that no one will take your crown." This requires, first of all, faithfulness in whatever we have received from the Lord, especially the words of Scripture. Deep spirituality is not enough; it can lead us astray. We must be faithful to Scripture, willing to be judged by it, rather than judging it. His word must be treated with respect. Without faithfulness to the Bible we will stray from God and lose our crown.

These words of our glorified Lord are a timely Advent admonition. We must hold on to the words of the Bible or we will suffer great loss.

8 / Christ Rescues from Hell

*"For the message of the cross is foolishness to those who
are perishing, but to us who are being saved it is the
power of God"* 1 Co 2:18.

HELL IS the lot of those who reject the message of the cross.
But, it does not wait until after death; many people experience
hell already here and now. Their inner life is hell; family life
becomes hell; work is a curse; interpersonal relationships are a
tragedy. Things do not improve by being touched up or by adding
entertainment. If we reject the word of the cross, hell is
inevitable --temporal hell first and then eternal hell.

Paul says that the message of the cross is the power of God
"to those whom God has called" 1 Co 1:24. Whoever is distressed
by his sinfulness and yearns for renewal is experiencing God's
call. As a Finnish hymn states, the person who is called by God
"finds hell in his own bosom."

It is futile for a sinner to try to put away sins that have not
been forgiven. Our affairs are not changed until we become
God's friends. Satan tries his best to keep a sinner from
accepting grace. First, by leading him into sin and corrupting his
life, and then doing his level best to keep the sinner from
accepting forgiveness as a sheer gift of grace.

"Let God change you from enemies into his friends" 2 Co
5:20 (TEV). Refuse to listen to Satan's arguments that grace is
not for sinners. Despite the feelings of worthlessness that still
cling to you, trust in the promise of Christ's forgiveness. In doing
so, you become a friend of God and are freed from the tyranny of
Satan. At one time you were far away, but you have now "been
brought near through the blood of Christ" Eph 2:13. The cross
has become God's life-renewing power for you.

9 / Help Is on the Way

"By his wounds we are healed" Is 53:5.

WHAT WILL I DO with my wickedness? Even though I cannot
know the depth of my sins, I experience my wickedness every
day. It constantly surprises me, so that people for whom I wish
only the best have to suffer because of my wickedness. An

awakened soul must complain with Paul: "What I want to do I
do not do, but what I hate I do" Rom. 7:15.
    Others advise: "Don't take it too seriously. People simply are
like that. You're no different. Forget it; others will forget it too!"
But the awakened soul knows all too well that forgetting will not
take care of his wickedness. The Lord's eyes are upon him. He
sees the wickedness others see, as well as our secret sins.
    Someone else suggests: "Overcome your wickedness; get rid
of it!" But what happens when I try? I am like the man who tried
to roll a boulder up a hill. As soon as he paused, it began to roll
back. Many of us carry on such a hopeless struggle with our
wickedness. Exhausted, we give up the struggle, realizing its
futility.
    There is a third way: talk to other people about your
wickedness. That may do good, for it helps us to experience the
shame of our wickedness. Such confession deprives sin of some
of its power, but it does not really help.
    There is a better way. We can bury our wickedness. The
burial place of our sinful nature is at the foot of the cross. No
matter how great and invincible the power of wickedness,
Christ's wounds are still bleeding! For this reason, wicked
people need to take the road of the cross in order to find
forgiveness.

10 / How Shall I Receive Him?

*"Godly sorrow brings repentance that leads to salvation
and leaves no regret"* 2 Co 7:10.

ADVENT IS a time of joyous expectation. Christmas, lying just
ahead, casts a spell of anticipation. The many pre-Christmas
celebrations serve as appetizers for the coming feast. But, in the
midst of such festivities we easily overlook the other side of
Advent. Since ancient times, Advent has been a time for quiet
self-examination. It has been a time of repentance and prayer to
prepare to receive the wonderful message of Christmas. Roman
Catholic Christians, for example, are devoting these weeks
before Christmas to various forms of fasting.
    We all have our sorrows, especially now as we wait for
Christmas. Money problems are only the beginning of sorrows
for many. But, "godly sorrow brings repentance that leads to

salvation and leaves no regret." Not all sorrow "leaves no regret." It can happen, therefore, that we are left without the blessing of Christmas, even though we have had plenty of sorrow.

God wants to deepen our sorrow, so that it will bring repentance. Paul says that godly sorrow produces earnestness, eagerness to clear oneself, indignation, alarm, longing, concern, and readiness to see justice done (2 Co 7:11). A person experiencing godly sorrow begins to abhor his sins, fear God, and want to escape hell. He begins to long for freedom from sin; he fights against wickedness, especially his own; he is willing to discipline himself; he is ready to be humbled.

All of this God wants to bring about in us during this Advent season. Christmas will bring no blessing, unless we are prepared to receive it in the right spirit.

11 / When God Is Absent

"My soul thirsts for God, for the living God" Ps 42:2

IT HAS BEEN said that the present age suffers from a lack of God. We seldom meet people whose very being witnesses to their having met the living Lord. Many people can talk about their religious experiences, but their pious words do not convince us. The abundance of religious language can be like spiritual cosmetics covering up an inner emptiness.

Where are the people who have met the living God, whose whole being radiates the Holy One, whose souls tremble before God, who are filled with holy delight? Where are people who can say to us, "Thus says the Lord?"

When God hides Himself, people increase their own activity and begin to feel important. Consider the important roles people have assumed in religious matters. But, God wants people who are spiritually poor, who know nothing about their own spiritual capital. We need people who pray in their rooms and wait for power from above before they take up their work. Is the church today a praying church?

The central thought of the gospels is faith in the living God. Are we searching and struggling to know such a God? Is it our goal to have our whole life witness to the Holy One? Perhaps we should not be asking so many questions. Perhaps we should be crying out: "My soul thirsts for God, for the living God."

12 / Christ Is Coming Again

"Therefore keep watch, because you do not know the day or the hour" Mt 25:13.

MISCALCULATIONS can be fatal. The more important the matter, the greater the loss. The Bible says that people make a serious miscalculation if they fail to reckon with the Lord's return, warning us: "Therefore keep watch, because you do not know the day or the hour."

One of the consequences of the failure to keep watch is that we begin to oppress each other. When the servant thinks to himself, "My master is staying away a long time," he "begins to beat his fellow servants and to eat and drink with drunkards" Mt 24:48f. Likewise, when the return of Christ is not expected, Christians begin to argue, find fault, and judge each other. They have forgotten that they are servants who must give an accounting, not masters who can lord it over others. A similar spirit takes hold of our homes and lives when the Lord's return is forgotten. With good reason the Bible says, "Don't grumble against each other, brothers, or you will be judged. The Judge is standing at the door" Jas 5:9.

Keep in mind another Bible passage: "Fathers, do not embitter your children, or they will become discouraged" Col 3:21. When a father forgets his own responsibility and accountability to the Lord who is coming, he begins to lord it over his children. He will leave deep impressions on their sensitive souls that will hurt them the rest of their lives.

Giving up on the Lord's return also allows the spirit of the world to take over our hearts. In the words of Jesus, the absence of anticipation of the Lord's return desensitizes the conscience of the Christian in its dealings with the world and "he begins to eat and drink with drunkards" Mt 24:49. Christians begin to fellowship with the world in various ways, and soon the world has gained the upper hand.

A Christian who does not watch stumbles inwardly at first, and then publicly. Christ is returning! His return is closer than we think!

13 / Love and Justice

"*God is love*" 1 Jn 4:8.

AN INWARDLY awakened person sees justice as one of the fundamental laws of life. He is aware of the many injustices that prevail in all areas of human life. Interpersonal relationships, social structures, political dealings, and private lives are all based on lies. As a result, he desires to fight for justice, both in his own life and the lives of others.

When genuine and sincere, this endeavor is sacred. God, who is fair and just, is behind this struggle for justice. "He has showed you, O man, what is good. And what does the Lord require of you? To act justly and to love mercy and to walk humbly with your God" Mic 6:8. Fear of the living God creates the imperative for justice. The fear of God provides moral backbone in the struggle for justice.

However, justice is not the primary factor in life. If the heart of the universe were justice, if the final word of God to individuals and nations were justice, what would happen to us?

Keep this in mind when you witness injustice around yourself and in other people. Do not be too quick to judge others. When your conscience compels you to speak a hard word or to resort to harsh means in behalf of justice, do not forget, even then, that God is love. The fundamental law of the universe is love. Love upholds you; love has been patient with you; love has not become bitter because of what you have done; love suffered on the cross for you.

A proud person would rather talk about justice than love; but a person who has been awakened, and knows who he really is, cannot live if God is not love. God's love makes His justice holy and precious. He who has been awakened no longer sees a need to choose between justice and love. For him it is both love and justice, in that order.

14 / God Is Love--and Just

*"Correct me, Lord, but only with justice--not in your
anger, lest you reduce me to nothing"* Jr 10:24.

HUMBLING is essential; "God opposes the proud but gives
grace to the humble" 1 P 5:5. It is impossible to praise humility
too highly; it is a rare human quality.

But the road to humility is not a scenic route. No one sets
out on this road on his own initiative. God must start us on the
road. We argue and resist, but afterwards we admit that it was
the best thing that could have happened.

Consider the remarkable prayer of the prophet: "Correct me,
Lord, but only with justice--not in your anger, lest you reduce
me to nothing." Even the godly are afraid of being reduced to
nothing. The prophet asks that this not happen to him, but he
acknowledges that the correction is deserved. God has already
humbled him under His mighty hand (1 P 5:6), leading him to
acknowledge his guilt and ask for God's grace to cover his own
lack of merit. He seeks to crawl from under God's anger to God's
grace.

This remarkable prayer encourages all who, in full
awareness of their imperfection, anxiously cry for help. We have
permission to appeal from God's wrath to His mercy, asking to
be corrected with justice, lest we perish.

Jeremiah has preserved for us the Lord's answer: "I will
discipline you but only with justice; I will not let you go entirely
unpunished" Jr 30:11. Christ has truly borne the punishment of
our sins and paid in full our penalty. The Lord promises to be
just, but we still must carry the marks of our sins in order to be
humbled.

15 / Good Children Need No Gifts

"I must stay at your house today" Lk 19:5.

WE ASSUME that peace and love prevail among good people. A
familiar Advent hymn says:

There peace and love do always dwell,
Where Jesus makes his home.

An idealistic view of things assumes that Jesus makes his home with good people. But things are different in reality. "There is no one who does good, not even one" Ro 3:12. This is the bitter truth, experienced even in happy homes. Now and then things come up that cause even a good person to do something evil and corrupt. Peace and love disappear. If it were true that Jesus dwells only with good people, what chance would we have of getting him into our homes?

But the Lord does not dwell with good people. "I have not come to call the righteous, but sinners" Mk 2:17. Sinners need Jesus. How desolate we would be this Advent season, listening to the cries of "Hosanna! Hosanna!" if Jesus were on his way only to good homes! But, he is the Savior of those who are not good! He does not avoid us because we are bad. We keep him away with pretended goodness.

Wherever the Lord Jesus has won for himself even a single member of the family who needs him because of the pain of inner corruption, a new spirit will enter that home. Under Jesus' care cold hearts will begin to thaw. He who has received much forgiveness will forgive much. Having discovered his own unworthiness, he will admonish and instruct others with mercy and patience. Through such a family member, peace and love will enter the home. Just remember that these are not qualities of the person himself, but gifts of Jesus Christ.

As we long for spiritual renewal in our homes, and fear that in the midst of the Christmas rush we may offend and hurt each other, we need to be aware of the true source of the spirit in our homes. Ask Jesus, the source of love and peace, and he will give you living water (Jn 4:10).

16 / Christians Have Convictions

"We take captive every thought to make it obedient to Christ" 2 Co 10:5.

WHAT A STRANGE way to talk! Christ wants to control our thoughts? As a matter of fact, he alone has the right to do that, for he is the truth and the way to truth. We are not capable of seeing things in their true light. We cannot distinguish between right and wrong, truth and lies. We must submit to Christ's leadership in all our thinking.

When this happens, Christian convictions are born. As long as we direct our own thinking, we will pick and choose. What we choose and reject depends on our taste. When Paul talks about people "blown here and there by every wind of teaching" Eph 4:14, he has in mind people who lack convictions. But if our thoughts are obedient to Christ we have given up our right to decide and have convictions. We travel our own road, right behind Christ.

A Christian with convictions has a certain ruggedness about him. He does not fit everywhere. He cannot approve everything. He wants to be faithful to his Lord; feeling captive to the truth as it has been revealed to him.

This does not imply that a person with Christian convictions is called to lord over and judge people who think differently. On the contrary, he loves them; but he is bound by the truth. His path is narrow and he cannot accept everything that is labeled Christian. His thoughts are captive to Christ!

17 / To Watch Is to Love

"What I say to you, I say to everyone: 'Watch!'" Mk 13:37.

CHRISTIAN watchfulness begins with giving God's word due honor. "Blessed is the man who listens to me, watching daily at my doors, waiting at my doorway" Pr 8:34. A spirit of drowsiness has overcome us; our eyes are too droopy to read God's word. When God awakens a person to watchfulness, it always happens when the word comes alive.

Secondly, watchfulness means that a person is alert to the presence of the powers of sin in his own being. The spirit may be willing, but the flesh is always weak, easily causing us to stumble. The Lord says, "Behold, I come like a thief! Blessed is he who stays awake and keeps his clothes with him" Rev 16:15.

Thirdly, a Christian watches in behalf of others and their salvation. He feels responsible for those around him. Certain individuals are especially entrusted to him.

Finally, a Christian who is awake waits for the Lord's return. Most of the New Testament passages that urge watchfulness have to do with waiting for Christ's coming again. It's not easy to stay awake as we watch through the night. But the Christian bears in mind that dawn is near and he remains alert.

All things must be in readiness for him who is coming. Included in a special way is service to our neighbor, whenever and wherever he needs our help. The best way to be a watchful Christian is to love and serve others.

18 / Satan Fosters Foolishness

"Everyone on the side of truth listens to me" Jn 18:37.

THE BIBLICAL concept of truth differs essentially from common conceptions. People ordinarily assume that truth is arrived at by thinking. The Bible, however, teaches that truth is like a country in which we must live in order to get to know it. It is not enough that I approach truth with my thinking. I must surrender to truth with my whole being; I must live in truth.

Rational thinking will not lead anyone to faith, nor will it lead any one away from faith. But if a person does not live in truth, Paul says he becomes foolish (Ga 3:1). If we do not have a living faith, we will be susceptible to the spells of Satan which are rampant in the world. Under Satan's spell we will become foolish and do foolish things.

There are innumerable examples of this in recent history. Wise people have strayed into foolish ventures under Satan's spells, with tragic results for all humankind. The Bible says that when people did not honor God and believe in Him, "their thinking became futile and their foolish hearts were darkened. Although they claimed to be wise, they became fools" Ro 1:21f.

Whoever desires to guard against foolishness, let him watch and strive to live in truth. Pray for a living Christian faith!

19 / The Lord Puts Christ in Christmas

"You may ask me for anything in my name, and I will do it" Jn 14:14.

A CHRISTIAN'S sense of responsibility is intensified as God's Spirit takes over in his conscience. He discovers new tasks, which demand ever greater faithfulness and obedience. God's holy will compels him.

Our natural tendency is to increase our efforts to accomplish the tasks we feel are assigned to us, especially in these days before Christmas. But, Jesus' plan is different. "You may ask me for anything in my name, and I will do it." Jesus does not say that he will give us strength to do it; he says, "I will do it." We will never become people capable of doing God's works in the world on the basis of our own ability. But if we are aware of our limitations and practice true prayer, Jesus promises to do what needs to be done. He will, in fact, use us and other people as tools.

What a liberating thought! No matter how you may have failed, no matter how bitterly you have experienced your limitations and inabilities, all options are open, for the road of prayer has not been closed. God's Spirit comes to those who have reached a dead end on the road of their own possibilities. Prayer is how we stand before God with our impossibilities, acknowledge our bankruptcy, and beg for His help.

In the midst of our preparations for Christmas, let us not forget that Christmas is not our doing but the Lord's. It is not up to Christians to put Christ back into Christmas. But if we acknowledge our helplessness to the Lord in persistent prayer, the Lord will make Christmas for us.

20 / Life Is a Healing Process

"Heal me, O Lord, and I will be healed; save me and I will be saved" Jr 17:14.

HEALING is not something that I do; the Lord is the Healer. Let all Christians who have failed to save themselves impress this upon their minds. Let them not persist in their self-help but rather call on the Lord to do His work in them.

How does the Lord heal or save us? The cross directs our attention to the word of the Lord, leading to healing and salvation. The Lord heals us by placing us beneath the cross of Jesus. The Lord sits down as a refiner to purify us like gold and silver in the fire of suffering (Ml 3:2f.) He keeps us in the fire until He can see His own reflection in us, just as the goldsmith purifies and refines the gold until he can see his own image in it. Let us not complain when afflictions overtake us. Their purpose is to uncover and remove the dross in us and to draw us into God's word.

In trying to heal ourselves, our goal is always to recover as quickly as possible from the wounds and bruises of sin. But it often happens that wounds heal prematurely, before they have been properly cleansed. We must be patient and stay in the care of the Lord so that He might lance and cleanse our sins.

There is no magic potion. The Lord Himself must use the healing power of his sacred blood to cleanse our sins. As Luther remarked, the whole life of a Christian is a healing process. Let us stay in his care without trying to break away into attempts at self-healing. The blood of Jesus Christ, God's Son, "purifies us from all sin" 1 Jn 1:7.

21 / True Christmas Joy

"I sing in the shadow of your wings" Ps 63:7.

WE SELDOM find true joy in life; and yet it's joy that we long for. The Bible says, "The joy of the Lord is your strength" Ne 8:10. Why do we find so little of this true joy?

"I sing in the shadow of your wings." When we read this verse of Psalm 63 we learn about a man who seemed to lack joy. He had sought and yearned for God: "O God, You are my God; early will I seek You; my soul thirsts for You; my flesh longs for You in a dry and thirsty land" Ps 63:1 (NKJ). This man knew about the riches of life, but he still longed for joy. "Your love is better than life" Ps 63:3. He sought love and grace, for these alone could fill him with joy. Finding God was a gift of grace for him and he could not take it for granted. He was fully aware of the enemies that dogged his every step. For that reason he sought refuge in the shadow of the wings of the Almighty. Reaching their safety, he experienced heartfelt joy.

Is it possible that we lack true joy because we have not felt the need for the safety of the wings of God? Have we tried to get by on our own? We are not safe by ourselves, for we live in a wicked world, whose ruler is the devil. The evil one robs us of our joy. Even now as we wait for Christmas, the evil one is at work in us, our homes, and all around, keeping us from finding the joy of Christmas. If, in our temptations and tribulations, we find refuge in the shadow of the wings of our Lord, we will know true joy in spite of the evil around and within us.

How wonderful that the shadow of God's wings is a living reality! We do not have to prepare a shelter for ourselves. God in Christ has prepared a place of refuge for all who are hounded by the prince of darkness. Let us pray that with our loved ones we may celebrate Christmas in the shadow of the wings of our Lord.

22 / The Frame and the Picture

"For God has revealed his grace for the salvation of all mankind" Titus 2:11 (TEV).

THERE IS such a thing as "criminal's grace." Many people have found grace only by taking their place alongside the criminal who was crucified with Jesus. But have we always remembered that the criminal was a contrite criminal? He rebuked his fellow criminal: "We are punished justly, for we are getting what our deeds deserve" Lk 23:40. Only a contrite heart finds grace.

It is so difficult to lower oneself to true contrition. By nature we want to defend ourselves. When we suffer, we blame others. In one way or another we try to bolster our own cause. But even our piety does not qualify us for grace. "God opposes the proud but gives grace to the humble" Jas 4:6.

What your Christmas will be like depends on whether you take your place with the contrite. Too many Christmases have gone by where the picture of our Savior in the manger has not spoken to our consciences. We have seen only the glittering frame. A contrite heart is the best preparation for Christmas. Only those who need the Savior will find joy in his manger.

"God has revealed His grace for the salvation of all mankind." Without our need for salvation there can be no Christmas and no joy.

23 / The Glory of Christmas

"The Word became flesh and made his dwelling among us. We have seen his glory" Jn 1:14.

CHRISTMAS is at the door! In the midst of Christmas preparations the Christian sighs, "Would that this year's Christmas were truly Christmas! Would that Jesus were born for me too!"

When people have truly experienced Christmas they can say, "We have seen his glory." We all need to see Christ's glory; it is not enough to hear about him from others.

Which road leads to the place where I can see Christ's glory? Can I find that road, even if the sorry sounds of my sins have continued during these days before Christmas? Can one who is unholy and unclean see the glorious? The fog of sin is very real, dimming our inner vision, and keeping us from recognizing the presence of Christ. Sin becomes a very comfortable home. In our better moments we sense that things are not as they ought to be, but we are not moved to seek that which is missing.

"We have seen his glory." The gospel does more than tell us about glory; the gospel guides us along the road leading to the place where we can see it for ourselves. The gospel reveals Christ. Thomas Wilcocks writes in *A Choice Drop of Honey*, a devotional book popular in Finland, "Seek Christ daily in the Bible, as gold in the hills, for that is where Christ's heart is hidden." Or, as Luther said, "The gospel is not a book of laws but a message about Christ's good works."

Luther also wrote, "He who would find Christ must first find the church. How would we know where Christ is, unless we know where his believers are?" We see Christ's glory when we are in living fellowship with the Lord's people. Whoever has glimpsed Christ's glory will yearn for the fullness of heaven. He will not find peace until he has reached the heavenly home. He will live his life as though he were in the waiting room of the great hall where the wedding dinner of eternity is being served.

24 / Merry Christmas

"I bring you good news of great joy" Lk 2:10.

WHEN JESUS was born, the indifferent world celebrated the pagan Roman winter festival with its ungodly entertainment. Today, the greater part of Christendom continues to observe Christmas with indifference. What most people mean by Merry Christmas seems strange to the awakened Christian.

What makes Christmas Christmas? Is it the tree, the gifts, Christmas dinner, or the family gathering? Partly, but not really! The Christmas message makes Christmas. If this message is missing, Christmas is sadly impoverished, no matter the abundance of other things. Remember that we do not maintain the Christmas tradition, the message does.

Our thoughts, in the midst of our busyness, must be directed to the Christmas message: "A Savior has been born to you, he is Christ the Lord" Lk 2:11. The Savior was born also for the indifferent; he wants, and is able, to free us from indifference "into the glorious freedom of the children of God" Ro 8:21. It makes no difference what you and I think of the Savior; he remains Christ the Lord.

The reason for Christmas joy is not some special quality we may have as Christians, but the special character of our Lord Christ as the Savior of sinners and the indifferent. Let us celebrate Christmas by hearing the amazing and wonderful message of Christmas.

Already on this Christmas Eve we may greet each other by saying "Merry Christmas!" Remember, the angels greeted the shepherds on the first Christmas eve with the words, "I bring you good news of great joy."

25 / How to Celebrate Christmas

"You are to give him the name Jesus, because he will save his people from their sins" Mt 1:21.

DURING CHRISTMAS it seems that we should be able to think and talk about Jesus, the true treasure of Christmas. Everyone may not have amazing things to tell about him. You yourself may not have had remarkable experiences that you might relate to others. Would it not be better to remain silent? You might feel like a hypocrite if you began to talk and converse about Jesus.

Do not think that way! Everyone is able to talk about Jesus. If nothing else, we can ask others what Jesus has done for them. The wonderful thing is that when people talk about Jesus, he himself is present to bless his friends. When we talk about him, he finds his way to people to tell them what he did for us on Golgatha and what he continues to do today to save us from our sins. Christ did not come to save just angels, special people, or the elite. He is everyone's Savior. The news of his birth was to be announced to all the people. This keeps happening when people talk about him whenever and wherever they meet. Where difficulties are the greatest, he is needed the most.

Let us celebrate Christmas by talking about the Savior. After you have read these words, talk about them with at least one other person. More than that, take the message of Christmas with you wherever you go. He wants to bless you this Christmas. You need the Savior and so do others.

If we celebrate Christmas in this way, we experience the reality of salvation from sins. New life, new riches, and new joy become ours. Let us continue our conversation about Jesus throughout the new year and experience a new blessing from God.

26 / The Prince of Peace and the Sword

"I did not come to bring peace, but a sword" Mt 10:34.

JESUS TELLS US that he is among us as the Savior of the world. We live in a fallen world, which is in rebellion against its Creator and Lord. In our own way we are all involved in this rebellion, arguing constantly against God and rejecting His holy will.

Christ has no interest in enabling the world to continue in its rebellion. He came to destroy the works of the devil, to bring back the rebels, and to establish the kingdom of God in place of the kingdom of evil. But Satan will not give up without a fight. The coming of Christ, therefore, means war that will continue until every thought is captured and made obedient to Christ (2 Co 10:5).

If you celebrate Christmas in the right way, and Jesus has become your Savior, war has broken out in your life. It is the same war that Paul describes in Romans 7:14-25 and to which he urged his friends in Ephesians 8:10-17. Often the fighting appears hopeless; there are serious wounds and bitter defeats. The cause may seem lost. Then Christ shows himself as the victorious hero to those who hoped in him when there was no hope.

If you find yourself in a hopeless condition, even in the midst of your Christmas celebration, remember that Christ "did not come to bring peace, but a sword." Yet in the midst of battle, he is still the Prince of Peace!

27 / Good Will Toward Others

"Let your gentleness be evident to all. The Lord is near"
Phil 4:5.

WE HAVE CELEBRATED Christmas, which for a good reason is called a festival of good will. People are right to sing Christmas carols about good, warm, and tender feelings. But let us not assume that people will become good when they are taught to think good thoughts and do good things. The heart is wicked; it cannot be changed by nice words or good feelings, nor even by the radiance of Christmas lights.

Luther instructs us in the explanation to the eighth commandment to apologize for our neighbor, to speak well of him, and to interpret charitably everything he does (*Small Catechism*). Our hearts are wicked and our will corrupt, but we are not excused from wrestling with this problem. We must defend our neighbor when others attack him, but we must also defend him from ourselves, when suspicions and doubts about his intentions threaten to dominate our thoughts about him.

How differently we would talk with each other, dish out advice, and correct the erring, if we tried to interpret charitably everything our neighbor did. This is not easy, but we must try, willingly confessing our failures, though our pride will object.

When the angels sing about good will, they mean primarily God's good will toward fallen humanity. The Christian on whom God has had mercy will strive to be a person of good will toward his neighbor in the sense in which Luther explained it. "The great love she has shown proves that her many sins have been forgiven. But whoever has been forgiven little shows only a little love" Lk 7:47 (TEV). Good will toward others is possible only for the person who has been shown God's good will.

28 / The Post-Christmas Celebration

"But Mary treasured up all these things and pondered them in her heart" Lk 2:19.

THESE WORDS describe the right kind of post-Christmas celebration, calling attention to two things.

First, "Mary treasured up all these things." God had spoken to Mary. His words must be cherished, for it is the word of God's love that makes Christmas. We must store up and treasure the special word we received from the Lord this Christmas. But that may not have happened. Words of the Christmas gospel have been heard again and again, but they have gone with the wind, quickly forgotten.

Surely you don't want to let Christmas go without receiving something! Celebrate the right way: prayerfully reread the Christmas gospel, recall the messages you heard, and read once more the devotional articles that you may have only glanced at. You will certainly find a word from God addressed especially to you.

Secondly, Mary "pondered them in her heart." Conflicting thoughts filled Mary's mind, bouncing off each other. But, they were combined in her soul. A similar situation arises in the person who receives a word from heaven. The inner equilibrium is disturbed, questions arise that must be faced and pondered.

Once before Mary had been called to decide, saying to the angel, "I am the Lord's servant. May it be to me as you have said" Lk 1:38. Even though everything seemed impossible, she had yielded to the word, denying her own wishes.

That is the way it goes for those who live in the Lord. The road ahead seems impossible; the festive days are over, and the gray dullness of everyday life threatens from every side. But something remains: the word, the conflict-producing word, the incomprehensible word. But, it is the word in which God speaks. We must be satisfied with it; we must ponder it in our hearts.

God gives abundantly. At Christmas He gives good gifts, words of grace. We must "treasure up all these things and ponder them" in our hearts. That is what our post-Christmas celebration is all about.

29 / No Need to Boast

"Do not think of yourself more highly than you ought" Ro 12:3.

SELF-LOVE leads us to imagine great things about ourselves. We think that we are somebody. Even if we have been battered by the world, we still entertain exaggerated ideas about ourselves.

We become dissatisfied and bitter when the circumstances of life do not correspond with our self-evaluation. Only God's Spirit can teach us to think soberly and humbly about ourselves.

Paul demonstrated true self-knowledge on his first missionary journey in Lystra, where he and Barnabas were greeted as gods. The people of Lystra were pagans, but that did not give Paul reason to look upon his Christian faith as a special privilege that elevated him above them. Paul said, "Men, why are you doing this? We too are only men, human like you" Ac 14:15.

God's Spirit shows us that we are human. In doing so He unites people with each other, for true unity is created on the lowest level, that is, among sinners. If Christianity is seen as a human achievement, even partially, then competition is inevitable. Comparison of achievements ensues and true fellowship becomes impossible. But if Christianity is a pure gift and if righteousness is only by grace, people will discover that no one is more special than another. True unity is born only where people bear in mind that God's friends have no reason or need to boast.

30 / Don't Stop Too Soon

"Let us run with perseverance the race marked out for us"
He 12:1.

TRAVELER, do not stop! Don't stay too long at the rest stop; you
are not yet at your destination. Christ promises rest; but he
promises to be with those who follow him. Now is the time to
follow Christ; our journey is not over.

Don't complain about travel pains; they are a part of the
picture. Once when I complained to an elderly, experienced
Christian, he reprimanded me, "We must not complain; we must
swallow!" Put away petty whining! All it does is add pain to our
struggle. Let us be of good courage, seeking patience to do God's
will!

Don't give up; every pilgrim that has gone before you has
experienced what you are experiencing. We must endure
hardship on life's journey. Who has told you that life without
hardships would be richer and more peaceful? The happiest
people are often those who have borne the heaviest burdens. The
Christian could not make it all the way without his cross!

But useless and unlawful baggage must not be dragged
along. Many of us are smugglers. We try to be Christians, but at
the same time we carry with us things that do not belong to
Christ's followers. "Let us throw off everything that hinders us
and the sin that so easily entangles us" He 12:1. Simplicity and
modesty belong in our baggage.

Keep your home in mind, it is your destination. If the world
is dear to us, we will miss heaven. Heaven must be our goal;
otherwise we'll never get there.

Seek the company of those who are on their way to the same
home. Let us reflect together on our common journey, helping
each other stay on the right road and overcoming the inevitable
obstacles. Traveling together makes it easier for all.

We must not become satisfied with what we have. "Not that
I have already obtained all this, or have already been made
perfect, but I press on to take hold of that for which Christ Jesus
took hold of me" Phil 3:12. A Christian must press on.

Travel blessings for the year ahead!

31 / Time to Give Account

"Everything is uncovered and laid bare before the eyes of him to whom we must give account" He 4:13.

THE END of the year is accounting time; life stops for a moment and we consider what has gone before.

We usually avoid giving account. We do not want to see how things really are. It may be that during the year we failed to pay some bills, perhaps even taxes, when we were short of funds. Our conscience is disturbed, and it will not leave us in peace until we have paid in full.

That's how it is in our inner world. Our life is chaotic. We may not even be fully awaye of what is troubling us. Closing the account clears the air. We must have the courage to examine our books for there is no other way to gain peace of soul.

If we look at the credit side, we marvel at God's inexpressible goodness and patience. We take it for granted that we are healthy, that our daily bread is provided, that our country has been at peace, that good people have supported us. All these things are God's gifts. If we overlook this, we become ungrateful and lose the most important gift. Gratitude multiplies the gifts. As the psalmist said: "Praise the Lord, O my soul, and forget not all his benefits" Ps 103:2.

On the debit side are our sins. Sins of omission are numerous. "Anyone, then, who knows the good he ought to do and doesn't do it, sins" Jas 4:17. Sins of omission would not have piled up so high, if we had thought more often about God's will. God has reminded us often enough through His Spirit, but we have muffled His voice and disobeyed His will.

As we give account, we do well to remember the words of the hymn:

> O, close Thou my account.
> And wipe away the debts,
> Which I have incurred.
> O, Jesus, won't you pay
> For all the many sins
> You know that I have done.